New Perspectives in Physics

New Perspectives in
PHYSICS

LOUIS DE BROGLIE

translated by
A. J. POMERANS

Basic Books, Inc., PUBLISHERS, NEW YORK

Preface

THIS BOOK CONTAINS A NUMBER OF PAPERS AND LECTURES on various aspects of theoretical physics and on the history and philosophy of science, all written during the period 1950 to 1956.

The papers on theoretical physics, which make up the first half of the book, are divided into two parts, in order to contrast my differences in attitude, before and after 1951, toward the interpretation of wave mechanics and of the wave-particle dualism. After the birth of wave mechanics, I strove for some years (1923 to 1927) to obtain an interpretation in keeping with traditional physics and the idea of causality, *i.e.*, to represent physical reality by means of precise images in space and time. The difficulties I encountered in these attempts, and the hostility they elicited from other theoretical physicists, persuaded me in 1928 to abandon all efforts in that direction and to range myself for the next 25 years with the probability interpretation of Born, Bohr, and Heisenberg, which became the official doctrine of the great majority of theoretical physicists. Most of the papers I have published in preceding volumes in this series* were devoted to developing this statistical interpretation—an interpreta-

---

* *Sciences d'aujourd'hui,* Albin Michel, Paris.

tion which is as subtle as its clear presentation is difficult. But during the academic year 1951–1952 I was led back to my earlier concepts, having asked myself whether they did not, in fact, lead toward a better understanding of the wave-particle dualism. In this way, my thoughts and my work assumed a new outlook during the years 1951 to 1955, and this is the subject of Part Two.

Those interested in the psychology of scientists may be curious about the reasons for this unexpected return to discarded ideas. No doubt the work of David Bohm and Jean-Pierre Vigier, which I shall discuss, has played a decisive role in my development since 1951, when I became acquainted with it, but there is equally no doubt that my mind was already somehow prepared for this change. I am thinking not so much of my constant difficulties in developing a statistical interpretation of wave mechanics, or even of my secret hankering after Cartesian clarity in the midst of the fog which seemed to envelop quantum physics, as of the following fact: As the subject of my lectures at the Henri Poincaré Institute in 1950–1951 I chose a critical examination of the statistical interpretation of quantum physics. I began the survey with a bias in favor of that interpretation and continued with a scrupulous examination not only of its faultless mathematical representation but also of Einstein's and Schrödinger's critiques and Bohr's counter-arguments. Despite my own tendency to favor the probability interpretation, I could not help being more and more struck by the force of the objections to it and by a certain obscurity in the arguments in its defense. I also examined von Neumann's theory of measurement, and while I admired its logical lucidity, I found it too abstract and based on too schematic an analysis of the conditions of measurement in the quantum domain. Moreover, von Neumann's carrying through his conceptions to the point of representing even macroscopic measuring instruments and observers by wave functions seemed highly questionable, for I could not agree that an observer's awareness of observable macroscopic events could in any way affect the course of microscopic phenomena. It gradually dawned on me that the partisans of the probability interpretation had passed, somewhat surreptitiously, from using the idea of a simple and subjective wave representation of probability to using the contrary idea of a wave with a certain physical reality, and that they managed to skirt around the difficulties of their doctrine by oscillating between the two opposite points of view. I realized that I myself, seduced by the current fashion, had, during the preceding years, unconsciously performed a similar set of dangerous mental acrobatics, and I began to understand why I had been so uneasy whenever I tried to give a lucid account of the probability interpretation.

Thus, toward the end of 1951 my mind was already fully prepared for my subsequent about-face, which was, in fact, no more than a sudden crystallization of my previous mental reservations. This is a psychological phenomenon whose importance in scientific research has been noted frequently, particularly by Henri Poincaré. To me, at least, it seems probable that whenever anyone takes an important but unexpected decision in any field, that decision must have matured gradually in the depth of his subconscious, suddenly to burst into consciousness.

No doubt I shall be asked to what conclusion I came after four years' re-examination of the question of the interpretation of the wave-particle dualism in wave mechanics. Before giving a definite answer, I should like to emphasize that, in the study of this problem, I have by no means been swayed by any philosophic bias in favor of determinism. What seemed to me to be eminently desirable was not a reestablishment of determinism but a return to precise space-time representations which could give a clear picture of what they were supposed to portray. Possibly such a return necessarily involves the re-establishment of determinism, which is, in fact, what happened in my 1927 theory of the double solution and in my recent endeavors. But I believe that it is extremely dangerous to fit physical theories to *a priori* concepts, or to deduce too highly extrapolated philosophical consequences from them. Many scientists have tried to make determinism and complementarity the basis of conclusions which seem to me weak and dangerous; for instance, they have used Heisenberg's uncertainty principle to bolster up human free will, though his principle, which applies exclusively to the behavior of electrons and is the direct result of microphysical measuring techniques, has nothing to do with human freedom of choice. It is far safer and wiser that the physicist remain on the solid ground of theoretical physics itself and eschew the shifting sands of philosophic extrapolations.

To summarize my present attitude toward the interpretation of wave mechanics, without entering into all the details here, I may say that, after a very careful re-examination—for I know the difficulties involved!—of the causal interpretation of wave mechanics I had first considered in 1927, I saw that some of the earlier obstacles receded or disappeared, and this encouraged my belief in the final success of this endeavor. Far be it from me to gloss over the remaining difficulties, but today I am convinced that a re-interpretation of wave mechanics, based on the substitution of "real" waves with singular regions for the usual continuous waves, will not only so rejuvenate quantum physics that it will be able to describe the structure of the different kinds of particles and to predict their properties but will also relate quantum theory to relativistic physics in the Einsteinian sense, *i.e.*, to a general field theory.

Now for a brief description of the arrangement of this book.

Part One contains a number of studies in theoretical physics which were independent of the interpretation of wave mechanics and were mainly written before my recent change of attitude. In my discussion, particularly of the nuclear field and of atomic particles, the reader will find a summary of ideas on the constitution of particles which I have developed for more than 20 years and also on the theory of the "subtractive field," to which I devoted particular attention between 1949 and 1952.

The second part contains, apart from a short reminiscence of my conversation with Einstein at the Solvay Congress in 1927, four papers dealing with my recent attempts to reinterpret wave mechanics. The first dates back to the eve of my change of attitude; the second was written for *Il Nuovo Cimento* at the beginning of the autumn of 1954, *i.e.*, only two years later. A comparison between these two papers will show the reader how greatly my ideas changed, particularly with regard to a more precise concept of a "real" wave with a region of singularity and its relevance to the explanation of interference phenomena and of the success of the usual method of calculating stationary states in quantized systems.

The paper entitled "The Wave-Particle Dualism in the Work of Einstein" requires special comment, because its subject is more dramatic than appears at first sight. In it I have tried to show that the effort to interpret wave mechanics by a theory of the double solution, which I developed from 1924 to 1927, is the natural extension of Einstein's discovery of light quanta and of his ideas on the relation of particles and fields. The rejection of that theory by the Solvay Congress, when Einstein apparently failed to pay sufficient attention to it, was to have an unexpected consequence for him. In effect, this setback, by initiating what appeared to be the final triumph of the statistical interpretation, to which Einstein never subscribed, was to force that illustrious figure to end his scientific life in sad isolation and—paradoxically enough—apparently far behind the ideas of his time. Perhaps the future will make some sort of posthumous amends to him.

The fourth paper of Part Two gives a somewhat different presentation of the ideas underlying the theory of the double solution and summarizes the weightiest objections to the current interpretation of wave mechanics.

Parts Three and Four contain a series of papers on philosophic and general topics, particularly on scientific progress and scientific history, past or present. Being less demanding on the reader than the two preceding parts, they may reward him for his patience in bearing with me that far.

LOUIS DE BROGLIE

September 1955

Contents

PART ONE

Particles
and Fields

ONE

The Uncertainty Relation
of Second Quantization

RECENT DEVELOPMENTS IN THEORETICAL PHYSICS HAVE LED TO
the adoption of concepts so radically different from those
held by classical physics and so original and abstruse that
neither philosophers nor physicists themselves have so far
managed to grasp their full significance. Forced to fit established, yet apparently contradictory, physical processes
into one and the same theoretical framework, modern physicists time and again have had to make a strenuous intellectual effort to revise all previous concepts and look at
physical phenomena anew.

One of the more recent attempts in that direction, on
which we shall concentrate in this article, involves an uncertainty relation which is far less frequently discussed than
the Heisenberg uncertainties, possibly because it is much
more difficult to grasp. Still, its importance and scope in
modern physics are very considerable. I am speaking of the
uncertainty relation which connects the "number" of Bose-
Einstein particles associated with a given wave and the
"phase" of that wave.

Before discussing this problem as such, I must first of
all remind the reader that atomic particles are divided into

3

two classes: those that obey Pauli's exclusion principle and are governed by Fermi-Dirac statistics, and those that do not obey the exclusion principle and are governed by Bose-Einstein statistics. While electrons, protons, neutrons, and certain atomic nuclei belong to the first class, alpha particles, photons, and certain atomic nuclei belong to the second. Dirac has called them *fermions* and *bosons*, respectively. There are good reasons for thinking that elementary, indivisible particles (of which electrons are a good example), as well as complex particles made up of an odd number of elementary constituents, are of the fermion type, while particles made up of an even number of constituents are bosons. This is not the place to develop this point, which is probably of great importance.

We shall first consider fermions, the most familiar example of which is the electron. When we say that fermions obey Pauli's exclusion principle, we mean that their wave-particle association is such that no more than one fermion can be attached to a given wave. The fermion is a savage; it remains isolated on its wave and refuses to do any collective work. From this it follows that aggregates of fermions are governed by Fermi-Dirac statistics. Applying these statistics to electrons, we can explain the electric conductivity of metals correctly, and, what is still more important, why every added electron plays a specific role, so that, as we pass from element to element in the Mendeleev system of classification, we encounter changes in chemical, spectroscopic, and sometimes magnetic properties, due to the individual role of the electron added in the outer shell of the atom.

Here we must stress an essential point: The waves associated with different fermions are completely independent, since every fermion forms a separate band. We are therefore unable to compare them; *i.e.*, their relative phases are completely indeterminate. Let me make myself clear. The differ-

ent parts of the wave of a given fermion have perfectly defined phase differences; this is what enables the waves of
electrons, for instance, to give rise to diffraction phenomena
in crystals (Davisson and Germer phenomenon) or at the
edge of a screen (Börsch's phenomenon). But, by virtue of
the isolation of the fermions, we cannot define the precise
phase difference between the wave of one fermion and that
of another. In wave mechanics this fact is expressed mathematically by saying that the phase of the ψ function always
contains an independent additive constant.

From this it follows clearly that the fermion wave is
quite unlike the classical wave. True, the square of the
modulus of its amplitude—its intensity—gives the probability with which the associated fermion will reveal its
presence at any given point, which is in agreement with a
classical energy distribution. Moreover, the spectral decomposition of the ψ wave associated with a given fermion will
give the respective probabilities of the different possible values of the energy and the momentum associated with the fermion, in agreement with the spectral decomposition of the
classical theory of light. But these agreements between the
properties of the ψ wave and those of the waves of classical
physics are due to the introduction of random (stochastic)
factors—which are altogether alien to the classical concepts
of position and momentum. Moreover, the analogies stop
there. It is impossible to liken these fermion ψ waves to true
"vibrations" propagated through space, such as the elastic
and electromagnetic waves of macroscopic physics, which
are capable of causing vibratory movement in sensitive receivers. It is equally impossible to add the amplitudes of
two fermion waves in the way in which the amplitudes of
macroscopic elastic or electromagnetic waves can be added
(vectorially), for the simple reason that every fermion and
its wave are characteristically isolated. The ψ wave is,

therefore, interpreted today as simply an element of prediction—the mathematical representation of the probability
of observable events and of the results of measurement.
Thus the amplitude of the ψ wave, determined by normaliza-
tion based on the principle of compound probabilities, has
no direct mechanical or physical significance.

The fermion ψ wave, therefore, appears to be only a
symbolic wave which merely enables us to predict the possible results of a discontinuous succession of measurements
performed on the associated particle. However, there are
other waves (*e.g.*, electromagnetic waves) which have the
character of genuine vibrations, the amplitudes of which
can be added, and which are capable of transmitting mechanical vibrations to a receiver. If we make the quite natural assumption that electromagnetic waves are the ψ waves
of photons, we may therefore say that there is a marked
difference between the ψ waves of photons and those of
electrons. To understand this difference, we must first remember that photons are bosons and not fermions. Let us,
therefore, turn our attention to bosons.

Unlike fermions, bosons are not subject to Pauli's exclusion principle and can therefore attach themselves to one
wave in fairly large numbers. This is expressed by the fact
that collections of bosons are governed by Bose-Einstein
and not by Fermi-Dirac statistics. The validity of Bose-
Einstein statistics for the case of photons, which, as we have
seen, are bosons, follows from Planck's well-known energy-
distribution law of black-body radiation, because this radiation can be likened to a "photon gas."

The study of boson groupings on one and the same wave
has led to the development of the theory of second quantization, the principles of which were clearly defined by Dirac
in the 1930's. Applied to the particularly important case of
photons, the second quantization leads to the "quantum

theory of electromagnetic fields" propounded by Jordan, Heisenberg, and Pauli; this becomes particularly clear in my development of this theory as the "wave mechanics of the photon." * The examination of the problems of groups leads to very important novel ideas, for it introduces new aspects of uncertainty and complementarity—concepts which Bohr and Heisenberg have made classical for the case of the single particle and its associated wave.

For greater clarity we shall concentrate on the photons of light, although our remarks are, in principle, applicable to other bosons as well. Let us consider the case of a single photon and its associated wave—as in the case of the emission of a photon by an atom in a Bohr quantum jump. In it, the associated wave, like the fermion wave, has no more than a mathematical sense of prediction, defining the possible positions of the photons by its local intensity and the probability of their possible momenta by its spectral composition. The wave attached to a single photon is never a true, observable, vibratory phenomenon. In the emission of a Hertzian wave by a radio aerial, on the other hand, the wave is indubitably associated with vibrating electric and magnetic fields of perfectly defined phase, capable of transmitting a synchronous vibration to an appropriate receiver. We can make this clear by considering a somewhat old-fashioned Hertzian transmitter—a high frequency alternator, from which a sinusoidal high-frequency current is sent into an antenna to produce Hertzian waves of the same frequency, their phase directly related to the movement of the alternator and to the arrangement of its circuits. Here the case is quite clear: the electromagnetic field is undoubtedly a real vibration, the phase relations of which are

---

* For a discussion of this subject, see L. de Broglie, *Mécanique ondulatoire du photon et théorie quantique des champs électromagnétiques*. Gauthier-Villars, Paris, 1949.

determined by the mechanical rotation of the alternator. But since Maxwell showed that an electromagnetic wave does not differ in any way from a light wave, we must suppose that it carries photons, and we are bound to wonder why this case differs from that of the emission of an *isolated* photon.

In the case just considered, the Hertzian wave must be looked upon as the ψ wave of the associated photons, even though it has the physical characteristics of a classical vibration (it has a well-defined phase; the amplitudes of two superposed waves can be added vectorially; the vibration can be transmitted to an appropriate receiver, etc.). Why, then, has this wave so different a character from the fermion or isolated photon wave? The reply to this question is as follows. Photons, being bosons, can be grouped on a single wave, and the usual Hertzian wave is precisely a wave with a very large number of associated photons. It is easy to ascertain that, because the quantum $h\nu$ is so small, every group of Hertzian waves carries a very large number of photons, and it is this grouping of photons on a single wave that gives the Hertzian wave a character altogether different from that of a ψ wave associated with an isolated particle. The emission of a Hertzian wave is due to the movement of an assemblage of electricity in the emitting antenna (and eventually in the high-frequency alternator); looked at from the quantum point of view, this combined movement amounts to an infinity of small coordinated and *coherent* quantal transitions. This process is, therefore, quite different from the emission of an isolated photon during an individual quantum transition; it is made possible only because photons, being bosons, can group themselves in large number on a single wave, which cannot happen during the emission of fermions.

A macroscopically detectable electromagnetic wave, such

as a Hertzian wave, is therefore characterized by two factors: the invariably large number of photons it carries, and the invariably well-defined phase of the vibration which it represents. Now—and this is the essential point—between these two quantities—"number of photons" and "phase of the wave"—the theory of second quantization and the quantum field theory derived from it have established the existence of a relationship of complementarity involving uncertainties altogether analogous to the well-known uncertainties holding between the position of any particle whatever and its momentum.

Let us first recall the nature of Heisenberg's uncertainty relations and the complementarity which they express. At a given moment, we can establish either the position of a particle or its energy and momentum, but we cannot simultaneously measure a coordinate (q_i) of the particle and the corresponding component (p_i) of its momentum. Every attempt to make a simultaneous evaluation of both these "conjugate" magnitudes introduces the uncertainties δq_i and δp_i into their exact value, such that the inequality

$$\delta q_i \times \delta p_i \geq h$$

(where h is Planck's constant and $i = 1, 2, 3$), may be satisfied. These are the Heisenberg inequalities, to which, however, a fourth inequality with a somewhat different significance must be added:

$$\delta E \times \delta t \geq h$$

(where E is energy).

The values of the coordinates (q_i) and of the time (t) accurately define the position of the particle in spacetime in accordance with its granular aspect; the values of p_i and of E define "the dynamic state" of the particle according to its "wave aspect," as formulated in wave mechanics. Thus—and Bohr has stressed this point—the Heisenberg uncertainties express the "complementarity" of the granular and wave aspects of the elementary physical entities which we call particles. The more we succeed in defining one of these aspects, the more uncertain the other becomes, and in this way the existence of these apparently irreconcilable aspects never entails a contradiction.

Let us now return to electromagnetic waves, bearing a large number of photons. The theory of second quantization shows that complementarity holds between the number of such photons and the phase value of the associated wave. For instance, we could estimate the photoelectric effects produced by the incident photons and thus determine the number of photons carried by an electromagnetic wave, but that determination would tell us nothing about the phase value of the wave. Conversely, we could establish the phase value by observing the electrical or mechanical vibrations produced in a receiver by an electromagnetic wave, but that determination would not tell us anything about the number of photons associated with the wave. More generally, every observation leading to the simultaneous evaluation of the number of photons and of the phase of the associated wave introduces the uncertainties δN and $\delta\Phi$, such that the uncertainty relation

$$\delta N \times \delta\Phi \geq 1$$

may be shown to hold. The "number of photons" and the "phase value" therefore appear as observable, but in Bohr's sense complementary, aspects of macroscopic electromagnetic waves. The sharper our definition of one of these aspects, the more uncertain the other becomes.

Thus again there is a relation of complementarity between the granular aspect and the wave aspect of photons. In fact, the possibility of "numbering" the photons is crucially related to their having the granular character of discontinuous entities, while the existence of a well-defined phase is inseparably bound up with the possibility of associating a wave with the displacement of photons. Nevertheless the wave-particle complementarity involved here is of a very special kind. In Heisenberg's relations, the granular aspect is defined by the localization of the particle and not by numbering the particles (since only one particle is considered at a time), and the wave aspect is defined by the momentum and energy, *i.e.*, by the wavelength and frequency, but in no way by the absolute phase value, since, as we saw, the phase of individual ψ waves always involves an arbitrary additive constant.*

The cooperative presence of a large number of photons (or, more generally, of bosons) in the same wave gives this wave the properties of a classical wave—a true physical vibration, propagated with a well-defined phase, additive amplitude, and the ability to transmit electrical or mechanical movements in phase to appropriate receivers. However, these classical properties can be demonstrated only if we refrain from breaking the wave down into particles and numbering them. Every enumeration of this kind invariably causes the classical wave properties to disappear.

The appearance of a macroscopic electromagnetic wave is therefore the result of the cooperation of a very large and undetermined number of photons. More generally, macroscopic wave fields of well-defined phase appear in association with particles of the boson type, which alone, by their ability to congregate on a single wave, make the appearance of macroscopic wave fields possible.

By applying the theory of second quantization to the quantum representation of electromagnetic fields, we have

---

* This also follows from the fact that for $N = 1$ and $\delta N = 0$, the uncertainty relation $\delta N \times \delta \Phi \geq 1$ gives $\delta \Phi = \infty$.

thus succeeded in giving a combined account of two physically certain but at first sight contradictory factors, the
emission of radiation by photons undergoing Bohr transitions, and the macroscopic existence of electromagnetic
waves with well-defined phases and with classical properties.
But, just as it has been impossible to account for the grain-
wave double character of particles on the atomic scale except by introducing the Heisenberg uncertainties and the
complementarity which they express, so the quantum and
classical wave aspects of electromagnetic radiation could be
reconciled only by introducing the uncertainy relation
$\delta N \times \delta \Phi \geq 1$; *i.e.*, by a new kind of complementarity between the number of photons associated with a wave and
the phase of that wave.

In philosophical accounts of the new physics, this uncertainty has been rather neglected, while that of Bohr and
Heisenberg has been stressed. Nevertheless, it is very important, since without it we should never be able to understand how quantum processes on the microscopic scale give
rise to important phenomena on the macroscopic scale. It
also emphasizes the distinction between fermions, which are
always isolated and associated with individual waves lacking classical properties, and bosons, capable of grouping
themselves on a single wave which then assumes the properties of classical waves.

One cannot overemphasize the importance of the quantum theory of electromagnetic fields in the development of
theoretical physics. It has become the basis of all the more
or less successful explanations of such atomic or nuclear
phenomena as the Lamb-Retherford spectral shift, which
caused so much ink to flow some years ago. But, immersed
in their calculations, theorists far too often ignore the basis
of their theory, despite its capital importance and its many
unsolved problems. When, in due course, we shall be in a

better position to take stock of the novel concepts introduced by contemporary physics, we shall no doubt discover that the complementarity between the number of bosons associated with a single wave and the phase of that wave has an altogether fundamental significance.

TWO

The Lamb-Retherford Experiment and Its Consequences

THE ACCURATE OBSERVATION OF VERY SMALL PHENOMENA HAS often been the basis of great advances in physics. A striking example has once again been provided by the many new ideas which have followed in the wake of the remarkable Lamb-Retherford experiment.

We know that the structure of the hydrogen spectrum, represented as a first approximation by Balmer's empirical formula, can be roughly explained by Bohr's famous atomic theory, which in 1913 enabled its author to rediscover Balmer's law and the numerical value of the so-called Rydberg constant. But in reality the hydrogen spectrum is far more complex than Balmer's formula suggests, since the Balmer lines can be broken down into many closely spaced lines. After Bohr's theory had proved successful, scientists endeavored to interpret the "fine structure" of these lines, which Bohr's theory had left unexplained. Thus, in an important paper in 1916, Sommerfeld introduced the relativistic idea of the variation of mass into Bohr's theory and managed to give a more detailed account of the hydrogen spectrum, which apparently explained its complex nature correctly. Sommerfeld's important contribution was rightly

14

considered a striking victory achieved by the theory of relativity and the quantum theory together.

Nevertheless, a closer study of the problem soon showed that Sommerfeld's theory was not as satisfactory as it had seemed to be. True, it appeared to explain all the observed hydrogen lines, but its classification of the quantized states of the hydrogen atom—that is, the energy levels from which the frequency of the emission lines can be derived in Bohr's theory—was not entirely satisfactory. Furthermore, the study of the optical spectra of elements heavier than hydrogen and of X-ray spectra had shown that the number of lines in these spectra was far greater than Sommerfeld's theory predicted: the theory failed to account for the full complexity of the fine structure and the energy levels which it defines. Thus the theory had to be supplemented by purely empirical considerations, and this was considered intellectually objectionable.

A new phase in the history of spectroscopy began in 1925, when Uhlenbeck and Goudsmit suggested that the electron should no longer be regarded simply as an electric charge but also as a magnet, with a magnetic moment and a related angular momentum, both quantized. This new characteristic of the electron—its *spin*—may be represented roughly (in classical terms) by imagining electrons to be small spheres of electricity rotating on one of their axes. Physicists quickly persuaded themselves that spin was an essential property and that its existence explained many of the previous anomalies. In particular, rough calculations showed that, by introducing spin, quantized levels could be classified more satisfactorily and completely than they could by the Sommerfeld theory, and at the same time, spectral lines which Sommerfeld's theory could not have interpreted could now be taken into account.

In 1929, combining the spin hypothesis with the principles of the new wave mechanics, Dirac developed his magnificent theory of the magnetic electron, one of the most brilliant contributions to contemporary theoretical physics. Applied to the hydrogen atom, Dirac's theory led to the same results as Sommerfeld's, though it went much further and corrected some of the shortcomings. For the past 15 years it has therefore been considered to give a perfect representation of the structure of the hydrogen spectrum.

Moreover, by introducing spin, scientists finally managed to interpret the anomalous Zeeman effect, which had so long eluded their analysis. In 1896 the great Dutch physicist H. A. Lorentz had suggested that a homogeneous magnetic field must produce a splitting of the lines emitted by a source of light, and the phenomenon soon afterward was observed by Zeeman. What Zeeman detected was, however, only the "normal" effect, which is really the exception rather than the rule, for it was by pure chance that Zeeman happened to be working with elements producing it. Although magnetic fields invariably exert an action on spectral lines, the action is generally far more complex than Lorentz suggested. Now these complex processes, the so-called Zeeman effects, eluded all attempts at interpretation by Lorentz' classical electron theory, by quantum theory, and even by wave mechanics, and therefore they were described by empirical laws. It was mainly Landé's introduction of the g factor (which gives the "degree of anomaly" induced by an external magnetic field on the atom for every one of its quantized levels) that led to a better understanding of the anomalous effects. Now the notion of electron spin was an integral part of Landé's solution of this obscure problem. Classical theories had wrongly assumed that all atoms behaved similarly in the presence of a magnetic field. In fact, since all atoms actually contain magnetic properties, they have specific field reactions. By considering the magnetic moment of the electron, which is equal to one Bohr magneton, scientists were enabled not only to explain the origins of the anomalous Zeeman effect but also to justify the empirical laws previously used and to elucidate the form and scope of the "Landé factor." The anomalous Zeeman effect, despite its complexity, seemed at last to have been completely interpreted.

Few scientists could have expected that such phenomena would play a part in atomic questions. Nevertheless it was work on radio frequency that revealed the details of the hydrogen spectrum. During the last 20 years or so, and particularly during World War II (we have only to think of radar), scientists have considerably developed the art of producing and measuring very short electromagnetic waves —down to decimeter and even centimeter waves. These are the so-called very high frequencies, though, judging by criteria of optical physics, they seem to be rather low. Now the hydrogen atom has quantized levels so close to one another that a Bohr transition between them stimulates the emission of a "high-frequency line"—*i.e.*, a line whose wavelength is too long to be studied by optical methods. The wavelength can, however, be measured precisely with recent radio techniques, and a new path has therefore been opened to detailed studies of the structure of the hydrogen levels and lines.

It was experiments of this kind that led Lamb and Retherford (1)* in 1947 to make a remarkable discovery about the hydrogen spectrum. For some considerable time, spectroscopists had been under the impression that even the most perfect theoretical formulas, such as, for instance, Dirac's, did not give a rigorous representation of the fine structure of the hydrogen spectrum. Since, however, the

* References are collected at the end of the chapter.

errors were very small, most scientists were not perturbed. However, measurements at very high radio frequencies enabled Lamb and Retherford to show conclusively that Dirac's formulas, though very much more satisfactory than all previous ones, nevertheless failed to fit the observable facts completely. More recently, Mack and Austern (2) came to similar conclusions about the spectrum of ionized helium.

What a shock to the theorists! They were unable to explain these very small but undeniable discrepancies. The apparent solution was offered by Bethe (3) in a beautiful and strikingly original paper. The question was immediately taken up by a number of scientists, including Tomonaga, Schwinger (4), and Feynman (5). We cannot go into all the many subtle and complicated details involved and shall therefore be content with giving the main conclusions.

The mass of the electron appears in the equations of Dirac's theory and also in the formulas that predict atomic energy levels. Now this mass is taken to be the observed mass of electrons moving in the absence of a field or in very weak fields. If, on the other hand, we suppose with J. J. Thomson that at least part of the mass of electrons is due to their interaction with the surrounding field, we realize that the mass of the electron in a strong field may differ from that in a weak or zero field. In the interior of the atom, close to the nucleus, we find a very strong electric field, and hence we know that the mass of an atomic electron must differ, however slightly, from that of a free electron, and, moreover, it will differ according to the region of the atom in which it is found, and thus depend upon its quantum energy state. For this reason, corrections must be made to allow for variations in the mass of intra-atomic electrons, with consequent small modifications of the Dirac formulas. This correction is precisely what Bethe (and subsequently Schwinger and Feynman) discovered to be the solution.

Nor is that all. As Schwinger was the first to show, the magnetic moment of an electron undergoes small changes as a result of radiation, so that it is no longer quite equal to one Bohr magneton. Thus the Landé g factor in the theory of the anomalous Zeeman effect must be corrected. Radio-frequency investigations of the Zeeman effect enabled Kusch and Foley (6) to demonstrate this phenomenon, while Jacquinot and Brochard (7) obtained similar results with optical measurements. The existence of an addition to the magnetic moment of the electron can also be deduced from the study of the hyperfine structure of hydrogen lines, as was shown by the experiments of Nafe, Nelson, and Rabi (8).

In short, the discovery by Lamb and Retherford, in the hydrogen spectrum, of very small discrepancies from the predictions of the Dirac theory triggered off a chain of important ideas which led not only to explanation of the observed discrepancies but also to predictions and precise demonstrations of similar errors. The study of very-small-scale phenomena has thus amply rewarded scientists for their patience and perseverance by throwing fresh light on the relationship between matter and radiation.

REFERENCES

1. W. E. Lamb and R. C. Retherford, *Physical Review 72* (1947), p. 241.
2. J. E. Mack and N. Austern, *Physical Review 72* (1947), p. 972.
3. H. A. Bethe, *Physical Review 72* (1947), p. 339.
4. J. Schwinger, *Physical Review 72* (1947), p. 339.

5. R. P. Feynman, *Physical Review 74* (1948), pp. 939, 1430.
6. P. Kusch and H. M. Foley, *Physical Review 72* (1947), p. 1256; *73* (1948), p. 412.
7. P. Jacquinot and J. Brochard, paper read to the *Société française de Physique*, November 19, 1948.
8. J. E. Nafe, E. B. Nelson, and I. I. Rabi, *Physical Review 71* (1947), p. 914.

THREE

A New Arrival in Physics: The Nuclear Field

THE FIELD CONCEPT, ONE OF THE MOST MYSTERIOUS IN PHYSICS, has gradually forced itself on the attention of scientists trying to interpret the interactions among different parts of matter. When mechanics was developed in the seventeenth and eighteenth centuries, it was assumed that small material particles (the material points of classical mechanics), of which all bodies were supposed to be constituted, were acted upon by forces attributable either to the interactions among the particles themselves or to the action of bodies external to the system. Force was considered as an "action at a distance," and it was as such that Newton introduced it into the idea of universal gravitation. However, the idea of action at a distance, unaffected by the medium separating the interacting bodies, caused physicists some measure of disquiet, which even Newton and his contemporaries shared. Gradually physicists became convinced that, if a body placed in an empty region of space is acted upon by a force, it is because that region of space is not really structureless but has a power of action of its own.

These new ideas were developed particularly in the nineteenth century, first by Faraday, in what was perhaps

21

a somewhat oversimplified form, and later by Maxwell in his elegant electromagnetic theory, in which the notion of the "field" is defined in precise mathematical terms as the capacity of action at each point and instant. In Maxwell's theory, which is restricted to electric and magnetic phenomena, the field is represented by the sum of two vectors: (1) the electric field, which acts on charges at rest or in motion, and (2) the magnetic field, which acts only on charges in motion—*i.e.*, currents. The propagation of these interactions through space with a finite velocity is accurately expressed in electromagnetic theory by those formulas that give the "retarded potentials"; that is, the state of the electromagnetic field at any point and instant depends not on the actual position and motions of the electric charges but on their position and motion at a prior moment, thus allowing for the time needed to propagate the action from the charge to the point in space under consideration. Thus to Maxwell and his successors the field idea and the concepts of force and potential energy assumed a much more satisfactory form than they had in classical mechanics, with their actions at a distance.

Let us add that light and other radiations, which range from radio waves to X-rays and gamma rays, are regarded in electromagnetic theory as disturbances of the electromagnetic field which are propagated freely in space. Thus all the many types of radiation are lumped together under the general concept of the "field."

Electromagnetic field concepts cannot be applied directly to gravitation; consequently, gravitational forces continued to be looked upon as Newtonian actions at a distance. It was only after the new interpretation given to gravitation by Einstein's generalized theory of relativity that gravitational attraction was introduced into the general field framework and considered as propagating itself through space with a finite velocity.

The new field theory thus contrasted matter, formed ultimately of well-localized elementary particles, with the continuous field covering the empty spaces between these elementary particles. Field and granular matter now symbolized the essential antinomy—continuity vs. discontinuity —in which the material entities were the "sources" of the fields they created around them. However, this clear-cut distinction, so intellectually appealing by its very simplicity, was to be demolished by the findings of the theory of wave mechanics, corroborated by a host of experimental work; this showed that elementary particles and fields alike involve a wave-particle duality. This duality necessarily introduces the concept of quanta, and it can be expressed only in terms of probability. Henceforth, a new kind of continuous field, the ψ wave, must be constantly associated with all particles of matter, whereas the fields of the classical radiation theory must now be associated with particles which, in the case of the electromagnetic field, are called photons and symbolize the discontinuity of energy exchanges between radiation and matter. In future, therefore, there will be a much greater symmetry between matter and radiation, since both involve continuous waves and discontinuous particles.

How, then, can we characterize the difference between fundamental material particles and field particles of the photon type? A first important difference is that material particles cannot appear or disappear except in pairs, whereas field particles, such as photons, can be emitted and absorbed singly. A second difference, of a mathematical kind, is that electromagnetic fields associated with photons are represented by vectors, while the ψ wave of elementary particles (*e.g.*, electrons) must be represented by "spinners." A third difference is explained by the fact that elementary particles are governed by Fermi-Dirac statistics, while photons obey Bose-Einstein statistics. All these contrasts can be summarized by the following fundamental distinction: material corpuscles have a *spin* (internal rotation) which, expressed in the unit $h/2\pi$ (where h is Planck's constant), is equal to $\frac{1}{2}$, whereas the spin of field particles, expressed in the same unit, seems always to be an integer: 1 for the photons associated with electromagnetic waves and 2 for the "gravitons" associated with gravitational fields. On the basis of their spin, we can construct a theory of particles which allows us to coordinate all the facts and to explain the essential differences between particles of matter and "field particles" in the old or restricted sense of the word.

We have therefore been given a highly significant new means of contrasting material corpuscles and their ψ waves with the field, in which particles appear and disappear singly and in which the waves are of the vectorial type.

We now come to the fundamental question: How many types of field can be distinguished? Forty years ago the reply would most probably have been that only two—the gravitational and electromagnetic fields—could account for all the observed phenomena.

These two fields were quite distinct. The gravitational field, represented at each point by a single vector, was closely associated with the existence of the masses from which it apparently emanated. In consequence of the strict proportionality between inert mass and gravitational mass, the movements resulting from its presence were thought to be independent of the nature of the bodies submitted to its action. The electromagnetic field, on the other hand, was represented at each point by two vectors, one of an electric and the other of a magnetic nature. It was bound to the existence of electric charges, and the electrified bodies submitted to it moved differently according to their nature or, more precisely, according to the value e/m, that is, the ratio of their charge to their mass. A great many attempts were made to explain both fields by a single theory.

As for the gravitational field, we know that Einstein's generalized theory of relativity has led to an interpretation which connects the field with the space-time curve induced by the very presence of material bodies, thus providing a remarkable explanation of the previously mysterious fact that inertial and gravitational masses are proportional, and that the trajectories of different bodies placed in the same gravitational field are the same, notwithstanding the difference of their masses. As to the electromagnetic field, which can easily be fitted into the framework of the restricted theory of relativity, no such explanation has been found. In order to construct "unitary" theories of gravitation and electromagnetism, it has therefore been necessary to bring in new ideas—for instance, variation of the standards of length when measuring closed circuits in space-time (Weyl), a fifth dimension (Kaluza), torsion of space (Einstein *et al.*), etc. The very variety of these attempts shows that no single one has been truly satisfactory. Moreover, any acceptable theory of the electromagnetic field must be quantal today and must take account of the existence of photons, particles of spin 1; similarly, the gravitational field, too, probably is quantized in the form of gravitons, which probably have spin 2. In any case, the development of a genuine synthetic theory of the gravitational and electromagnetic fields remains a task for the future.

Meanwhile the scope of "fields" has been widened by the discovery of a new type of field—the nuclear field—the importance of which is as great as that of the two others.

This field acts only at very short distances—up to the order of 10^{-12} centimeter, the order of magnitude of nuclear dimensions—within which it has an essential effect on the internal cohesion of atomic nuclei. But it has no influence once the distances between the interacting particles reach the still microscopic order of magnitude of atomic dimensions (10^{-8} to 10^{-9} centimeter). For this reason it merits the term "nuclear field."

The existence of nuclear fields was brought to light (without its importance being fully appreciated) by Rutherford in 1910, when the great English physicist realized that the deflections of alpha particles in the close vicinity of atomic nuclei could be explained only by a law of interaction differing from the Coulombian law. Nuclei and alpha particles, being positively charged, exert an electrostatic repulsion on one another, and we can use this repulsion to calculate the deflection that must ensue when an alpha particle passes near a nucleus. The calculation is completely confirmed by experimental results when the impact is not too close—that is, if the particle does not approach the nucleus within distances of the nuclear order. If it does, the calculations are proved wrong, which indicates the presence of forces other than Coulombian.

Long after Rutherford's experiments, when, around 1930, nuclei were discovered to consist of protons and neutrons (or, in modern terms, of positively charged and uncharged nucleons), it became evident that there must be an attraction between these constituents—even those not electrically charged. In other words, a proton and a neutron, or even two neutrons, must be mutually attracted, despite the fact that there are no electric interactions between them. Similarly, two protons must experience, along with the Coulombian electrostatic repulsion due to their electric charges, an attraction of another kind, independent of the charge on the particles. Physicists were thus brought back to the idea of the nuclear field in order to explain the stability of atomic nuclei. Moreover, various reasons (which I cannot develop here) bore out the belief that this field acted exclusively at distances of the order of the nuclear dimensions.

But what is the nature of this new field? Must we suppose that, like the electromagnetic field, it is associated with particles, and, if so, what are these particles? The answer was provided by Yukawa in 1935, when he stated his reasons for assuming that the nuclear field was connected with the existence of particles with a mass roughly 200 times greater than that of the electron. The general theory of particles leads to the view that the potential created by a particle around itself must be of the form

$$V = \frac{\epsilon}{r}e^{-k_0 r}$$

where $k_0 = \frac{2\pi}{h}\mu_0 c$,

    h is Planck's constant,

    c is the speed of light in a vacuum, and

    μ_0 is the mass of the particles connected with the field created by the particle.

In the case of an electromagnetic field set up by an electrified particle at rest, ϵ is the electric charge e of the particle, μ_0 is the mass of the photon, which can be taken as zero, and the potential V is reduced to the electrostatic potential in e/r. If the particle sets up a nuclear field around itself, ϵ will be the charge with respect to the nuclear field, and k_0 must be sufficiently large for the exponent to approach zero at a distance of 10^{-12} centimeter from the particle. It follows that the mass of the field particle must be at least 100 times that of the electron. Yukawa therefore took the bold step of proposing the existence of particles of a mass intermediate between that of the electron and that of the proton. A little later he added that these particles, being field particles, probably had the same spin as photons $(h/2\pi)$. The subsequent discovery, in cosmic rays, of particles with a mass roughly 200 times that of the electron brought an unexpected confirmation of Yukawa's daring hypotheses. The name mesons was coined for these particles.

Following in Yukawa's path, other physicists have constructed a complete theory of nuclear fields by considering them as mesic fields. While these theories are extremely interesting, it must be admitted that they still rest on rather weak foundations. The complexity of nuclear physics and the gaps in our knowledge of the properties of mesons are such that the theory of meson fields and the calculations of the interaction between nucleons produced by them are still far from established. The problem has been further complicated by the discovery that mesons are of at least two types with different masses: the mu meson, the one originally isolated in cosmic rays, with a mass about 200 times that of the electron, and the pi meson, more recently identified, with a mass about 275 times that of the electron. Moreover, there are other types of meson, particularly the tau meson, with a mass roughly 1000 times that of the electron. Some uncertainty as to the exact value of the spin of these particles only increases a little the soundness of our interpretation of the nature of the nuclear field. It seems that the mu meson, the first discovered, has a spin of $\frac{1}{2}$, which would mean that it could not play the role of a field particle, for that role calls for a meson of spin 1. Still, the whole subject is subject to revision.

In any case, the nuclear field certainly exists, and there are good theoretical reasons for thinking that it is associated with particles of the meson type. Possibly we may even have to allow for the existence of different kinds of nuclear fields associated with mesons of different mass. Since charged nucleons (protons) set up a Coulombian field in their vicinity, they must have an electromagnetic as well as a meson field (or perhaps even a number of meson fields). The question then arises whether the electromagnetic and the meson fields are to be considered independent of each other or not. A "unitary" theory of these two fields (which must be carefully distinguished from unitary theories covering electromagnetism and gravitation, for gravitation is not involved) has been considered by a number of physicists, particularly by Stueckelberg.

Let us take the case of a proton, and let us suppose, for simplicity, that there exists no more than one type of meson field with constant k_0. If the electromagnetic and the meson fields are independent of each other, the electrostatic field of the proton will be due to the Coulombian potential $V_1 = e/r$, and the meson field to the potential

$$V_2 = \frac{\epsilon}{r} e^{-k_0 r}$$

where e and ϵ are the electric and meson charge, respectively, of the proton. The unitary theory to which we have referred consists in blending the two fields and in assuming that they are due to the potential

$$V = V_1 + V_2 = \frac{e}{r} + \frac{\epsilon}{r} e^{-k_0 r}$$

with the supplementary hypothesis that $\epsilon = -e$.

This relation expresses the fact that the fields are opposed, which allows us to speak of a "subtractive field theory," since a meson field is "subtracted" from the Coulombian field. The moment the distance r from the proton is greater than the nuclear dimensions, the exponential term

$e^{-k_0 r}$ in V becomes negligible, and V is reduced to the Coulombian potential. But at distances of the order of the nuclear dimensions, the meson term makes itself felt and counteracts the Coulombian field, so that, as r approaches zero, V remains finite. The theory becomes more complex if we assume the existence of more than one type of meson field, an essential assumption for explaining the finite mass of neutrons.

I myself think that this fusion of the electromagnetic field with the meson field reflects a physical reality and that it must be carefully considered. In 1949 I tried to show that a unitary conception of the two types of field should help to remove the well-known difficulties of quantum field theories, particularly in respect of the value of the intrinsic energy of electrified particles. The solution of all these problems has only just been attempted, but we can already glimpse its remarkable interpretative possibilities.

In concluding this brief survey of the nuclear field, I should like to stress the danger that always threatens theorists: the temptation to consider our current knowledge as final. Almost instinctively our intellect tends to make apparently complete syntheses based on knowledge which is, and, no doubt, will always remain, fragmentary. Such syntheses are often extremely valuable in guiding scientific research, but we must always be careful not to attribute to them a permanency which they lack. Instances of such "final" interpretations abound in the history of science, and I shall cite a few examples.

The successes of classical mechanics in explaining the motions of stars and of the terrestrial bodies misled nineteenth century physicists into believing that all physical phenomena could be explained in purely mechanical terms. Having served them well for a time, this belief nevertheless had to be discarded when the discovery of, and research into, electromagnetic phenomena showed the important role these phenomena played in nature and made clear that they could not be explained in classical terms. Physicists then tried to reconcile classical notions with the laws of electromagnetism, a reconciliation which was effected by the theory of relativity. After a few notable successes, this synthesis in turn crumbled after the discovery of quanta, which could not have been foreseen by electromagnetic theory. The discovery of the "wave aspect" of material particles (diffraction of electrons, etc.) forced another revision of all previous conceptions.

More recently still, when the structure of the nucleus was first being investigated, the only recognized elementary particles were protons and electrons, which alone were thought to form the nucleus. But the quite unexpected discovery of the neutron in 1931 forced physicists to revise their attitude once again: the nucleus was now thought to be made up of protons and neutrons (nucleons), electrons being created when a nucleon passed from the uncharged state to the positively charged state or vice versa.

Similarly, the appearance of the nuclear field, which plays as important a part in the structure of matter as the electromagnetic and gravitational fields, has seriously upset previous attempts to reduce all fields to only two, the electromagnetic and the gravitational. Nuclear physicists are now attempting a new synthesis of the electromagnetic, nuclear, and (in this domain, less important) gravitational fields.

Thus with every advance in our scientific knowledge new elements come up, often forcing us to recast our entire picture of physical reality. No doubt, theorists would much prefer to perfect and amend their theories rather than be obliged to scrap them continually. But this obligation is the condition and the price of all scientific progress.

FOUR

Particles on
the Atomic Scale

ATOMIC THEORY, AS DALTON RESURRECTED IT FROM ITS ASHES some 150 years ago, tells us that all compound bodies are formed of molecules, which in turn are combinations of simple elementary atoms. It was thought that atoms were the elementary constituents of matter, and that, by combining in various ways, they gave rise to the entire wealth of known material structures, thus fully satisfying man's intellectual quest for the hidden unity behind all manifest phenomena.

Nevertheless this intellectually pleasing picture was not quite so satisfactory as it appeared at first sight. As Lavoisier and his immediate successors well knew, there were many elements, and nearly every year chemists kept discovering new ones. Advances in physics were able to fill the gaps in Mendeleev's classification of the chemical elements, and the discovery of isotopes, of natural and artificial radioactive elements, and of transuranic elements led physicists to acknowledge the existence of hundreds of simple bodies, and consequently of hundreds of different atoms. Had physicists continued to look upon the atom as the elementary particle of nature, they would have been very dis-

appointed indeed as they saw the beautiful simplicity of the
old atomic hypothesis vanish into thin air. In fact, by this
time they had ceased to look upon atoms as the simple
bodies that their name implied. Instead, atoms themselves
were now said to be complexes of more subtle elementary
particles.

From Rutherford's and Bohr's famous results (1910 to
1913), we know that all atoms consist of a central nucleus
which carries a positive electric charge and of negatively
charged electrons revolving around the nucleus. If we desig-
nate the negative charge of the electron by $-e$, an atom
(which is normally electrically neutral) must be made up
of a nucleus with the positive charge Ze (Z being an integral
number) and of Z electrons around it. The integral number
Z is called the atomic number; it ranges from $Z = 1$ for
hydrogen, the lightest element, to $Z = 92$ for uranium, the
heaviest. (Actually, it goes higher than 92, when we include
the unstable transuranic elements produced by nuclear
physics.) However, the atomic nucleus is not characterized
solely by its electric charge Ze, for it also has mass. Now
for a given value of charge, that is, the atomic number Z,
the mass of the nucleus can have several distinct values,
because a given chemical element is made up of a number
of isotopes of different mass.

While the nucleus of the hydrogen atom, called the
proton, has appeared to be an indivisible, elementary, particle, the nuclei of the heavier elements seemed from the
beginning to be increasingly complex "compounds" of protons and electrons (in which the number of protons always
exceeds the number of nuclear electrons, since the net charge
of the nucleus is always positive). Simplicity seemed once
again to have been re-established, since all matter, however
complex, appeared to consist of only protons and electrons.
This was a most pleasing intellectual picture, even though

these two constituents were known to lack perfect symmetry. For, though their charges were equal and opposite, the proton had about 1840 times the weight of the electron. Quite inexplicably, positive electricity seemed to be very much more intimately bound up with mass than negative electricity did. Another cloud on the clear horizon was the discovery of the photon, a somewhat ethereal particle found in all radiation. Still, physicists consoled themselves that even with three particles the atomic framework was far from being intellectually dissatisfying.

Then, about 1930, further particles were discovered, and elegance was dealt a severe blow. First there was the neutron, an electrically neutral particle with a mass very close to that of the proton. Then came the positive electron, the positron (whence the negative electron became known as the negatron); this was an unstable particle with the same mass as the negative electron but with an equal though opposite charge. Later still, there was discovered in cosmic rays a particle whose mass fell between those of the electron and the proton—the meson. At present we are familiar with two kinds of mesons, which sometimes are positively charged, sometimes negatively charged, or may exist also in the neutral state: the mu meson, with a mass roughly 210 times the electron's, and the pi meson, with a mass roughly 275 times. But in addition to these, in the last few years a whole host of further mesons and hyperons have been detected—some with greater certainty than others. More intensive research of cosmic rays and the construction of ever more powerful particle accelerators in which transmutation effects can be produced are bringing to light an ever increasing number of mesons, without, however, helping to explain why these masses have certain well-defined values.

To the list of these new particles we shall probably have to add the somewhat enigmatic neutrino. The theoreti-

cal interpretation of the continuous beta radiation of radioactive bodies has led physicists, in their attempts to preserve
the principles of the conservation of energy and momentum,
to postulate the existence of an electrically neutral particle
of extremely small mass (*i.e.*, very much smaller than that
of the electron).

If, in addition to protons, electrons, neutrons, positrons,
several kinds of mesons, neutrinos, and photons, we also
consider gravitons (particles probably associated with the
gravitational field), we see that the list of fundamental
particles has once again grown far too long to provide an
intellectually satisfying picture.

In order to take full stock of this setback (perhaps
temporary) to our intellectual ambitions, let us now see
which of the new particles have a right to be considered
truly fundamental, *i.e.*, which cannot be broken down into
smaller ones.

The electron is one of these, unless a quite unforesee-
able discovery proves the contrary, and the same is true of
the proton. Still there is one qualification we must make:
it seems certain that the neutron, which has equal claim to
the title of fundamental particle, is related to the proton in
such a way that both can be considered as two different
states of one and the same elementary particle. This "two-
faced" particle, called the nucleon, can appear in either
form: the proton changes into a neutron with the emission
of a positron and no appreciable change of mass, and the
converse transition from neutron to proton is accompanied
by the emission of an electron (*i.e.*, negatron). This hypothesis, which seems to fit the known facts extremely well,
allows us to consider that all atomic nuclei consist only of
positive or neutral nucleons, that they do not contain electrons, as was formerly thought, and that the negative and
positive electrons (beta particles) emitted by radioactive

nuclei are created whenever one of the nucleons changes its state.

As for the positive electron, it must be considered the counterpart of the negative electron. This was appreciated in theoretical terms by Dirac, who, by a shrewd interpretation of certain unexpected solutions to his equations, explained the relationship between the two types of electron and predicted the existence of the positron. Recently a young American physicist, Richard P. Feynman, has suggested that the positive electron is a negatron which "reverses the course of time," with most interesting theoretical consequences. Whatever we may think of his theoretical views, it seems certain that the two kinds of electron are so closely related that we may look upon them as a single kind of elementary particle. It would therefore appear that, at least provisionally, the designation of fundamental particle belongs exclusively to electrons (whose two aspects are the positron and the negatron) and to nucleons (whose two aspects are the proton and the neutron).

What of the photon, the several mesons, the neutrino, and the graviton? Must we take it that all these particles, and those yet to be discovered, are one and all fundamental? Our intellectual need to simplify and unify natural phenomena balks before such a plethora of elementary entities. Before proposing the solution to which I have devoted much attention over the past 20 years, I must first say a few words about the notion of spin.

The spin of particles

Modern descriptions of particles, instead of being based on simple and traditional concepts, involve the wave-particle dualism of wave mechanics. It would take us too far afield to give a full account of the theory of wave mechanics here, but it must be stressed that the following discussion would not be possible without it.

One of the greatest achievements of modern microphysics was the introduction of spin into the description of atomic processes. Spin, which is as fundamental a property of particles as charge and mass, may be likened to an internal rotation endowing the particle with an angular momentum. This momentum is quantized; that is, it cannot assume values other than $n(h/4\pi)$, where n is an integer and h is Planck's constant. If $h/2\pi$ is taken as the unit of spin, two categories of particle can be distinguished: those with "half-integral" spin ($\frac{1}{2}, \frac{3}{2}, \frac{5}{2}, \cdots, (2n+1)/2$ times the unit) and those with "integral" spin ($0, 1, 2, \cdots, n$ times the unit). Now experiment has shown that these two categories have very distinct physical properties, notably in respect to their statistical behavior. Particles with half-integral spin are governed by Fermi-Dirac statistics and obey the Pauli exclusion principle, whereas particles with integral spin obey Bose-Einstein statistics.

The study of atomic nuclei has revealed the existence of a simple and important relation between the numerical value of a particle's spin and the number of its constituents. We have seen that nuclei consist entirely of nucleons (protons and neutrons), and from the atomic number and the mass of a nucleus we can deduce the number of its constituent nucleons. If, in addition, we determine the value of its spin (and thus the statistics by which it is governed), we come to the following conclusion: nuclei made up of an odd number of nucleons have half-integral spins and follow Fermi-Dirac statistics, whereas nuclei made up of an even number of nucleons have an integral spin and follow Bose-Einstein statistics.

It also emerges that all the particles which scientists

have been forced to call "fundamental" (*i.e.*, electrons and nucleons) have half-integral spins. If a number of these particles combine into a complex particle, their several spins arrange themselves parallel to one another, in an equal or opposite sense, and the resultant spin of the complex particle is the alegbraic sum of the individual spins. It follows that a complex particle made up of an odd number of constituents with half-integral spin will itself have a half-integral spin, while a particle formed of an even number of constituents with half-integral spin will have an integral spin. We can illustrate this by means of a simple diagram. In a particle containing two constituents with half-integral spin, the constituent spins can line up in one of two ways (the absolute direction or order of the arrows is immaterial):

(*a*)   ↑↑   ↑↓

The total spin in these combinations is 2 and 0, respectively. In a particle containing three constituents of half-integral spin, the constituent spins can also line up in one of two ways:

(*b*)   ↑↑↑   ↑↑↓

The resultant spin here is $3/2$ in the first case and $1/2$ in the second. More generally, particles with an even number of constituents with half-integral spin will have the resultant spin n, $n-1, \cdots, 1, 0$; and particles with an odd number of constituents with half-integral spin will have the resultant spin $n/2$, $n/2 - 1, \cdots, 1/2$. Thus there is a clear relation between the number (odd or even) of constituents of a nucleus and the value (integral or half-integral) of its total spin. If we apply these considerations not only to atomic nuclei but also to particles in general, we arrive at very interesting conclusions which enable us to set up a rational classification of all particles.

Elementary and complex particles

We shall assume that, like the electron and the nucleon, all other elementary particles have spin ½, that is, an internal rotation of $h/4\pi$. Any particle with a spin other than ½ therefore must be a complex particle, with its spin depending only on the number of constituents and on the direction of their individual spins. It must, however, be stressed that complex particles with an odd number of constituents may also have total spin ½ [see (b) in preceding section], so that spin value alone is not a characteristic of "fundamental" particles.

If we grant these very simple hypotheses, we can say of other particles what we have said of nuclei: every complex particle made up of an even number of elementary particles must have an integral spin and obey Bose-Einstein statistics, whereas every complex particle made up of an odd number of elementary particles must have a half-integral spin, be subject to the Pauli exclusion principle, and obey Fermi-Dirac statistics. An important theorem of wave mechanics, the theorem of Ehrenfest and Oppenheimer, provides a solid mathematical basis for all these assumptions.

We are now in a position to reduce the number of truly fundamental particles. Thus photons assuredly have a spin equal to 1 (which is borne out fully by the polarization of light); it is also probable that certain mesons have a spin equal to 1, and gravitons, we have good reason to believe, have a spin equal to 2. These, then, must be complex particles, each of whose several constituents has a spin equal to ½; the latter could be electrons or neutrinos. The idea that photons are made up of two particles of spin equal to ½ was basic to my own attempts (1934) to advance a new theory of light by developing the wave mechanics of the photon (1) and enabled me to formulate general wave equations for particles of spin 1. The same general idea, namely, that all particles of spin other than ½ must be complex, was discovered independently and more recently by the Russian physicist Frenkel (2). The Italian scientist Enrico Fermi tried to apply it more specifically to mesons (3).

If we wish to give precise expression to this hypothesis by means of modern wave mechanics, we encounter difficult mathematical problems. We must, in effect, begin by expressing the complex particle as a collection of two or more elementary constituents, each of spin equal to ½, and each expressed by the Dirac equations. Only then can we set up the equations which, by other methods, have been shown to represent the properties of complex particles correctly. In writing the new equations, the spins of the elementary constituents are transferred to the center of gravity of the complex particle, with due regard being paid to their individual orientations. I first tackled this problem as early as 1935, in a paper to the *Académie des Sciences* (4), but my first attempt, although on the right lines, was inadequate. More recently, encouraged by the work of Frenkel and Fermi, I have returned to the old problem with the able assistance of Mme. Tonnelat. In two papers submitted to the *Académie* and in a number of articles in the *Journal de Physique*, we were able to treat the problem anew and, I fancy, more successfully (5).

In any case, no matter what difficulties are still to be surmounted, I feel certain that the idea of looking upon particles with spin other than ½ as complex particles, formed by the direct combination of elementary corpuscles each with spin of ½, is correct, and that it is bound to lead toward a rational classification of the various sorts of particles and toward decreasing the number of those which must be considered fundamental.

The general theory of particles

But though we may be enabled to classify particles, we are far from having a general and complete theory of them. Such a theory must show first of all how particles can be represented by some sort of singularity—by a singular region in an extended field or in any other suitable way. Attempts in this direction were made even before the discovery of quanta. Thus in Lorentz' electron theory the electron appeared as a small sphere of negative electricity with a finite radius, within which the electricity was distributed in a certain way. But the nature of this distribution was interpreted in a variety of ways by different writers, and there was an even stronger objection to the theory in the fact that the negative constituent parts must repel one another and the electron would have to "explode." Henri Poincaré had shown in 1905 that, in order to ensure the stability of the electron, it was necessary to assume that a pressure of unknown origin counterbalanced the electrostatic "explosive" pressure. Now this counter-pressure, the so-called Poincaré pressure, is not of electromagnetic origin and cannot be fitted into the framework of Lorentz' theory, which therefore fails to provide an accurate image of the electron. On the other hand, if we assume that the electron, far from being an extended distribution of electricity, is an exact particle, we run into another difficulty—its electromagnetic energy, and hence its mass (related to electromagnetic energy by the principle of the inertia of energy), would have an infinite value. This difficulty might have been resolved within the framework of classical physics by the ingenious theory put forward by Max Born, who, by developing certain of Mie's ideas, assumed that for strong fields Maxwell's equations must be replaced by nonlinear expressions. However, by that time (1934), it had become abundantly clear that such classical descriptions of the electron were inadequate and that quantum considerations had to be taken into account.

Now in wave mechanics, at least in its current form, the general theory of particles causes greater difficulties than it ever did before. Based on probability considerations alone, the modern wave-mechanical interpretation is forced to describe particles exclusively by means of a continuous ψ wave, and thus to exclude all localizations of particles, together with all structure involving extension or radius. The modern analytical interpretation is thus forced to assume that, at least as far as its interactions are concerned, the particle behaves as if it were a point, so that we are back with the old paradox, namely that its specific energy and mass must be infinite. Heisenberg, Yukawa, Pauli, *et al.* have put forward a number of hypotheses to overcome this difficulty, and we shall discuss a related solution—that of the theory of the subtractive field—below.

One may wonder if the difficulties are not entirely due to the purely statistical approach of modern wave mechanics, and if a return to the more classical concepts suggested by me in 1927 and recently developed by Bohm and Vigier might not lead back to the older image of particles conceived as singularities or as singular regions in a field (see Part II). However, there are a great many reasons for retaining the purely statistic approach, and until these reasons are fully countered, it would be premature to claim that the older path would lead to a more satisfactory solution. In any case, any general theory of particles will have to resolve the very difficult problems of classifying particles, of explaining why their masses have discrete and distinct values, and why the same is true of their electric charges (which, apparently, have no values other than 0 and $\pm e$). The value of their spin will probably be explained in accordance with our previous discussion, and there is no doubt that no full explanation will be able to ignore the problem of spin, which may well prove *the most essential* property of particles. Moreover, such an explanation will also have to account for the magnetic moment related to the spin, a value which, in the important instances of protons and neutrons, has already led to anomalies.

Since such a general theory, which may well call for yet another change of theoretical front, must still be formulated, I shall conclude this chapter with an account of some personal work connected with what one may call the theory of the subtractive field. One of the chief advantages of this theory is that it establishes a correlation among the constants characterizing the various types of particle by "unifying" the fields considered by current theories. Quite possibly the concepts thus introduced, when suitably extended or modified, may one day take their place within a general theory of particles.

The theory of the subtractive field

We have already shown how particles can be classified according to the numerical value (integral or half-integral) of their spin. At the moment, the only known particles with spin other than $\frac{1}{2}$, apart from atomic nuclei, are particles of integral spin, but these are extremely important. The principal example of these is the photons, which not only constitute visible light, but also the entire range of electromagnetic radiation, from radio waves right up to X-rays and gamma rays. Another, more recently discovered, particle with integral spin is the meson, or rather, certain types of meson. Although the spin of all mesons has not yet been established with absolute certainty, we have good reason to think that at least some of them have integral spins.

Now the theory of particles shows that, in the case of particles with spin 1, the structure of the associated wave is quite different from that of the wave associated with particles, like the electron, of spin $\frac{1}{2}$. In contradistinction to what happens in particles of spin $\frac{1}{2}$, the wave associated with particles of spin 1 is represented by vectors, and it is analogous to Maxwell's electromagnetic wave. This explains why the photon, *i.e.*, the particle associated with electromagnetic waves, must be a particle with spin 1, since the wave associated with it is none other than Maxwell's electromagnetic wave. Now we have good reason for believing that the wave associated with certain mesons must be analogous to an electromagnetic wave, which would agree with our claim that these mesons have spin 1.

Just as the electromagnetic field is associated with photons, a field similar in form but not in nature, namely, a meson field, must be associated with every kind of meson with spin 1. Now it is certain that nuclear cohesion, that is, the stability of the nucleons constituting the nucleus, cannot be due to an electromagnetic field, which does not act on these neutrons. Contemporary physicists therefore assume that nuclear cohesion is ensured by meson fields which act on nevtrons and protons alike. If their assumption is correct, interaction between particles can take place either by means of a photon (electromagnetic) field or by means of a meson field. A study of the interactions of elementary particles in these two types of field is therefore essential.

The analysis of the interaction between a particle and

the electromagnetic field is found in every good textbook. We know that the intensity of this interaction depends on a numerical coefficient characteristic of the particle, called its electric charge, which can be positive or negative. It can even be zero, which would be true in the case of neutrons, since there is no interaction between a neutron and the electromagnetic field. If the charge is assumed to be a point charge, we have seen that the interaction between the particle and the electromagnetic field results in the energy of the particle at rest, and hence its mass (according to the principle of the inertia of energy), having an infinite value, which is inadmissible. With classical concepts, this difficulty is easily avoided—we simply assume, as Lorentz did in his electron theory, that charged particles, instead of being concentrated at a point, occupy an extended region of space. In that way we obtain a finite value for their energy, but, on the other hand, we are forced to introduce a pressure of unknown origin—the Poincaré pressure mentioned earlier— to assure the stability of the particle.

In quantum theories the problem is posed in quite a different way. Indeed, since the interpretations of wave mechanics exclude all structural images of particles, the quantum theory of the electromagnetic field has been forced to postulate implicitly the existence of electric point charges, and hence to re-endow them with infinite energy at rest, and thus with infinite mass. This difficulty has been haunting quantum theory since the thirties, and though the greatest theorists of our time, like Dirac and Heisenberg, have offered various suggestions for overcoming it, it seems that no truly satisfactory solution has been found.

The same problem is met with again in the theory of meson fields. The interaction between a particle and a meson field depends on a characteristic coefficient of the particle, which plays the same role as that of the electric charge in the interaction of a particle and an electromagnetic (photon) field. This coefficient, which may be positive, negative, or even zero, is the meson charge of the particle with respect to the meson field considered. The presence of a meson charge surrounds the particle with a potential, somewhat different from that of the classical Coulombian electrostatic potential. This is called the Yukawa potential after the Japanese physicist who first introduced the idea of meson fields. But here, too, we find that the energy of the particle interacting with the meson field is infinite, since the quantum theory of meson is forced to consider particles as point charges, so that we come back to infinite energies with their inherent difficulties.

To avoid such infinite values of energy various physicists, particularly Stueckelberg, Bopp, Pais, and Feynman (6), have introduced a hypothesis which I shall call the "hypothesis of the subtractive field." In its simplest form, it assumes that every charged particle always interacts with both a photon and a meson field, and that the meson charge of the particle, measuring the intensity of its interaction with the meson field, is equal and opposite to its electric charge measuring the intensity of its interaction with the photon field. In short, the field surrounding a charged particle, instead of reducing to a simple electromagnetic (photon) field, is, in fact, a combination of two opposing fields, a photon field and a meson field.

For a number of years, I have put forward and developed this new idea in a series of papers (7). The crucial point of the new concept is undoubtedly its discarding of the autonomy of the electromagnetic and of various meson fields, at least in respect to the interaction of these fields with particles, and that it considers instead a total field formed by the superposition of electromagnetic and various meson fields of spin 1. Following Podolsky, we can then develop a Lagrangian scheme, which gives in compact form the equations of this total field for any number of meson fields of spin 1 (8). We shall now enumerate some of the consequences that can be derived from this theory.

First, let us return to the simple case of a charged particle, which we shall assume to be an electron, interacting with an electromagnetic and a single meson field. This means that should there be more than one meson field corresponding to mesons of spin 1 with different masses, all the meson charges of the electron except one are zero. The electric charge of the electron being $-e$, its meson charge must be $+e$. Then the total potential created around the electron is

$$V = - \frac{e}{r} + e\frac{e^{-kr}}{r}$$

where k is the constant of the meson field related to the mass μ of the associated mesons by the relation

$$k = \frac{2\pi}{h}\mu c$$

We can obtain the specific energy of the electron from the energy-momentum tensor of the general Lagrangian scheme. It is simpler to calculate it, by noting that it ought to be expressed by

$$W_0 = \frac{1}{2}\lim_{r \to 0} (-eV) = \frac{ke^2}{2}$$

Since, according to the principle of the inertia of energy, $W = mc^2$, where m is the specific mass of the electron, we find

$$\mu = 2 \frac{hc}{2\pi e^2} m$$

Now $2\pi e^2/hc$ is the well-known fine structure constant, whose reciprocal is very nearly equal to 137; whence

$$\mu = 274m$$

a value very close to that of the pi meson. This is a curious coincidence, and probably no more than that.

Another strange result, shown by Bopp, is the following. We saw that the "explosive" electrostatic pressure of the electron had to be counterbalanced by the Poincaré pressure to assure the electron's stability. Now this counter-pressure is automatically introduced by the theory of the subtractive field. In other words, the centrifugal pressure that the electrostatic field would exert by itself is cancelled by its combining with the meson field. In other words, the failure of classical electron theories to explain the stability of the electron was due to their failure to recognize the role of the meson field. The automatic resolution of the classical difficulty, expressed in the Poincaré counter-pressure, is therefore one of the most fascinating aspects of the theory of the subtractive field.

We might try to apply the same theory to neutral particles like the neutron. For the neutron, whose interaction with the electromagnetic field is zero, to have a finite mass, it would have to interact with two different meson fields, that is, with fields associated with mesons of different mass. Furthermore, the meson charges of the neutral particle would have to be of equal and opposite sign. Once we know the value of these two charges and that of the masses of the two types of meson with which the neutron interacts, we can calculate its mass and thus obtain a finite value. What is interesting about the neutral particles is that their very existence seems to prove the existence of at least two types of meson of spin 1, but of different mass.

Naturally, we could generalize our theory to cover the case of interactions between a particle and more than two meson fields of spin 1, on the legitimate assumption that there exists a great number of mesons of spin 1 but of different mass. Moreover, there is no reason why we should not consider photons as a particular category of meson with specific mass zero, or very nearly zero. We can then state, quite generally, that a given particle interacts with a certain number (n) of meson fields, one of which may be the electromagnetic photon field, in which case the meson charge would correspond to the usual electric charge. This generalization, which I have developed more fully in a recent paper (9), shows that the n masses and n charges of the mesons involved in this interaction must satisfy a number of conditions if the specific energy of the particle is to remain finite. These conditions increase with n, and are expressed quite generally by

$$\sum_{1}^{n} \epsilon_i \mu_i^{2(p-2)} = 0 \qquad 2 \leq p \leq n$$

where μ is the mass of the meson of type i. For $n = 2$, we have only $\epsilon_1 + \epsilon_2 = 0$, which we have already met. For $n = 3$, we have the two relations $\sum_{1}^{3} \epsilon_i = 0$, $\sum_{1}^{3} \epsilon_i \mu_i^2 = 0$. For $n = 4$, we have $\sum_{1}^{4} \epsilon_i = 0$, $\sum_{1}^{4} \epsilon_i \mu_i^2 = 0$, $\sum_{1}^{4} \epsilon_i \mu_i^4 = 0$, etc. The condition that the sum of the meson charges be zero is therefore quite generally satisfied, but further relations are added for $n > 2$. For any n, we have $n - 1$ relations between the n meson charges and masses. We can therefore say that of the $2n$ constants of charge and mass, there are $n + 1$ which can take any values whatever, and that the others can be obtained from them by the above relations. *

Only if we could compile an accurate list of the masses of neutral mesons of spin 1, and only if we could evaluate the interaction coefficients of particles like the electron or neu-

---

* Mesons of spin 1 are in principle neutral mesons. The meson charges which we have been discussing are the interaction coefficients of a particle and a meson field, and not the electric charges of the mesons.

tron and the corresponding meson fields, could we verify the above relations. But although our knowledge of mesons is growing rapidly, it is still too inadequate to permit putting the theory to that test.

I have said enough to show the attractiveness of the subtractive field theory, particularly as it affects the relations between the masses of various particles. Still, even if, by assuming that all particles of spin other than $\frac{1}{2}$ are complex, we can establish a reasonable classification and thus reduce the number of fundamental particles, and even if the theory of the subtractive field, possibly in a modified and extended form, opens up new horizons and enables us to verify the relations between the constants ascribed to the various particles, a complete theory of particles has not yet been offered, and remains one of the most urgent and most difficult tasks of physics. If, in the performance of this important task, we should once again be forced to revise all our present notions, we dare not shirk this danger, for it is only a general theory of particles which would enable us to plumb the secret of the atomic structure of matter and of radiation, and to understand the causes of the discontinuous values of the parameters which characterize their elementary units.

REFERENCES

1. Louis de Broglie, "Une nouvelle théorie de la Lumière." *Actualités scientifiques 181*, Hermann, Paris, 1934.
———, "Nouvelles recherches sur la théorie de la Lumière." *Actualités scientifiques 411*, Hermann, Paris, 1936.
———, *Une nouvelle théorie de la Lumière: la Mécanique ondulatoire du Photon*, Hermann, Paris (2 vols.) 1940-1942.

———, *Théorie generale des particules à spin,* Gauthier-Villars, Paris, 1943.

2. J. Frenkel, *Journal de Physique de l'U.R.S.S. 9* (1945), p. 1943.

3. E. Fermi and C. N. Yang, *Physical Review 76* (1949), p. 1739.

4. Louis de Broglie, *Comptes rendus 200* (1935), p. 361.

5. Louis de Broglie and M. A. Tonnelat, *Comptes rendus 230* (1950), p. 1329.

   Louis de Broglie, *Comptes rendus 230* (1950), p. 1434.

   M. A. Tonnelat, *Journal de Physique 12* (1951), p. 509.

   ———, *Journal de Physique 12* (1951), p. 516.

6. E. G. G. Stueckelberg, *Nature 144* (1939), p. 118.

   ———, *Helvetia Physica Acta 14* (1941), p. 51

   F. Bopp, *Annalen der Physik 36* (1940), p. 345; *42* (1943), p. 575.

   A. Pais, *Verhandelingen der Nederlandschen Akademie,* Part I, Section 19, Amsterdam, 1947.

   R. P. Feynman, *Physical Review 74* (1948), p. 939.

7. Louis de Broglie, *Comptes rendus 229* (1949), pp. 157, 269, 401.

   ———, *Portugaliae Mathematica 8* (1949), p. 37.

   ———, *Journal de Physique 11* (1950), p. 481.

8. Louis de Broglie, *Comptes rendus 232* (1951), p. 1269.

   ———, *Comptes rendus 234* (1952), p. 20 [cf. also Daykin, *Canadian Journal of Physics 19* (1951), p. 459].

9. Louis de Broglie, *Comptes rendus 234* (1952), p. 1505.

FIVE

The Philosophical Meaning and Practical Consequences of Cybernetics

THERE HAS BEEN MUCH TALK OF A NEW BRANCH OF SCIENCE called cybernetics, founded by the American mathematician Norbert Wiener. Cybernetics has become most fashionable, not least because its novel concepts bridge hitherto separate fields: chemistry, physics, physiology, psychology, and possibly even sociology. Its scope is therefore such that the *Conservatoire des Arts et Métiers*, anxious to play its traditional role of keeping the public in touch with scientific developments, has felt the need of devoting a number of lectures to this new subject, bestowing on me the great honor of opening the discussion with a general survey of cybernetics.

It is none too easy to give a precise definition of cybernetics. Its name, first used by Ampère in his classification of the sciences, is derived from the Greek *kybernos*, from which, in turn, our own *governor* was derived, and therefore it may be called the science of control. We might equally well call it the science of trigger effects, that is, of small-scale actions involving negligible quantities of energies but unleashing appreciably larger phenomena. A good example is the governor of a steam engine, which, though small in size, assures the even speed of a colossal machine. Or, if we take an example from quite a different field, we might consider a telegram instructing the commander of a large army to start a major offensive on which the outcome of an entire war might depend. I have deliberately chosen two such dissimilar examples, the better to illustrate the variety of phenomena covered by cybernetics. For while most of the individual branches of science with which it deals were studied separately long before cybernetics was first expounded, cybernetics has revealed the subtle connections between them all.

No wonder, then, that cybernetics has stressed the fundamental role of "information," which scientists had previously chosen to ignore. The "trigger effects" studied by cybernetics are, in fact, always set off by the arrival of information from other parts of the system, or else from the outside. For instance, the governor of a steam engine, whose flyballs are deflected too much when the speed of the engine increases above normal, uses up a minimum of energy to "inform" the steam inlet, which thereupon contracts until normal speed is re-established. Similarly, when outposts or scouts inform their commander by field telegraph or telephone that one of the enemy sectors is undefended, the commander may launch a violent attack in this sector in order to breach the enemy lines.

One of the main branches of cybernetics is therefore concerned with the theory of information and communication—that is, with the scientific study of the means of transmitting information by mechanical, acoustical, optical, electrical, radio-electrical, and other means. Telecommunication, with all it involves—namely the analysis and development of control devices, of servomechanical procedures, electronic circuits, etc.—is thus a special case considered by cybernetics.

Cybernetics also covers the development of calculating machines. More than three centuries ago Blaise Pascal, then scarcely more than an adolescent, invented the first arithmetical machine in order to help his father, whose duties as Commissioner of Normandy entailed laborious calculations in the imposition of taxes. It is not, however, because the assessment of taxes is infinitely more complicated today than it was in 1640, that calculating machines have become so important in our day and age. The reason for these developments must rather be sought in scientific and technical advances involving ever more accurate solutions to ever more complicated problems. Using all the resources of precision engineering and of modern electronics, designers of calculating machines are today producing veritable marvels of ingenuity. While some of these machines code all their information into a set of 1's and 0's (digital computers) and must therefore be considered the direct descendants of the seventeenth century arithmetic predecessor, others, the so-called analog computers, are of an entirely new type. Drawing on the knowledge that all physical phenomena can be described by algebraic, differential, and integral equations, these analog computers solve the equations by assuming certain initial or limiting conditions to hold for the physical quantities under investigation. Though less accurate than digital machines, analog computers have the advantage of speed and lower cost. In any case, analog and digital computers alike can now carry out a host of difficult calculations much more surely and, above all, much more rapidly than the human brain can hope to do. The brain is therefore outstripped by the product of its own invention.

The theory of calculating machines, that is, the theory of the transmission of signals, and more generally all the aspects of communication covered by modern cybernetics, might be expected to throw a great deal of light on the normal and pathological nervous processes, and in particular on reflexes. Some scientists, like Couffignal in France, have shown how cybernetics can help us to understand the nature of logical thought, and Wiener has stressed that even social phenomena can be better interpreted by means of his new technique.

In this way the scope of cybernetics seems to be vast, though some of the expectations placed in it seem to be a little exaggerated. In order to gauge its true significance, we shall first examine the actual achievements of cybernetics, and then try to define its possible scope and limits.

One aspect of cybernetics is the mathematical study of telecommunication, based on the propagation and distortion of "signals" (a term with a precise connotation). Recent mathematical developments have significantly introduced quantum considerations into cybernetics (cf. particularly the contributions by Gabor and Ville), representing signals by a complex function somewhat similar to the complex wave functions of wave mechanics. In this function, the important inequality

$$\delta v \cdot \delta t \geq 1$$

expresses the fact that, the shorter the duration of the signal, the greater the number of its Fourier components, and inversely. Here, many theorists have seen an analogy with Heisenberg's fourth uncertainty relation. We shall discuss the relevance of these analogies more fully below, and, for the moment, note that they have given a great impetus to recent developments of the theory of information.

Since the production, transmission, and reception of signals are subject to a variety of accidents, probability counts have become an indispensable adjunct of cybernetics. Some very important and very interesting work on this subject has been pursued. I draw attention only to the work of the young French scientist André Blanc-Lapierre. The concept of "correlation" which plays so important a role in probability theory has been applied to cybernetics with great success, and, in particular, the elegant theory of self-regulation, which was developed a few years ago, has proved most fruitful in communication problems. Some of the results were anticipated some twenty years ago by the late Bernamont in the course of his original work on fluctuating currents. The theory of self-regulation has a direct bearing on, among other things, the behavior of signals.

In the course of their studies of the theory of information and related problems, a number of scientists, particularly Wiener and Shannon, coined the related terms "quantity of information" and "speed of information," and showed that information as defined by them played a role in their theory of information similar to the role of entropy in thermodynamics. The unexpected discovery of this similarity has rightly aroused the keen interest of physicists, since, of all the novel contributions of cybernetics, this is certainly one of the most striking.

Although this is not the place to give a full mathematical account of this aspect of cybernetics, I should nevertheless like to discuss the analogy between entropy and information at greater length. We know that in the current statistical interpretation of thermodynamics, the entropy of a system is directly related (by Boltzmann's formula: $S = k \log P$) to the probability of the system being in a given state. The second principle of therodynamics, the Carnot-Clausius principle, which expresses the fact that, if any physical system is allowed to distribute its energy in its own way, its entropy will increase, is thus given a simple and almost intuitive interpretation—every system tends toward the most probable state. True, this statistical interpretation of entropy is not devoid of serious problems. More than once, scientists (this is the paradox of Loschmidt) have objected that the original attempts of statistical mechanics to derive an irreversible principle like that of Carnot from the reversible laws of classical physics is quite illogical. But quantum mechanics holds out some promise of solving the paradox, and it seems certain that the irreversibility of time, an essential point of human experience, is always associated with an increase in entropy. In any case, whatever the final conclusions of heated discussions about the irreversibility of natural phenomena involving a privileged sense of time, it is quite certain that the statistical interpretation of entropy has enabled us to fathom the real meaning of the second law of thermodynamics.

Let us take a simple case of signal transmission such as sending a telegram in Morse code along a conducting wire. Now, a series of intelligible symbols traveling along this wire is highly improbable *a priori*. Since Morse signals consist of either dots or dashes each with the probability $\frac{1}{2}$, the most probable sequence of signals would be that in which the signals travel at random, much like a message sent by a demented operator hitting the keys just anyhow, and ignorant of the significance of the dots and dashes. Hence a meaningful message is an improbable phenomenon, due only to the intervention of a rational operator and the correct use of language. Obviously then, there must be some inverse relationship between the information transmitted by means of signals and the probability of these signals being received as a meaningful sequence in time; the information is greater, the smaller the probability and consequently the entropy of that sequence of signals. Adopting Léon Brillouin's concept of "neg-entropy" (negative entropy), we may say that neg-entropy diminishes as the probability of a sequence of meaningful signals increases, *i.e.*, that the quantity of information is a sort of neg-entropy. This conclusion is borne out by a consideration of the possible distortions of signals during their transmission as a result of accidental disturbances and of other disturbances dictated by physical factors, or, occasionally, by the difficulties of transcribing the message correctly at the receiving or sending end. The final message is not usually identical with the message sent out, and generally contains a number of errors decreasing the quantity of information. Clearly, that quantity can never be *increased* in this way. If I wire you the complicated proof of a mathematical theorem, it may happen that an error of transmission, by changing essential points of my argument, will prevent you from understanding or from reconstructing my proof, but if I were to wire you the reason why I am not coming to prove the theorem, there is never any chance that errors of transmission will provide you with the required proof. This is just one illustration of the fact that the quantity of information has a tendency to decrease, just like the neg-entropy of thermodynamics. The most favorable case, corresponding to reversible transformation of an isolated system in thermodynamics, is that in which there is a conservation of neg-entropy. This case has been expressed quantitatively by Shannon *et al.*, who were able to show that information can be expressed by a formula of the type

$$\sum_i p_i \log p_2,$$

where p_i gives the probability of a given succession of signals. Apart from its sign, this formula is identical with Boltzmann's well-known H function, which enabled him to express entropy in statistical terms. Hence there is an extremely suggestive mathematical analogy between information and neg-entropy.

Comparisons between entropy and information have drawn the attention of physicists to an old bugbear: Maxwell's demon, which like Ampère's *bonhomme,* might be called a skeleton in the cupboard of theoretical physics. Maxwell imagined an enclosure kept at a fixed temperature, divided into two compartments by means of a partition with a tiny hole. Once the enclosure is filled with gas, the molecules of the gas will be able to pass from one compartment to the other through the hole in the partition until the gas had reached a state of thermodynamic equilibrium, *i.e.,* until both compartments are at the same pressure and temperature. Now Maxwell introduced a molecular being endowed with intelligence, who would keep watch over the tiny hole, opening and closing it at will, and with a minimum of energy. In this way, if it chose, it could allow the most rapid molecules to pass from the left into the right compartment, and the slowest molecules to pass from right to left. After a while, it would therefore have filled the right compartment with rapid molecules, and the left compartment with slow molecules; and if, as a result of collision, the two categories of molecules would have reached their several states of thermal equilibrium separately, the right compartment would be filled with a hotter gas than the left one. In other words, in defiance of the second law of thermodynamics, a system in thermal equilibrium would have been transformed into one in thermal disequilibrium—and with a negligible expenditure of energy! Moreover, there is no reason why Maxwell's demon should not allow any molecules to pass from the left to the right compartment, merely preventing all passages in the opposite direction. After some time, all the gas would then be concentrated in the right compartment, retaining its original temperature, while the left compartment would have become completely evacuated. In this case, the entropy of the gas would have decreased spontaneously—

another result that is contrary to the Carnot principle. Thus Maxwell's obstreperous little demon has managed what we, poor mortals, can never hope to do—it has dethroned the sacrosanct laws of thermodynamics. It could do that precisely because it was molecular and could act on individual molecules while our cruder methods absolutely exclude that possibility—we can only affect vast aggregates of molecules over what, in molecular terms, are vast time intervals.

It has long been held that Maxwell's demon is a serious challenge to the laws of thermodynamics. But is that claim strictly correct? Before setting to work, the demon must be plunged into a medium in thermal equilibrium, one having isotropic black radiation; under such conditions the demon would be quite blind, and unable to distinguish between individual molecules. Moreover, our molecular demon would itself be subject to molecular agitation and be unable to perform its task of "umpire" without being attacked by the two sides. The problem is, therefore, much more subtle than Maxwell would have had us believe, and requires further analysis. Several writers have undertaken this analysis, notably Léon Brillouin, who is continuing the valuable work on statistical thermodynamics begun by Szilard around 1930.

In order to discriminate between molecules, the demon, even supposing that Brownian movement does not prevent it from doing its work, would have to carry a torch, which, according to Brillouin, would have to be at a higher temperature than that of the gas, and hence would upset the thermal equilibrium. By means of this torch, our demon would then be able to scrutinize the approaching molecules and to estimate their velocity. It would therefore be receiving essential information and this is where cybernetics comes in, for analysis has shown that this information can be gained only at the expense of the external medium's neg-entropy—Maxwell's demon, just like the physicist in his laboratory, cannot acquire information except by borrowing neg-entropy from the external medium—another confirmation of our contention that information is merely one form of neg-entropy. Once it has gained the required information, the demon will be able to manipulate the shutter so as to increase the neg-entropy of the moving gas, but in the end this increase of neg-entropy has to be made good with a decrease of the entropy of the external medium, in such a way that there will have been no increase in total neg-entropy. By calling the act of manipulating the shutter a "decision," we may say that the process runs through the following cycle: neg-entropy → observation → information → decision → neg-entropy, observation transforming neg-entropy into information, and the decision changing the information back into neg-entropy. In other words, the neg-entropy has merely changed its form and not its quantity during the cycle.

I have dwelt on the question of Maxwell's demon at such length because it is a good illustration of the analogy between information and neg-entropy, and because it shows to what extent cybernetics can throw new light on even very old problems.

The theories of servomechanism, and of radio-electrical reaction phenomena, may also be considered as branches of cybernetics, for, although they can perfectly well be developed quite independently, cybernetics has a great contribution to make to them.

Again, cybernetics has been very successful in physiology, and particularly in the physiology of the nervous system. Norbert Wiener, although first and foremost a mathematician, has done a great deal of work in this field also, and has applied for a research fellowship at the National Institute of Cardiology in Mexico. The reader will forgive me for neglecting this aspect of cybernetics—it falls outside my province.

All I can say is that the neurons of the central nervous system are known to receive "information" from the surroundings, and that this information is transmitted from the peripheral receptors by means of nervous impulses. The nerve centers of the brain or of the spinal cord can react to this information by sending voluntary or reflex impulses back to the periphery where they are translated into actions. Conditioned reflexes, so brilliantly studied by Pavlov, evidently enter into this general process. Certain organic dysfunctions, such as ataxia, by impairing the nerve paths cause a disturbance similar to a failure of signal transmission, thus showing clearly the important role which cybernetics may play in physiological studies of the nervous system.

In a closely allied field, there has recently been a great deal of discussion about the similarity between the workings of calculating machines and the human brain. Modern calculating machines not only calculate but also solve difficult analytical problems. We have seen that they work with much greater certainty and rapidity than our brains. Since their operations are associated with logical processes, we might say that these machines are endowed with logical faculties. But we can also endow them with a memory, that is, with the ability to store previous results and to act accordingly. Clearly then, all these "faculties" are very reminiscent of our own thought processes, so much so that it has been suggested that even man's highest intellectual operations can be fully explained by analogies with calculating machines. Later I shall give my reasons why this opinion strikes me as somewhat exaggerated, but there is no doubt that the whole subject offers much scope for reflection.

But cybernetics not only throws new light on the functioning of the nervous system and on the processes of mental

activity, but it also impinges on life as such. Life being a
most complicated series of actions and reactions, the transmission of signals and information and neg-entropy are
bound to play a most important role in it. One might even
ask oneself, though I would not perhaps go so far, whether
living organisms are not simply automatons whose mechanism cybernetics will one day be able to explain fully on the
basis of physical and chemical laws.

How delighted would de Vaucanson have been to see
science returning to his eighteenth century mechanical duck!
Automatons, once the fashion, were relegated to the toy cupboard, only to return to favor centuries later, when the
Spaniard Torres y Quevedo developed his famous chess
player, a robot that could take on any human rival and
beat him, and, moreover, ring a bell whenever the opponent
broke the rules of the game. Far more recently, Gray Walter,
the famous Bristol physiologist, presented an astonished
world with his automatic tortoises whose conditioned reflexes are comparable to those of living animals. For where
animals react to hunger by going in search of food, the tortoises go in search of a source of energy, whenever they are
"run down." Is not the animal *homo sapiens* just another,
though particularly complex, robot? Recent advances in the
construction of automatons might well incline us to give an
affirmative answer to this question, and to offer a purely
mechanical interpretation of vital processes.

Having outlined some of the most interesting notions
and some of the most striking achievements of cybernetics,
I should now like to discuss its explanatory scope more fully.

First, cybernetics in its current form is basically a
branch of classical physics, that is, its concepts and laws
are those of classical mechanics. In other words, it completely disregards quantum theory and wave mechanics, and

is therefore incapable of giving an exact interpretation of any but large-scale phenomena. Hence it has no bearing on phenomena on the atomic scale, which, as we know, form the basis of all physics.

We might add that cybernetics is not quite as original as one might believe. The theories of information, of regulating devices, of servomechanism, etc., were largely developed long before the birth of cybernetics, and may be considered as autonomous branches of science, based directly on classical physics. Thus the chief role of cybernetics has been to unify apparently independent theories into a coherent framework and to show their inner connection. In so doing, cybernetics has undoubtedly opened up fascinating new horizons, but this is a far cry from making such fundamental and radically new contributions as, for instance, those of quantum theory.

I should like to dwell a little on the relationship between quantum theory and cybernetics. The fact that modern cybernetics profits from a complex representation of signals (the analytical signals of Gabor and Ville), and that it employs the inequality $\delta \nu \cdot \delta t \geq 1$, which shows that the Fourier analysis of a signal of duration δt contains spectral components covering an interval of frequency $\delta \nu$ which cannot be smaller than $1/\delta t$, has occasionally been adduced as proof that there is a direct connection between it and quantum physics. This is far from being the case. The use of complex functions, of Fourier series, and of the inequality $\delta \nu \cdot \delta t \geq 1$ has been known to mathematicians outside the context of any particular physical theory. What characterizes quantum physics is not so much the use of these notations as the introduction of the quantum of action h by means of which the geometric and the dynamic aspects of atomic phenomena are fundamentally related in a way quite unexpected by classical physics. Now none of the current theories of cybernetics involves the quantum of action.

However, there is no reason why the quantum of action should not be introduced into cybernetics, and in particular into the theory of information, as an external experimental datum. This is precisely what Gabor has done in his paper to the Cybernetics Congress mentioned earlier. Gabor has rightly insisted that no true theory of information can ignore the physical nature of signals, and of their emission, propagation, and reception. On closer investigation, all these processes prove to be the results of quantum transitions and thus involve the constant h, at least in principle. In this way quantum concepts are automatically introduced into the theory of information and consequently into cybernetics.

A characteristic phenomenon of communications is what physicists have termed "thermal noise." Take the case of an ordinary receiving aerial, which, as it does not emit a current, is in thermal equilibrium with its environment. Thermal agitation of the electrons inside the aerial will lead to an emission of radio-electric energy which will affect radio sets in the neighborhood in the form of thermal noise. As the movement of electrons is quantized, we see that all strict analyses of this phenomenon are bound to introduce the constant h. Gabor has investigated this question in connection with his theory of the elements of information $\delta\nu \cdot \delta t$. Beyond that, he has also investigated the way in which a beam of electrons absorbs part of the energy of an electromagnetic wave in its path, and he could thus show how elementary quantum absorptions give rise to the continuous absorption of classical electromagnetic theory. His conclusions have great relevance to future developments of quantum physics and particularly to the quantum theory of electromagnetic fields. They also show how necessary it is to introduce quanta into certain aspects of cybernetics. It must, however, be remembered that quantum theory is the donor and cybernetics the recipient, and that it would be wrong to expect cybernetics as such to make original contributions to the theory of quanta.

We must also stress that the analogy between information and neg-entropy, instructive and attractive though it is, is full of pitfalls. First of all, the very definition of "quantity of information," which would have to be precise for any similarity with negative entropy to be established, is far from being so. In his paper on the transmission of information to the Cybernetics Congress, Aigrain expressed grave doubts whether "quantity of information" can be defined irrespective of the use to which it is being put—a serious obstacle to any attempts to prove the analogy between information and neg-entropy. Moreover, Léon Brillouin, who recently made a critical study of all these problems, has revealed a further serious difficulty. We know that if thermodynamic transformations occur in an isolated system, the entropy of the system must increase (or, as a limiting case, remain constant for reversible transformations). Hence, its neg-entropy must decrease. We might therefore say that, whenever one body transfers neg-entropy to another, the neg-entropy acquired by the recipient can never be greater than the neg-entropy lost by the donor. This is easily demonstrated. Therefore every acquisition of neg-entropy by one body is necessarily accompanied by a decrease of neg-entropy of another body. In the case of information, the process is not entirely analogous. When a lecturer teaches the laws of physics to his pupils, he gives them information without becoming less knowledgeable himself—he does not forget the laws, the moment he has taught them to others. Similarly, if I send you a telegram announcing the fall of the government, I do not immediately forget what I know about the ministerial crisis.

Clearly then, the analogy between information and neg-entropy is not an unqualified success. Since the analogy seemed to hold for the case of the *transmission* of information by physical techniques, in the course of which the quantity of information is bound to decrease, we might put it that the analogy breaks down the moment living beings are brought into play. However, that would be an over-simplification since it can be shown that calculating machines with a built-in "memory" are quite capable of imparting the results of their calculations, that is, information, without forgetting any part of it. Léon Brillouin has stressed this point as being a crucial challenge to the correctness of the analogy between information and entropy, one of the most striking results of cybernetics. Perhaps this difficulty may be resolved one day, but meanwhile it certainly continues to dog the footsteps of cybernetics.*

We have seen that cybernetics has thrown new light on physiology, particularly on the physiology of the central nervous system. It might therefore be reasonable to expect to throw new light on the nature of human intelligence and reason as well, and possibly on the mystery of life as such. After all, Gray Walter's tortoise is the nearest thing to a living being, and modern calculating machines to functioning brains.

I believe that here, also, we must tread softly. True, calculating machines can arrive at specific results with much greater certainty and rapidity than our own brains can ever hope to do, but this certainty and rapidity are the direct results of their mechanical nature, which precludes any creative faculty. The ability to go beyond acquired data is, in fact, characteristic of human thought, and Léon Brillouin has done well to emphasize that calculating machines, themselves the products of human genius, can never go beyond

* The difficulty has meanwhile been overcome, or so it would appear. See the Postscript at the end of this chapter.

the purpose for which scientists and engineers have constructed them. Moreover, to function smoothly, the machines require maintenance and repair, whereas human beings manage far more effectively to maintain themselves. The machines also lack another essential characteristic of living brains—consciousness of their existence and individuality—and this lack precludes even the most perfect calculating machine from being equated to a real mind. The very term "machines" makes clear that they are products and not producers of intelligence, mere links in the chain of tools which humanity has slowly improved from the primitive stone axe of pre-history to the most refined instruments of modern technology. Machines are inherently incapable of making the kind of creative effort involved in scientific discoveries. To use Léon Brillouin's expression, human intelligence creates "absolute information," and absolute information involves consciousness. Clearly this type of consciousness cannot be attributed to a machine.

The hope of certain cyberneticists that they might one day be able to explain not only all the functions of the nervous system but also man's total intellectual activity by means of the theory of information or its consequences seems to be akin to earlier hopes that all biological phenomena could be explained by the known laws of physics and chemistry. This brings us to the great problem of life, and although this problem falls somewhat outside the chosen field of cybernetics, I should nevertheless like to devote a few remarks to it, if only because recent developments of quantum theory and of cybernetics have led a great many physicists, including Schrödinger, Pierre Auger, and Léon Brillouin, to pay attention to it.

It would seem that all scientists are agreed on one point implicit in Bergson's philosophy—biological phenomena have a tendency to postpone increases in entropy. Now the second principle of thermodynamics states that, as the universe continues, its entropy must inexorably increase, but it tells us nothing about the rate at which this increase occurs. If it were possible (which, in practice, it is not) to halt all irreversible phenomena for some time, the increase in entropy would be halted as well, if only for a brief interval. Now just as certain catalysts, by triggering irreversible reactions, accelerate the normal increase of entropy, there are other, negative, catalysts which slow down normal developments and thus increase neg-entropy. It is characteristic of life that it produces just such negative catalysts. A pessimist has said that life is a struggle whose inevitable outcome is defeat. That sardonic expression contains a profound truth, since, in fact, life is a hopeless struggle to preserve the highly improbable state represented by the living organism from experiencing the inevitable increase of entropy which tends to bring us to the most probable state—the return to that dust whose molecules are no longer combined into an organic structure. And yet life has known how to counteract this inevitable process, by reproducing itself, thus keeping entropy at bay. Thus life with its faculties of assimilation, spontaneous repair, and reproduction, and, in its highest form, of conscious intelligence and reason, is an altogether extraordinary phenomenon.

This remarkable property of life has recently been the subject of a fascinating book by an eminent physicist. In his *What Is Life?* Erwin Schrödinger puts forward the idea that only the existence of quanta can explain the continued existence of living beings. We know that if the classical picture were exact, matter itself would have to be unstable— only the existence of quantum discontinuities can explain the stability of atomic and molecular structures, and hence the stability of inert matter. But living matter is another striking example of stability, the stability of living organisms during their entire existence, involving the stability of the cells and cellular organizations of which they are made up, and, moreover, the stability of species over millenia, and hence the remarkable stability of the genetic cells which retain their character for millions of successive generations. As in the case of inert matter, this stability is assured by quantum discontinuities. Like atoms, cells and genes remain stable only because they are subject to sudden and finite transitions and not to the continuous variations postulated by classical physics, and because these sudden transitions alone enable them to make good possible damages or dislocations. The discovery of sudden mutations, mainly by De Vries, and the consequences that this discovery has had on biological concepts, are surely additional corroboration of the fact that cells, just like the atoms and molecules of inert matter, cannot be changed except by sudden jumps, i.e., by quantum transitions.

These brief remarks on Schrödinger's contribution should suffice to stress the great relevance of quantum concepts to biological phenomena. Even supposing that a quantum biology of the future would be able to solve all the secrets of life, cybernetics, which is not, in fact, based on quantum theory, will have little share in the credit.

Schrödinger has very good reason to suppose that biological phenomena can be explained only by introducing quantum concepts, but Léon Brillouin, for one, doubts Schrödinger's assumption that life can be *fully* explained in that way. According to Brillouin's view, which, by the way, I fully share, it is a recurring and dangerous illusion to believe that the science of a given age is complete, and can explain every possible phenomenon. Lagrange is said to have complained 150 years ago that, since Newton's cosmology was so perfect, no new discoveries could ever be made. We know how greatly mistaken he must have been, and that, had he lived to see the spectacle of modern astronomy and physics, he would have been sorry for his rash conclusions. But we are always in danger of committing the same error of believing that, while our predecessors knew nothing, we ourselves know everything. There is no doubt that our present picture will change again tomorrow, and undeceive us about our present assumption. I agree with Léon Brillouin that, if ever we manage to understand the true nature of life, it will be only on the basis of entirely new knowledge about the laws of nature and, doubtless, of new points of view and mental processes that are still beyond our present intelligence. Who knows but that these laws of biology—and Léon Brillouin seems to suggest just that—might not one day strike us as the most general natural laws, of which the laws of physics and chemistry are no more than particular instances!

While not wishing to become too speculative on these issues, I think we are on safe ground when we affirm that it is not cybernetics that will give us the master key to biological phenomena.

As for the economic and social applications of cybernetics, which may well become very important one day, they are only so many suggestions today. Moreover, what Wiener has to say about them strikes me as rather vague.

And now I should like to give a quick summary of my conclusions.

Cybernetics has given us all much valuable food for thought. It has provided us with new methods and original points of view, which in itself is laudable enough. Though it has not created new scientific disciplines—all the individual topics treated by it were known before and could easily have developed without its assistance—by combining them it has been able to verify their mutual validity. Since certain of the branches of science which it covers, for example the theory of information, are of great technical importance, cybernetics is not only a remarkable product of the human mind but it can also initiate advances of great practical scope.

The most important and most striking idea suggested by cybernetics is unquestionably its emphasis on the similarity between information and entropy, an idea which has clarified many previously obscure problems, like that of Maxwell's demon. Though its fruitful contribution to scientific thought still meets with many objections, it seems probable to me that cybernetics, possibly in a suitably modified form, will eventually assume its rightful place in our scientific heritage, and that it will continue as a spur to many branches of science.

But we have no right to expect more of cybernetics than it offers. To my mind, it holds out no hope of supplying, in the foreseeable future, the solution of the triple mystery of life, consciousness, and thought.

Postscript

Since the above chapter was written, the objections to the analogy between information and neg-entropy (see p. 66) seem to have been completely overcome by the postulate that the *sum* of information and neg-entropy can never increase. If the information shared among a group of people and the neg-entropy of the enviroment have the original values I_1 and N_1 and the final values I_2 and N_2 respectively, we have

$$I_1 + N_1 \geq I_2 + N_2$$

In a series of beautiful analyses Brillouin has been able to demonstrate (1) that human beings can only transmit a given quantity of information by borrowing from the environment a quantity of neg-entropy at least equal to the quantity of information transmitted. This is in accordance with the above inequality.

Let us now re-examine the case of our lecturer. Though the total information has been increased—the pupils have acquired new knowledge while the lecturer has lost none—it follows from Brillouin's argument that, in order to impart knowledge to his pupils, the lecturer must have borrowed a quantity of neg-entropy, at least equal to the final increase of information, from his environment. The problem is thus solved, and information appears to be only a specific form of neg-entropy. This conclusion, moreover, agrees with our interpretation of the action of Maxwell's demon.

REFERENCE

1. Léon Brillouin, *Journal of Applied Physics 24*, pp. 1152–1163; *25*, pp. 595–599, 887–893.

SIX

Crystal Structure and the Study of Radiation

I FEEL SOME NATURAL EMBARRASSMENT IN ADDRESSING A BODY of crystallographers [the Congress of Mineralogy, Paris, 1954], since I myself am rather unfamiliar with this branch of physics. I hope I shall therefore be forgiven if I restrict my remarks to only one aspect of crystallography: the use of crystals in demonstrating the nature of radiation and in measuring wavelengths.

The first experimental indication of the effect of crystals on the propagation of luminous waves and hence of the scientific significance of their essential symmetry was probably the discovery by the Danish physicist Bartholin of double refraction in Iceland spar (calcite) in 1669. At that time, however, nothing was known about the real structure of crystals, and though Huyghens soon afterwards related double refraction to his undulatory theory of light, the influence of crystals on the propagation of radiation for a long time was neglected by the scientific world.

By the nineteenth century, however, many new facts had come to light. The work of Romé de L'Isle, of De Haüy, of de Bravais, and others had led to a classification of crystals into systems according to their essential symmetry,

74

and hence to an understanding of their structure. Moreover, Thomas Young's work on interference persuaded Fresnel to repeat experiments on diffraction with crystals, whence he was able to show that the results could be explained only on the basis of the undulatory theory. Some years earlier, in 1807, Malus had first described the polarization of light and Arago has made this phenomenon the subject of further study. Fresnel, after first interpreting polarization by assuming that all light waves are transverse vibrations, then adopted Huyghens' theory of double refraction and developed the complete theory of the propagation of light waves in crystalline media as we know it today. With its subsequent developments, notably the remarkable introduction of conical refraction by Hamilton, the discovery of rotatory polarization (which is accompanied by the magnificent spectacle of chromatic polarization), Fresnel's crystalline optics, which must be considered one of the most remarkable branches of classical physics, has given a host of striking demonstrations of the influence of the internal structure of crystals and their elements of symmetry on the propagation of light. Crystalline optics was the basis of the profound observations by Pasteur and Pierre Curie on the importance of symmetry in physics and even in biology.

But although the effects of symmetry, particularly in crystalline media, on radiation had been clearly demonstrated, none of the earlier theories introduced the effects of the regular and reticular arrangements of the crystalline nuclei explicitly. It was only as a result of Max von Laue's great discovery of the diffraction of X-rays and its subsequent developments by a number of physicists, particularly Sir W. H. Bragg and his son W. L. Bragg, that the close relationship between the structure of crystals and the undulatory nature of the radiation which they diffracted could be fully demonstrated. There is no need to recall the theoretical interpretation of X-ray diffraction by crystals by the classical Laue-Bragg formula, and its many aspects and subsequent developments. The essential point is to note that it expresses a close relation between the regular arrangements in three-dimensional space of the material centers that do the scattering and the various spectral elements of the radiation, when the wavelengths involved are of the same order of magnitude as the lattice spacings of the crystals.

This formula, which has a close mathematical relationship to the Fourier series, can be employed in one of two ways depending on whether we apply it to the spectroscopic study of X-rays or to the study of crystalline structures. In the first case, we take the lattice spacings and the essential symmetry of the crystals as given, and arrive at a very exact estimate of the wavelength of the scattered radiation; in this way we can determine the wavelengths of X-rays, and a host of other spectral phenomena, such as the width of spectral bands, while simultaneously confirming the undulatory nature of X-rays and the Laue-Bragg theory, which, of course, requires no further confirmation today. In the second case, we send X-rays of known wavelengths into the crystals whose structure we wish to investigate and establish that structure accordingly. There is no need to insist on the great and essential services which this method is rendering to mineralogy and to other scientific or technical disciplines like metallography or the study of surface states.

I shall neglect the second application of the Laue-Bragg formula since, no doubt, it will be the subject of a great many papers and discussions during the present congress, and shall dwell rather on the contribution to science of the first application. Undulatory considerations alone show that material structures with periodic arrangements and with spatial planes of the order of the wavelengths of a given radiation should enable us to measure these wavelengths and at the same time to demonstrate the undulatory nature of the radiation. The construction of suitable periodic obstacles in the path of waves is a simple matter when it comes to fairly long wavelengths, such as those of the waves studied in mechanics, hydrodynamics, and acoustics. The problem becomes far more delicate when we are dealing with wave phenomena like light waves, whose wavelengths are of the order of a fraction of a millimeter. To demonstrate the undulatory character of this radiation by interposing a regular structure, we must construct such instruments as optical gratings, in which a series of very fine slits are ruled at intervals of the order of a hundredth of a millimeter or even less. Such gratings could not have been constructed before the nineteenth century, for it was only then that techniques of mechanical ruling became accurate enough. However, mechanical procedures, no matter how perfect, can never enable us to rule solids with slits fine enough to demonstrate the undulatory nature of X-rays and gamma rays, whose wavelengths are of the order of 1 angstrom and even less. Here, only nature herself can provide us with fine enough structures for analyzing this radiation, and it is von Laue and his successors' great merit and lasting contribution to physics that they recognized the suitability of crystals for this purpose in 1912. Their studies led to our present knowledge of the nature of crystals and they themselves felt convinced that they had provided high-frequency physics with the indispensable key to future discoveries. This is one of the main reasons why, quite apart from its great contributions to the study of symmetry in nature, crystallography merits the gratitude of all physicists.

Just like the discovery of X-ray diffraction by crystals in 1912, the discovery of electron diffraction by crystals in

1927 marked a milestone in the history of science. The latter discovery was a direct consequence of the former, since it was only the prior demonstration of the regular structure of crystals which enabled physicists to show that electrons have associated waves. Measurements of their wavelengths by means of the Laue-Bragg theory then gave the experimental proof of the accuracy of the basic concepts of wave mechanics. Since the corpuscular aspect of the electron had been demonstrated long before, the diffraction of electrons by crystals brought physicists face to face with the problem of wave-particle dualism, a problem that has not been resolved to this day, unless the rather imprecise notion of complementarity is considered to be its solution. In fact, the wave-particle dualism was already implicit, though unrecognized, in the discovery of wave interference and diffraction in X-rays and gamma rays, where quantum considerations had led to the introduction of the photon. But while the photon's lack of charge and insignificant mass hide its existence (except during its actual emission or absorption), electrons (like other particles) reveal themselves far more concretely and less fleetingly, and therefore emphasize the wave-particle dilemma particularly clearly.

Once the concepts and formulas of wave mechanics had proved their validity in interpreting the waves associated with electrons, it was easy to attribute a precisely determined wavelength to a homogeneous beam of electrons emerging from an electron gun, for since the momentum was known from the drop in potential which the electrons underwent in the electron gun, all that was needed was to calculate the wavelength from a well-known formula of wave mechanics which states that the wavelength is equal to the quotient of Planck's constant and the momentum. As in the case of X-rays, we can then use the diffraction of the wave (of known wavelength) associated with the electrons to determine unknown crystalline structures. Once again, we see very clearly how the diffraction of waves by crystals can be applied in two ways: to the determination of wavelengths once the crystalline structure is known, and vice versa. While the first method has fully established the validity of wave mechanics, the second provides a powerful instrument for determining the structure of crystalline bodies and of surface layers. Here, electron beams give superior results to X-rays, and have enabled many scientists of different disciplines to study a host of very important phenomena. We need only recall the remarkable work which Jean-Jacques Trillat is currently pursuing in France.

We all know that diffraction by crystals is by no means restricted to photons and electrons, and that experiments with homogeneous beams of protons and various ions have shown that these particles are diffracted as well. Although such experiments are extremely difficult to set up, and have therefore not been repeated often enough, it might be very rewarding to continue them. The diffraction of neutrons, too, has been demonstrated by means of highly ingenious methods. Neutron diffraction is particularly significant since it proves the general validity of the concept of wave mechanics. Moreover, it may lead to important applications in the study of nuclear forces, because the diffraction of neutrons by the nuclei of a crystal is not due to Coulombian electric fields, but to nuclear forces acting at very small distances from the nuclei.

Before concluding my lecture, I should like to make what I think is an interesting comparison between what we have learned from the diffraction of X-rays and gamma rays on the one hand, and that of particles on the other. The X-ray and gamma ray method, by enabling us to measure the wavelengths of high-frequency radiation emitted by the atoms of the anticathode (or possibly by the nuclei of a body undergoing radioactive transmutation) has taught us a great deal about the constitution of the atoms of the various elements and about their stationary (quantized) levels, and possibly also about the constitution of atomic nuclei and their quantized stationary levels. In this way, it has greatly contributed to the development of atomic and nuclear physics. As for the diffraction of material particles, particularly electrons, by crystals and the consequent determination of their associated wavelength, its main role has been to provide scientists with a very accurate verification of the basic concepts of wave mechanics, and, by establishing justified confidence in this theory, it has enabled them to derive many fruitful consequences in various fields, for example atomic physics, nuclear physics, quantum chemistry, and electron optics.

Clearly, contemporary physics owes many of its most striking advances and the solution of some of its most vital problems to the study of crystalline symmetry and its application to the analysis of periodic wave phenomena, and this, quite apart from its practical usefulness in mineralogy and in many other branches of science, constitutes the just fame of crystallography. This is one of the reasons why you are to be commended for your efforts during this Congress to further the remarkable science of crystallography by a fruitful exchange of ideas and experimental results, and thus to consolidate its integral place in the framework of natural philosophy.

PART TWO

*Essays on the
Interpretation of
Wave Mechanics*

SEVEN

Will Quantum Physics
Remain Indeterminist?

IN AN ARTICLE WHICH FIRST APPEARED IN THE *Revue de Métaphysique et de Morale* under the heading "Personal Memories on the Beginnings of Wave Mechanics," and was subsequently published in my *Physics and Microphysics,* I traced the development of my attitude to wave mechanics between 1923 and 1928, and explained how, after first having tried to work out a concrete and determinist interpretation largely in accordance with classical concepts, I was finally driven to adopt the indeterminist view of Bohr and Heisenberg. For the next 25 years, I shared that viewpoint with most theoretical physicists, and expounded it in lectures and books. In the spring of 1951, I received a personal letter from a young American physicist, David Bohm, in which he sent me a paper, subsequently published in the *Physical Review* of January 15, 1952. In this paper, Bohm returned to one of the aspects of my 1927 ideas and developed it in a most interesting way. Subsequently, J. P. Vigier drew my attention to the similarity between Einstein's concept of the motion of particles in general relativity and my theory of the double solution, developed independently in 1927. All these circumstances have recently forced me to re-examine my earlier ideas and, while I do not claim that science can return to my original determinist conception of wave mechanics, I am convinced that the whole question must be reopened. In so doing, we must take great care to avoid all preconceived philosophical notions, and concentrate only on the possibility of a coherent interpretation of all the well-established facts. Before presenting the whole question in its current form, I feel that I must outline the historical development of the concepts of quantum physics.

The most dramatic development in contemporary microphysics was the discovery of the wave-particle duality, which first emerged during the study of the properties of light. Scientists had quite naturally looked upon light as consisting of particles in rapid motion. In this way, they were able to give a simple explanation of the facts that light rays traveled in straight lines through homogeneous media, that they rebounded from mirrors, much as balls rebound from walls, and that they were refracted in passing from one medium to another. Quite intuitively, therefore, most physicists, including even Newton, adopted the corpuscular theory of light and adhered to it right up to the beginning of the nineteenth century. Even so, as early as the seventeenth century, the great Dutch scientist Christian Huyghens had propounded an undulatory theory of light, and made it the basis of a remarkable explanation, which remains classical to this day, of reflection and double refraction, without, however, being able to give a satisfactory account of the existence of light rays. It must also be noted that Newton, after having discovered the interference phenomenon known as Newton's rings, attempted to combine the corpuscular and undulatory theories in his remarkable "theory of fits" which, unfortunately, remained embryonic and was rapidly forgotten. At the beginning of the nineteenth century, the work of the English physician Thomas

Young once again drew attention to interference phenomena, and a little later Malus was able to demonstrate the polarization of light. After repeating earlier experiments on interference and diffraction, Augustin Fresnel showed that these phenomena, which eluded the corpuscular hypothesis, could be fully interpreted by the wave theory of light. Developing Huyghens' ideas on this subject, Fresnel also showed how the wave theory could be used to explain the rectilinear propagation of luminous rays in homogeneous media. When, after a very bitter struggle, he had won over his adversaries, Fresnel introduced the hypothesis that luminous waves are in transverse vibration to the direction of their propagation, and presented a complete theory of the phenomena of polarization and double refraction. In 1827, when Fresnel died of consumption at the age of thirty-nine, he had apparently placed the wave theory of light on a very solid footing. Forty years later, when Maxwell interpreted Fresnel's waves as electromagnetic waves of a special type, he made all optics a subdivision of electromagnetism. But while Maxwell's remarkable synthesis changed all previous ideas of the nature of luminous waves, he did little to shake the conviction of physicists that light is formed of waves with a continuous energy distribution.

It was only toward the end of the nineteenth century that the dramatic developments which I am discussing really began. Hertz's discovery of the photoelectric effect in 1887 could not possibly be explained by the wave theory. In 1905, Albert Einstein (who had just propounded his theory of relativity) showed that the photoelectric effect could be partially interpreted by a return to the corpuscular theory, *i.e.*, by assuming that, in all luminous waves of frequency v, the energy is concentrated in "bundles" of energy hv, where h is Planck's constant. These bundles of light which Einstein called light quanta are known as photons today. Einstein realized that his new hypothesis could not be strictly called a corpuscular theory, since it introduced the concept of frequency which is typical of waves. Moreover, a strictly granular theory cannot interpret interference and diffraction, so that Einstein rightly insisted on retaining the undulatory theory, inasmuch as he postulated a statistical correspondence between corpuscles and waves. This, as we shall see, was a most far-reaching assumption.

Einstein's theory met with a great deal of criticism, and its shortcomings were, in fact, easy to point out. Its great merit was that it was part and parcel of that great trend of ideas that was to revolutionize the whole of atomic physics —the theory of quanta. To give a brief account of the developments leading up to quantum physics, I shall remind the reader that the experimental study of black-body radiation had shown that its spectral composition was not what classical theories had thought it to be. Realizing that this was a basic and irremediable contradiction, Planck introduced his quantum theory in 1900. This theory, quite alien and opposed to all classical ideas, enabled him to establish a law of spectral distribution for black-body radiation which was in accordance with the experimental facts. The quantum hypothesis introduced a sort of "atomicity of action" which seemed to run counter to all our physical intuitions. Moreover, his experiments enabled Planck to assign a precise value h to his quantum of action. Very soon his hypothesis, which had seemed so strange at first, proved its tremendous worth in explaining phenomena on the atomic scale. Einstein used it in his theory of light quanta, and also showed its relevance to specific heat. Shortly afterward, Bohr and his immediate successors, particularly Sommerfeld, were able to show that by introducing quanta into the theory of the atom—which, after Rutherford, was looked upon as a miniature solar system—a remarkable interpretation of the properties of atoms and, in particular, of the laws which governed their spectral emissions could be obtained. From these theories, on which I do not wish to dwell here, it followed that electrons and other material particles did not, as was previously believed, obey the laws of classical mechanics but existed in discrete stationary states governed by certain quantum conditions described by the quantum h and certain (integral) quantum numbers. The appearance of integers in problems of micromechanics might have struck one as very surprising were it not that integers occurred commonly in wave theory, as in calculations of interference and of resonance phenomena. This was a hint that electrons and other material particles, like photons, were somehow associated with waves. This association was one of the basic ideas that guided me in my first researches on wave mechanics.

Around 1920, when after many years in the army, I returned to scientific research, I found the following situation. On the one hand, the existence of photons, which was soon to receive further confirmation by the discovery of the Compton and Raman effects, seem to be beyond doubt. On the other hand, wave theory could not be dispensed with, since the frequency ν was an integral part of the definition of the photon. Moreover, interference and diffraction phenomena, the laws of which had been established with extreme accuracy, made the adoption of a synthetic wave-particle view of light unavoidable. Again, as I have said earlier, the existence of quantized movements of particles on the atomic scale had suggested to physicists that the wave-particle duality applied not only to photons but also to the elements of matter. It therefore seemed clear to me that there was a need for a general synthesis, applying equally to matter and to light, which necessarily involved Planck's constant h.

I laid the foundations of this synthesis in a paper published in the *Comptes rendus de l'Académie des Sciences* at the beginning of the autumn of 1923, which I later developed in my doctoral thesis of November 1924. Basing my ideas on relativity concepts and also on concepts which Hamilton had developed a century earlier, I managed to associate the momenta of all particles with the propagation of waves whose frequency and wavelength were related to the energy and the momentum of the particle by formulas containing the constant h, and I showed how this synthesis could be used to explain the quantized behavior of atomic electrons. I shall not enter into any technical details here, and shall merely stress the following point: To the rectilinear and uniform motion of a particle in the absence of a field, I associated the propagation of a plane monochromatic wave of constant amplitude and linear phase in $xyzt$. By relating the energy and the momentum of the particle to the frequency and wavelength of the wave, I had, in fact associated the momentum of the particle with the phase of the wave. But how was it possible to reconcile the idea of a wave with the fact that particles are localized, when plane monochromatic waves have the same amplitude throughout space, and cannot, therefore, help to define the privileged point represented by the position of the particle at any moment? This difficulty, together with some relativistic considerations which I shall pass over in silence, persuaded me to think that, though the phase of the plane monochromatic wave has some physical significance, its constant amplitude has not; the uniform distribution of that amplitude in space simply signifies that the particle has an equal *a priori* probability of being found in any point of space whatsoever. Thus the amplitude would have only a statistical significance, and does not represent the true position of the particle (for I never doubted that the particle must have a given position at any moment). Hence I termed the wave which I had introduced the "phase wave," to emphasize the fact that it was essentially its phase which had a physical significance.

The ideas which I developed in my thesis, and which were first received with a mixture of astonishment and skepticism, were soon to be confirmed in an unexpected way. In 1926, Schrödinger completed and extended my ideas and, in particular, showed how one could obtain a general expression for the propagation of the associated wave and how, on the basis of this expression, the stationary levels of the electron in atomic systems, corresponding to the stationary forms of the associated wave, could be calculated accurately. In this way he made it clear that Heisenberg's quantum mechanics, developed in 1925, was only a mathematical transposition of wave mechanics. Then came Davisson and Germer's remarkable discovery in 1927 that electrons are diffracted by crystals in much the same way as X-rays. These remarkable experiments, which were soon repeated by a great many other physicists—so much so that they became everyday laboratory practice—provided decisive experimental proof of the validity of the concepts of wave mechanics and supplied a quantitative verification of its formulas. The momentum of an electron had been shown to be clearly associated with the propagation of a wave, and we know today that the same is true of the other constituents of matter as well (protons, neutrons, atomic nuclei, etc.), since they, too, can produce diffraction phenomena whose quantitative expression is given by wave mechanics.

From November 1924, when I submitted my thesis, until October 1927 when the Fifth Solvay Congress met, I quite naturally followed the successive stages of wave mechanics with keen interest, but I continued to be vexed by the physical interpretation of the new formalism and by the real meaning of the wave-particle dualism. To my knowledge, three possible interpretations of this dualism have been offered. One interpretation, which seems to be the one favored by Schrödinger, simply denies the reality of the dualism, claiming that waves alone have a physical significance in the classical sense. While the propagation of waves may occasionally give rise to corpuscular appearances, these are, in fact, no more than appearances. At first, Schrödinger tried to develop this idea by likening particles to small trains of waves, but this interpretation had to be rejected if only because a wave train must tend to spread continuously into space, and hence cannot provide a representation of particles with a lasting stability. Although Schrödinger apparently continues to hold fast to interpretations of this kind, I, for one, doubt their validity and prefer to take the wave-particle duality as a physical fact. Now, the other two interpretations to which I have alluded are, in fact, based on this duality but look at it from quite different points of view.

The one to which I myself subscribed until 1928 attaches a concrete physical meaning in the traditional sense to the wave-particle dualism, and considers the particle as a sort of central singularity within a continuous wave phenomenon. The problem then arises why wave mechanics can successfully operate with *continuous* waves lacking the singularities of the continuous, classical waves. I shall outline my attempted solution to this problem below.

In the second interpretation of the wave-particle dualism, particles and continuous waves are considered as being complementary facets of reality, in Bohr's sense. Later, I shall give a summary of this novel approach, which for the past 25 years has formed the "orthodox" interpretation of wave mechanics, and which is so radical a departure from classical physics.

For the moment, I shall return to my historical account. In 1924, just before submitting my thesis, I was so taken with classical concepts that I tried to fit my new ideas into the established framework, the one of Cartesian coordinates. I was convinced that a particle must have a given position and momentum in space at every instant, so that it describes a trajectory in space-time. But I was equally convinced that the particle must be associated with a periodic undulatory phenomenon with a definite frequency and wavelength. Hence I was naturally led to look upon every particle as a sort of singularity within a continuous wave, all forming one single physical reality. The movement of the singularity associated with the propagation of the wave, of which it constituted a part, would then depend on the physical nature of the propagation. For this reason, the particle would not obey the laws of classical point mechanics, according to which a particle is acted upon exclusively by forces which it meets along its trajectory. In my conception, the movement of the singularity would be affected by any obstacle that could influence the propagation of the associated wave of which it is an integral part. In this way, I could explain interference and diffraction.

But, my difficulty then was to explain why wave mechanics had proved so successful by considering only continuous solutions to wave equations, the so-called ψ waves, and why it could ignore singularities. I first came up against this difficulty when I tried to associate the rectilinear and uniform motion of particles with the propagation of plane monochromatic waves: while the phase of the wave which had enabled me to determine the frequency and the wavelength of the wave associated with the particles struck me as having a direct physical significance, the constant amplitude of the wave could not be anything but a purely statistical representation of the possible positions of the particle. Here there was a mixture of individual and statistical phenomena which greatly intrigued me and which I felt tempted to resolve.

Reference to my papers published on this subject between 1924 and 1927 will show how I was slowly impelled toward what I have since called the "theory of the double solution," a full, and the only complete, account of which I published in 1927 (1). In that paper I boldly postulated that every continuous ψ solution of the equations of wave mechanics had a kind of twin solution containing a generally mobile singularity (the particle!) having the same phase as the ψ solution. But while the phases of the ψ and u waves were the same function of $xyzt$, their amplitudes were quite distinct, since that of the u wave carries a singularity whereas that of the ψ wave is continuous. Assuming the same equation for the propagation of both ψ and u waves, I then enunciated a fundamental theorem: The mobile singularity must describe a trajectory in space-time such that the velocity at every point is proportional to the phase gradient. In this way, I was able to express the action of the wave propagation on the singularity which it contains. I also showed that this action could be expressed by considering the particle singularity as being acted upon by a "quantum potential," the mathematical expression of the action of the wave upon it. I was thus led back to a classical notion of light theory, namely that in being diffracted at the edge of a screen, a light corpuscle experiences a physical action which deflects it from its rectilinear path.

Since the u wave with its mobile singularity represented the particle and its surrounding wave, what possible meaning could be attached to the ψ wave? For me, it had no real physical significance at all, since the physical facts were fully represented by the u wave. But as the ψ wave was supposed to have the same phase as the u wave, and as the particle singularity was always displaced along the phase gradient, the possible trajectories of the particle could coincide with curves normal to the equiphase surfaces of the ψ wave. Hence I could easily show that the probability of finding the particle in a given point is equal to the square of the amplitude, which is the intensity of the ψ wave. This then was the first essential characteristic which could be attributed to the ψ wave: The square of its amplitude at any point gives the probability of finding the associated particle in that point. Now this original hypothesis of wave mechanics which was essential to the theory of electron diffraction was no more than a direct reformulation of an older postulate of optics. In fact, it had always been one of the essential principles of light theory that the density of light energy is given by the square of the amplitude of the luminous wave. If the idea of the photon is introduced into this principle, as Einstein realized clearly in his original work in 1905, the probability of finding a photon in a given point must be proportional to the square of the amplitude of the luminous wave with which it is associated.

Thus the ψ wave of modern wave mechanics struck me as a purely fictitious wave, a mere representation of probability, and hence subject to sudden modifications with every change in our knowledge of the state of the particle. This character of the ψ wave emerged more and more clearly from subsequent advances in wave mechanics. But for me, the ψ wave, as it were, merely hid the u wave which, with its singularity, actually describes the particle, the center of a continuous wave phenomenon. If the impression had arisen that the ψ wave alone gave a full interpretation of the experimentally observed behavior of the particle, it was only by virtue of the phase coincidence, the key to my theory.

Such was the complex interpretation of wave mechanics which I tried to develop in 1927. I did not overlook the fact that its presentation met with very great mathematical difficulties, since, even where the limiting conditions of a problem in wave mechanics and its ψ solution were known, it was necessary to establish the coexistence of u solutions with mobile singularities. Moreover, the theory of interference phenomena, for example Young's interference experiment, had to be explained by u waves alone, that is, without any reference to fictitious and continuous ψ waves, and u waves also had to supply the interpretation of the wave mechanics of systems of particles in Schrödinger's generalized space of n dimensions, etc. In fact, the mathematical difficulties were such that I could not resolve them with my u solution, however hard I tried.

At the present moment, a re-examination of my earlier ideas has led me to suggest a modification of the definition of the u wave, which in 1927 I considered as a singularity solution of the linear ψ equations of wave mechanics. Various considerations and, in particular, closer contact with the general theory of relativity, which I shall discuss below, have since persuaded me that the real equation of the propagation of a u wave must be *nonlinear*, like Einstein's gravitational equations. These nonlinear equations would approximate linear equations of wave mechanics with very low values of u. If this point of view is correct, we might even say that the u wave, instead of transporting a mobile singularity in the strict sense of the word, simply carries a very small singular mobile region (with dimensions of the order of 10^{-13} cm) in which the values of u would be so large that the linear approximation would no longer hold, though it would, of course, hold in all space outside this very small region. Unfortunately even this new viewpoint does little toward resolving the mathematical problems, since, if the singularity solution of linear equations is often difficult enough, that of nonlinear equations is considerably harder.

Let us return to 1927. In the spring of that year Lorentz had asked me to prepare a report on wave mechanics for the Fifth Solvay Congress, which was to meet in Brussels in the following October. Aware of the difficulties to be surmounted before I could give a reasonably satisfactory and mathematically rigorous account of my theory, I resolved to present the simple point of view that I had outlined at the end of my article in the *Journal de Physique*. At the time, I thought that the motion of particles was defined by the phase gradient common to the u and ψ solutions, so that, to all appearances, the particle was "guided" by the continuous ψ wave. That being so, I felt that it was legitimate to postulate the existence of the particle as an independent reality, and to assume that its velocity was proportional to the gradient of the ψ wave. I called this assumption the "theory of the pilot wave" and as such presented it to the Fifth Solvay Congress. I failed to realize that in adopting this kind of argument I was, in fact, weakening my own position. For while my theory of the double solution may have been beset with mathematical difficulties, it held the promise of a really satisfactory interpretation of the constitution of matter and of the wave-particle dualism and perhaps, as we shall see, of a synthesis with relativity theory. The simplified pilot wave theory, on the other hand, although an indirect consequence of the theory of the double solution, had none of these advantages. Because the statistical and fictitious character of the wave was well established and accepted by the majority of scientists, my colleagues objected that the pilot wave theory involved the determination of the momentum of a particle by the continuous ψ wave, which has no real physical significance and which depends on the respective state of knowledge of the observer, and must therefore be completely changed once new information modifies that knowledge. If these concepts of mine were ever to be resuscitated, it could only be in the form of the theory of the double solution, and not in the mutilated and unacceptable form of the pilot wave.

At the Fifth Congress in October 1927, my presentation of the pilot wave theory met with a very cool reception. Pauli raised serious objections to it, and although I could think of a possible answer to them, I was unable to present a fully satisfactory case. Schrödinger, who denied the existence of particles, did not follow me at all, and Bohr, Heisenberg, Born, Pauli, Dirac, preferred to develop the interpretation based on pure probability which I have previously called the orthodox interpretation. Lorentz, who presided over the Congress, put forward the minority view that theoretical physics must remain determinist and continue to employ clear images within the classical framework of space and time. Einstein, too, raised weighty objections to the probability interpretation, thus encouraging me in pursuing the path I was following without, however, taking my side.

When I returned to Paris after the Congress, I was very much disturbed by all these discussions, and, after much soul searching, I came to the conclusion that the theory of the pilot wave had to be discarded. Afraid to return to the theory of the double solution because of its mathematical difficulties, I therefore rallied to Bohr and Heisenberg's probability interpretation, which I have expounded ever since, though experiments have convinced me that it is full of pitfalls.

According to Bohr and Heisenberg's ideas, reality is completely described by particles and continuous ψ waves, neither of which can be represented in classical terms. In general, neither a position, nor a velocity, nor a well-determined trajectory can be ascribed to a particle, since only at the moment of observation or measurement can the particle be seen to have a given position or velocity. The particle may therefore be said to have a host of possible positions or momenta and only a given probability of manifesting itself at the moment of measurement. It is here that the associated wave comes in as a sort of representation of all possible positions and their respective probabilities. In this way, the dispersion of the ψ wave into space represents the uncertainty of the position of the particle, that is, the fact that the probability of finding the particle in a given point occupied by the wave train is proportional to the square of the amplitude of the wave in that point. Similarly for the states of motion: the ψ wave has a "spectral" decomposition which can be expressed in Fourier series or integrals and which represents all possible measurements of the momentums, in such a way that the probability of a given measurement is expressed by the square of the corresponding Fourier coefficient. This interpretation can be developed to apply to all measurable magnitudes—its elegant mathematical expression introduces all the resources of linear analysis, the theory of functions, series expansion, matrices, Hilbert space, etc. It can be shown that this concept necessarily leads to the Heisenberg uncertainties according to which the position and momentum of a particle cannot be determined simultaneously, since every observation that increases our knowledge of the position decreases our knowledge of the momentum, and conversely.

Bohr and Heisenberg's interpretation of wave mechanics have a great many philosophical consequences. The particle is no longer a well-defined object in space and time but has become a mere phantom which appears fleetingly in one of two aspects. Bohr, who, with his predilection for "obscure

clarity" may be called the Rembrandt of contemporary
physics, has described particles as "unsharply defined individuals within finite space-time limits." As for the wave, it,
too, has lost its classical significance to an even greater extent than the particle: it is no longer anything but a representation of probabilities (an element of prediction) which
depends on the knowledge of the observer. It is as personal
and subjective as the assessment of probability distributions
and, like it, it is suddenly modified with new information.
Heisenberg has called this phenomenon the "reduction of
the wave packet by measurement," and this reduction alone
is sufficient to demonstrate the nonphysical character of the
ψ wave.

Simultaneously, the determinism of classical physics
went by the boards and with it the possibility of forming
precise images of physical reality within space and time.
Future events can no longer be predicted with certainty,
since only the probabilities of possible phenomena can be
calculated. True, the probabilities between any two successive measurements are strictly governed by the wave equations, but every new measurement supplies new information
which breaks down our probability determinations.

Bohr and Heisenberg's interpretation not only forces
physics to embrace probability, but endows probability with
an entirely new meaning. While all great classical physicists from Laplace to Poincaré have always proclaimed that
natural phenomena are determined and that all probability
considerations introduced into scientific theories were no
more than the results of our ignorance or of our inability
to account for too complex but nevertheless determined
laws, the interpretation of modern quantum physics postulates the existence of "pure probability" which cannot be
overcome by greater knowledge. The statistical laws of
classical theories, like the kinetic theory of gases, were

thought to reflect the degree of our ignorance of the fully determined but disordered and complex movements of innumerable molecules; there was no reason, in principle, why these complex movements should not be fully understood, once hidden parameters had been brought to light. Now, the purely statistical approach of quantum mechanics utterly rejects this kind of interpretation—probability laws no longer reflect our ignorance of the hidden parameters, that is, the coordinates and the velocity of the particle, since, because such hidden parameters simply do not exist, the particle can manifest a clearly defined position or velocity only during the brief moment of its measurement. In quantum physics probability no longer results from our ignorance, but is the result of pure contingency.

By a well-known proof, von Neumann was able to show during the 1930's that the experimentally verified statistical law of wave mechanics is incompatible with the existence of hidden parameters. Thus the last links have been severed, and it will apparently be impossible to return to the classical definition of the particle, and hence to speak of hidden parameters in the formulas of quantum mechanics. Von Neumann's abstract and elegant proof is tremendously impressive, so much so that I considered it absolutely irrefutable. I shall explain later why I have doubts about its validity today.

Although the vast majority of physicists have shared Bohr and Heisenberg's probability theory for the past 25 years, there are nevertheless some notable exceptions. Thus Einstein and Schrödinger always put forward very serious criticisms of it. In particular, Einstein raised the following objection, as long ago as the Fifth Solvay Congress. Let a particle and its associated plane monochromatic wave fall normally on a screen pierced by a circular hole. The wave will be diffracted in passing through it and will form a spherical wave behind the screen. If a photographic film in the form of a hemisphere is placed behind the screen, the particle will reveal its presence by photographic action at a point P of that hemisphere. Now, according to wave mechanics the probability of the particle acting at P is given by the square of the amplitude of the ψ wave in P. But if a photographic effect is produced at P at the instant t, no other such effect can be produced anywhere else on the film, since our hypothesis considers only one particle. Hence, the moment the trajectory of the particle is known to have passed through P, the probability of its passing through any other point of the film becomes zero. Now, it is impossible to explain how a photographic effect at P can prevent a simultaneous action at a point Q, unless the particle is localized in space and occupies a definite point in the associated wave at each instant.

The argument of the probability theorists is that, before acting on the film, the particle is *potentially* present at any point behind the screen with a probability equal to the square of the amplitude of the ψ wave, and that, the moment the photographic impression is produced in P, the corpuscle becomes localized in P and the probability of its presence at any other point *instantaneously* drops to zero. This, according to Einstein, is quite incompatible with all our ideas on space and time (even in the relativistic form) and with the idea that physical actions are propagated through space with a finite velocity. Nor is the solution to consider that our concepts of space and time may not apply on the atomic scale—in effect the film has macroscopic dimensions (it might easily have a surface of a square meter), and what we have come face to face with is the inadequacy of our notions of space and time even on the *macroscopic scale*, a fact that is difficult to accept. This objection of Einstein's —to which, to the best of my knowledge, no one has given a satisfactory answer—was soon followed by other objections, notably by Schrödinger and again by Einstein. These objections were based on interaction phenomena and their resulting "correlated" states. I cannot go into all the details here, and merely mention in passing that, like Einstein's earlier objection, the new objections also led to paradoxical results and, in particular, ran counter to classical notions of space and time even on the macroscopic scale. Although Bohr has mustered some very shrewd and interesting counter-arguments, his replies are rather shrouded in the kind of "obscure clarity" we have mentioned earlier, and therefore strike me as somewhat unconvincing.

With minor modifications, the situation remained the same until January 1952 when Bohm published the article which I mentioned at the beginning of this paper. This article did not bring to light any essentially new facts, since it did no more than re-examine the theory of the pilot wave which I had presented to the Fifth Solvay Congress and which I had to abandon because of its mathematical difficulties. But, quite apart from having reopened the question, Bohm also made a number of interesting comments and, in particular, he suggested a new analysis of the measuring techniques which apparently meet Pauli's objections to my earlier ideas. Since the appearance of Bohm's paper and since I became acquainted with Vigier's ideas, which I shall discuss below, I have published two papers on their interesting viewpoints in the *Comptes rendus de l'Académie des Sciences* (September 1951 and January 1952). One of their suggestions which has interested me most is the following. Von Neumann's proof apparently forbids all interpretations of probability distributions in wave mechanics by means of a causal theory with hidden parameters. Now, the theories of the double solution and of the pilot wave, though unproved, nevertheless *exist,* and one might well wonder how their existence can be reconciled with von Neumann's theory. I was therefore led to re-examine the proof of that theory, and I realized that it involved this basic postulate: All the probability distributions assumed by wave mechanics have a physical existence *even before any experiment has been performed to introduce one of these distributions*. Thus the probability distributions, deduced from knowledge of the wave, of the position and momentum of the particle must exist before experiments establish the exact position or momentum. Now, one might equally well assume (and this is quite in accord with the essential role that all modern quantum physicists ascribe to acts of measurement) that these probability distributions, or at least some of them, are produced by the very acts of measurement and do not exist beforehand, that is, before the results of measurement are known. In the theories of the double solution and the pilot wave (which coincide in this respect), we assume that the probability distribution leading to a given localization and given by the square of the amplitude of the continuous ψ wave, exists before all measurement, but that other probability distributions, for instance of the momentums, are introduced by the measurements themselves. Hence von Neumann's postulate and conclusions do not apply to them. The purely statistical interpretation assumes the absolute equivalence of all probability distributions, and that is the reason why von Neumann assumed this equivalence as a postulate. But in so doing, he has simply shown that if one assumes a purely statistical basis of interpretation, one can no longer escape from its consequences. Here we have a kind of vicious circle, and von Neumann's theory now strikes me as not having quite the scope which I attributed to it in the past.

Following Bohm's suggestion, Jean-Pierre Vigier of the *Institut Henri Poincaré* made a very interesting attempt to combine the theory of the double solution with a theory of

Einstein's (also propounded in 1927 but quite independent of my work, since I was then immersed in quanta, while Einstein was concentrating on his general theory of relativity). To appreciate the importance of Vigier's attempt, it is essential to realize that theoretical physicists are at present divided into two apparently irreconcilable groups. On the one hand, Einstein and his followers are trying to develop general relativity theory, while by far the great majority of theorists, attracted by atomic problems, are trying to develop quantum physics quite independent of general relativity. True, wave mechanics has taken cognizance of the restricted theory of relativity and has tried to extend it. Thus Dirac's electron theory, and more recently the remarkable theories of Tomonaga, Schwinger, Feynman, and Dyson, have introduced the ideas of relativistic covariance. But in every case, they have considered only the restricted theory of relativity, though we know that that theory is inadequate by itself and that it must be generalized in the way shown by Einstein in 1916. It is quite incredible that the two great theories of contemporary physics, the theory of general relativity and that of quanta, should so utterly ignore each other. An agreement between the two would be extremely desirable.

After having developed the framework of general relativity, Einstein concentrated on ways of representing the atomic structure of matter by singularities in the gravitational field. He also concentrated on the following point: In general relativity we assume that the motion of a body is represented by a geodesic space-time curve. It was on that assumption that Einstein was able to reinterpret the motions of the planets about the sun, and to interpret, *inter alia*, the precession of the perihelion of Mercury. Now, if we wish to define elementary particles of matter by the existence of singularities in the gravitational field, we must be able to show from gravitational field equations *alone* that the motions of the singularities describe geodesics of space and time, without having to introduce that result as an independent postulate. This problem was finally resolved by Einstein and Grommer in 1927, and the solution was subsequently developed in various ways by Einstein himself and by his collaborators Infeld and Hoffmann. In fact, Einstein's solution bore some resemblance to my own attempts in 1927 to prove that the velocity of a particle is always directed along the phase gradient of the u wave of which it is a singularity. Vigier has since tried to pursue this resemblance between Einstein's and my own solution by introducing functions of the u wave into the definition of the measurement of space and time. Although these attempts perhaps may not have been entirely successful, it is certain that Vigier is pursuing a most interesting path that may well lead to a unification of general relativity and wave mechanics. By representing material particles (and photons) as singularities in the metrics of space-time, surrounded by an undulatory field of which they are a part and the definition of which would introduce Planck's constant, Einstein's conception of particles may well be shown to be in agreement with my theory of the double solution. Only the future can tell whether this far-reaching agreement of relativity and quanta is really possible.

In any case, I am convinced that this agreement would have to be in full accordance with all the results and calculations of current wave mechanics, including the idea that it is impossible to make general predictions of the results of microphysical measurements, the Heisenberg uncertainties, the quantization of atomic systems, etc. In that case it might be argued that there is no earthly reason for changing the current interpretation which accounts for all observable phenomena as it is, and for introducing all the unnecesary complications of the double solution, of a singularity solution, etc. The answer is simply that a return to clear Cartesian concepts, which pay due regard to the existence of space and time, would not only be most satisfying intellectually but would also meet Einstein's and Schrödinger's serious objections, and avoid some of the paradoxical consequences of the current interpretation, which, by trying to describe quantum phenomena uniquely by means of a purely statistical continuous ψ function, amounts to a sort of subjectivism and philosophical idealism, a tendency to negate the existence of objective physical reality. Now, as Meyerson has emphasized, physicists must be "realists" and for very good reasons; hence subjective interpretations must always make them feel somewhat uneasy, and I believe they would be only too happy to rid themselves of subjectivism.

Again, one might agree with Bohm that even if the current interpretation can predict phenomena on the atomic scale, it need not necessarily be able to do so on the nuclear scale where the zones of singularity of different particles can encroach on one another and hence cannot be considered in isolation. And, indeed, at the present moment the theory of nuclear processes, particularly of the forces which maintain nuclear stability, is in a very sorry state. Moreover, the lack of a theory of particles is felt to be all the more unsatisfactory as new mesons are discovered almost every month. It seems that physics is in urgent need of defining the structure of particles, particularly of introducing an electron "radius" like that of Lorentz' theory. But the exclusive description of particles by the statistical ψ wave, which effectively prevents the use of any kind of structural image of these particles, also prevents such a definition from being established. Therefore, there is good reason to believe that a change of approach and a return to spatiotemporal images would greatly improve the situation. True, at the moment, this is no more than a pious hope, a blank check as Pauli would call it, but this hope ought not to be dismissed *a priori,* or physics might well run the danger of remaining stuck in purely statistical interpretations and thus become completely sterile.

The ultimate question, which Einstein has often stressed, is whether the current interpretation with its exclusive use of a purely statistical ψ wave is a *complete* description of reality, in which case indeterminism would be a physical fact and we could never hope to give accurate descriptions of atomic events within the framework of space and time, or whether, on the contrary, the interpretation is incomplete and, like the statistical theories of classical physics, merely hides a completely determined and ascertainable reality behind variables which elude our experimental techniques. In my opinion, if this second hypothesis should turn out to be the correct one, it can prove fruitful only in the form of a (suitably amended) theory of the double solution related in an explicit way to the general theory of relativity. But I am fully aware (and a recent reexamination of the entire problem has made this clear beyond all doubt) that the theoretical and mathematical difficulties to be overcome are almost insuperable. In that case, we would willy-nilly be driven back to the purely statistical interpretation, but meanwhile a re-examination of the question could not possibly be amiss.

I have no doubt that, having apparently gone back on my first efforts and having apparently subscribed to Bohr and Heisenberg's view in all my writings during the past 25 years, only to go back on them in turn, I may be accused of inconstancy. I might quip back with Voltaire that only stupid men never change their minds, were there not a more serious reply. History shows clearly that the advances of science have always been frustrated by the tyrannical influences of certain preconceived notions which were turned into unassailable dogmas. For that reason alone, every serious scientist should periodically make a profound reexamination of his basic principles. The statistical interpretation of wave mechanics has certainly rendered physics yeoman service for a quarter of a century, if only because it has prevented it from becoming bogged down in arduous and apparently insoluble problems like those posed by the theory of the double solution, and has thus enabled it to march resolutely forward, with tremendous practical results. Today the explanatory value of wave mechanics seems largely to have vanished. This sad fact is, I think, generally agreed upon, and even the partisans of probability are striving, with little apparent success, to introduce new and ever more abstract concepts, farther and farther removed from the images of classical physics, for example S matrices and minimum lengths, etc. While admiring these attempts, one might wonder whether it would not be far better to return to the clarity of spatiotemporal representations. In any case, it is certainly most useful to re-examine the very difficult problem of the interpretation of wave mechanics, if only to determine whether the orthodox view is in fact the only possible one.

The scientist, like the writer, might do well to heed Boileau's injunction: *"Vingt fois sur le métier, remettez vos ouvrages . . .".*

REFERENCE

1. Louis de Broglie, *Journal de Physique 8* (1927), p. 225.

EIGHT

Is a New Interpretation
of Wave Mechanics Possible?

ALL PHYSICISTS ARE AWARE THAT FOR THE PAST 25 YEARS wave mechanics has been interpreted on the basis of pure probability. In this interpretation the wave associated with the particle is a probability function which varies with the respective state of our knowledge and is thus subject to sudden fluctuations, while the particle is said to lack a permanent localization in space and thus to be unable to describe a well-defined trajectory. This way of looking at the wave-particle dualism goes by the name of "complementarity," a very vague notion which some have tried to extrapolate from physics to other disciplines, often with dangerous consequences.

This interpretation of wave mechanics, so different from the one I anticipated when I first began to study the subject, is due mainly to Bohr and Heisenberg. Their viewpoint was quickly adopted by most theorists, even though such eminent physicists as Einstein and Schrödinger have raised weighty objections to it. I, too, renounced my earlier and quite different interpretation and rallied to the orthodox view, which I have ever since propounded. But about three years ago, mainly as the result of the work of Bohm and

Vigier, two young physicists, I was forced to ask myself if, after all, my original approach to the very complex problem of the wave-particle dualism had not, in fact, been the correct one. I do not wish to enter into a mathematical discussion of this problem, which I have developed elsewhere (1) but should merely like to summarize my original thoughts on the subject and my recent reflections on them.

In my original work on wave mechanics, which goes back to 1923, I had been fully convinced that wave propagation must be associated with the motion of every particle. The continuous wave of classical optics, which subsequently became the ψ wave of wave mechanics, did not strike me as portraying physical reality. Its *phase* alone, directly related to the motion of the particle, seemed to have deep significance, and it was for that reason that I originally called the wave associated with the particle the "phase-wave," a term which has unfortunately fallen into oblivion. Why did I attach so much more importance to the phase of the wave than to its amplitude? There were two good reasons for doing so. First, my work was based mainly on a relativistic analysis of the relationship between the frequency of a clock and the frequency of a wave. I had noted that these two frequencies could not be transformed by a Lorentz transformation, that is, a clock moving inside a wave will not remain in phase with that wave unless its motion is fully determined. Now, if we consider the particle as a kind of clock in phase with the surrounding wave, the phase agreement implies a definite relation between the propagation of the wave and the motion of the particle. Applying this idea to the most simple case, I realized that the propagation of a plane monochromatic wave must be associated with the rectilinear and uniform motion of the particle, and this prompted me to introduce the constant h from Einstein's theory of light quanta (photons), and I established the basic relations: $W = h\nu$; $\lambda = h/p$, which relate the energy W and the momentum p of the particle to the frequency ν and the wavelength λ of the associated wave. These equations, which I generalized in a number of ways and from which I derived many interesting consequences, have remained the basis of wave mechanics, and have been fully borne out by the discovery of electron diffraction. But since the equations related the motion of the particle to terms derived exclusively from the phase of the wave, I naturally attributed much more importance to the phase than to the amplitude.

In fact, and that was my second reason, this is why the continuous amplitude of the wave and particularly the constant amplitude of a plane monochromatic wave did not strike me as having as clear a physical significance as the phase. Since it did not mark any privileged point in space, the amplitude could never represent the position of the particle; at most, and this was assumed soon afterwards, the square of the amplitude gave the probability with which a particle could be located. This assumption did not satisfy me fully, and I hankered after a total wave phenomenon which, in the framework of space and time, would be able to give a unitary description of the wave-particle dualism.

Meanwhile the ideas which I had sowed had germinated, and the work of Schrödinger and Born led to great advances in wave mechanics. It became more and more apparent that the ψ wave with its continuous amplitude could give only statistical predictions, and hence scientists were slowly but inevitably driven toward the probability theory so ably propounded by Born, Bohr, and Heisenberg. Taken aback by this development, which seemed to agree with neither the explanatory "mission" of theoretical physics nor with my original ideas, I was persuaded about 1925–1927 that in all problems of wave mechanics there existed *two* solutions to the wave equations: on the one hand the ψ wave whose phase has a physical interpretation but which, by virtue of its continuous amplitude has no more than a purely statistical and subjective significance; on the other hand a wave which I called the u wave, which had the same phase as the ψ wave, but whose amplitude would have very high local values (or, as I put it at the time, would present a mathematical singularity in a point in space) and which, precisely by reason of this local concentration, could describe the particle objectively. In this way I obtained what had always struck me as essential, namely an image of the particle in which the latter appears as the center of a continuous wave phenomenon of which it is an integral part. By means of this postulated parallelism between the u wave, the objective reality, and the ψ wave, the subjective product of our mind, I now felt able to account for the properties of statistical prediction which had justly been attributed to the ψ wave.

I gave this hypothesis the suggestive name of the "theory of the double solution" and first presented it in its complete form in the *Journal de Physique* (May 1927). I subsequently presented it in a simplified and less highly mathematical form (notable in my lecture to the Fifth Solvay Congress in October 1927), but I now believe my simplification to have been mistaken. In it—the so-called pilot wave theory—I considered the particle as an *a priori* physical phenomenon that was "piloted" by the phase of the ψ wave. This presentation of my ideas, unlike the theory of the double solution, had the drawback that in it the particle, considered as an objective reality, was guided by the ψ wave, which I together with all other theorists knew to be a purely statistical and subjective phenomenon. This, I quickly realized, was a serious flaw. Discouraged by the rather unfavorable reception of my views by the majority of theoretical physicists who were carried away by the formal elegance and the apparent rigor of the statistical interpretation, I, too, joined forces with them, and it is only since 1951 that I have been wondering if my original trend was not, in fact, the better of the two.

In my paper of 1927 I had shown that, if the function of the u wave assumes very high values in a very small region, for example around a singular point, the mere fact that the u wave is governed by the same wave equation as the ψ wave necessarily implies that this region of singularity is displaced in time along one of the stream lines of the hydrodynamic image of the ψ wave. In my theory, the formula giving the velocity of the particle identified in this region of singularity, at every point of its trajectory, took the following simple form (when relativity corrections could be neglected):

$$\mathbf{v} = -\frac{1}{m}\operatorname{grad}\varphi$$

where $\mathbf{v}$ and m are the velocity and the mass of the corpuscle, φ the phase of the u wave, defined by putting $u = f e^{(2\pi i/h)\,\varphi}$ with f and φ being real. Since, by my hypothesis, the phase φ must be the same for both the ψ and the u waves, the formula which I have called the guidance "formula" would also allow us to consider the particle as being guided by its ψ wave, but, as I have said, this point of view is not really satisfactory.

The guidance formula had enabled me to show that the particle was governed by a dynamics which, side by side with forces of a classical type, contained a quantum force derived from a "quantum potential" which describes the action on the particle (in the strict sense of the word) of the continuous wave phenomenon in which it is *incorporated*, and of which it is a region of singularity. For that reason, the particle, unlike a particle in classical mechanics, is not uniquely acted upon by the forces along its trajectory; in my conception, the motion of the particle incorporated into the u wave would also, via the quantum potential, be acted upon by any barrier impeding the free propagation of the continuous wave of which it was a part. This approach struck me as offering a possible explanation of interference and diffraction phenomena.

The postulate of the identity of the phases of the u and ψ waves enabled me to show, subject perhaps to a more rigorous proof, that the intensity of the ψ wave (expressed by the quantity $|\psi|^2$) must give the probability with which the particle could be located in a point of space at any given moment, when we cannot say which of the trajectories defined by the guidance formula is actually being followed by the particle. (This lack of knowledge would appear to be imposed, through the intervention of the quantum of action, by the very nature of the observations that we are capable of making.)

In my paper of 1927, I also tried to explain the undeniable success of the wave mechanics of systems of particles in Schrödinger's generalized space. To my mind, every particle in such a system had to be considered as a kind of singularity within a continuous phenomenon spreading out through three-dimensional physical space. Now, since Schrödinger's fictitious space is described by coordinates of various singularities, clearly defined at every instant, the ψ wave of Schrödinger's theory is merely the representation in that fictitious space of the probability of localizing particles in real physical space.

All these questions were raised in my 1927 paper. I have said that I have been re-examining them for the past three years after I became acquainted, *inter alia,* with Bohm and Vigier's work. As a result, I have been able to develop my original ideas, and to extend my theory of the double

solution to the case of u and ψ functions with more than one
component, that is, the kind of functions which are considered in the wave mechanics of Dirac's electron.

Unfortunately, there were more serious difficulties as
well, which have discouraged me from pursuing my original
path for 25 years. Before discussing these difficulties and
the reasons which today persuade me that they may no
longer be insuperable, I shall first present a new idea which
I introduced into the theory of the double solution three
years ago, and which strikes me as being of very great importance, namely that the equation of the u wave is, in principle, nonlinear and hence different from the assumed linear
equation of the ψ wave, even though the two equations may
be considered identical in most space.

The idea of describing the u wave by means of a nonlinear equation was suggested to me by the similarity
between my guidance theorem and Darmois and Einstein's
conclusions about the motion of a particle.

In general relativity, the coefficients $g_{\mu\nu}$ of the space-
time metric obey nonlinear equations (even in the case of
a vacuum) and so do the quantities $\gamma_{\mu\nu} = g_{\mu\nu} - g_{\mu\nu}^{(0)}$, that
is, the difference between the space-time coefficients and
their constant Galilean values. Nevertheless, very small
singular regions of space and time apart (in which the $\gamma_{\mu\nu}$'s
assume very great values and which in Einstein's view constitute the world lines of particles), the $\gamma_{\mu\nu}$'s are approximately described by linear equations. Einstein and his
collaborators (2), arriving at a result which Darmois had
obtained earlier (3), have shown that singular regions must
be displaced in time and space in such a way that the very
slender world line representing their motion coincides with
a geodesic of the external field. This remarkable conclusion
enables us to deduce the momentum of a particle directly

from the field equations, without having to introduce the usual supplementary postulate of general relativity theory, namely that the world line of a particle is a geodesic of space-time. Admittedly, Darmois and Einstein's conclusions bear only on the gravitational field (and, moreover, on the nonquantized gravitational field in the absence of gravitons) but it is quite in line with Einsteinian ideas to hold that the u wave functions of various kinds of particles may one day be fitted into a suitably generalized framework of space and time. Hence it seems permissible to think that the u "fields" like the $g_{\mu\nu}$ fields must be governed by nonlinear equations.

Let us now try to introduce nonlinearity into the theory of the double solution. Clearly, the equation of the ψ wave, the fictitious symbol of probability, must remain linear because the principle of superposition, which is a necessary consequence of the statistical (linear) meaning of ψ, must be satisfied. The equation of the ψ wave must therefore retain the form wave mechanics has assigned to it. The theory of the double solution assumes that, apart from a very small region constituting the actual particle, the u wave obeys the same linear equation as the ψ wave, which does not prevent us from assuming that the true equation of the u wave is nonlinear, and that the nonlinear terms have no appreciable influence except in a very small, generally mobile, region of space, where the values of u become very large. Apart from this small region of singularity and perhaps also apart from the edge of the wave train where the derivatives of u may assume very large values, the nonlinear terms are small enough for the u wave to be governed by roughly the same linear equation as the ψ wave.

Einstein has stressed an important property of nonlinear equations. If the equations of a given field are linear, we can always find a singular solution to them, such that the singularity has a predetermined motion. Moreover, if we add a continuous solution to this singular solution, the addition would have no influence on the motion of the singularity. On the other hand, if the field equation is nonlinear, we can no longer obtain one solution by adding a number of solutions: nonlinearity creates a kind of solidarity between solutions that would have been independent had the linear approximation been generally valid.*

Let us apply these remarks to the theory of the double solution. Let us assume that the u wave obeys a nonlinear equation in a very small singular region of space, but otherwise reduces to the linear equation of wave mechanics. Beyond the region of singularity, we obtain the solution† u_0 which has a very low but rapidly increasing value in the neighborhood of that region. We can then find a continuous solution v in phase with u (which is of the usual type in wave mechanics) such that $u = u_0 + v$ at the exterior of the singular region. This solution would apply also to the nonlinear region of singularity but the resolution of u into u_0 and v would become meaningless here, since, as Einstein has shown, the function u cannot represent any real mathematical singularity in that region. Outside the region there would be a fusion of the u_0 and v waves, which would be independent were linearity to apply throughout space. This assumption explains how the region of singularity, defined by large values of u, may be guided by the v wave to follow

---

* In my paper of 1927, I assumed that wave equations were linear, and I considered two solutions, one regular and one singular, both of equal phase. Phase equality was a purely arbitrary postulate since, in principle, two solutions of a linear equation are independent. On the other hand, if the equation of the waves has a local nonlinearity, the solutions are no longer independent, which explains the phase equality.

† This solution is certainly valid in the absence of a field, and also in other cases recently studied by Petiau.

its stream lines. That is why, according to the guidance theorem, the u wave remains in phase with the surrounding v wave in the region of singularity. Now, once we equate the region of singularity with the particle, we are back with my original visual model: the very small region of singularity constituting the particle, which can be compared with a clock, would become displaced inside the v wave with which it is identical in such a way that the two are always in phase.

This new model of the u wave is much more precise than the model I constructed 25 years ago. It may be considered as containing a continuous "base," the v wave, which is a solution of the usual linear equations of wave mechanics, carrying a needle point, the extremely high values of u in the region of singularity. This needle point, which is joined to its base by nonlinearity, travels within the v wave in such a way that it always remains in phase with it. Moreover, since the ψ solution of the linear equation is a mental abstraction, we can make it proportional to v throughout space, by putting $\psi = Cv$. Because the u wave —and hence the v wave which coincides with it outside the region of singularity—is an objective fact, it must have a definite value. The ψ wave, on the other hand, may be "normalized" in any convenient way to allow the square of its modulus to play its generally acknowledged role of probability function. This can be done by the appropriate choice of a constant C. In this way, we have emphasized the marked difference between the u wave, which describes objective reality, and the ψ wave, which is a subjective representation of probability. This analysis confirms the original idea of the double solution, though in much more accurate and greatly improved form.

I shall now show how this new model resolves two important difficulties that stood in my earlier path.

The first of these difficulties arose from the success of the usual method of wave mechanics in calculating the stationary states (proper energy values) of a quantized system. Since 1926, this calculation has been based on Schrödinger's determination of the solutions (proper functions) of the linear equation of uniform and continuous ψ waves satisfying the limiting conditions of the problem under consideration. There is no doubt that this method enables one to calculate quantized energy very exactly. Now this fact is difficult to reconcile with a purely fictitious ψ wave and the assumption that the real wave is the u wave which, as such, does not obey conditions governing proper functions, since it either carries a singularity (this was my old hypothesis of 1927) or else fails to obey the usual linear equations throughout space (my current hypothesis). However, what we have said about the structure of the u wave shows the way out of this difficulty: since the v wave, which constitutes the base of the u wave, is proportional to the ψ wave, its stationary forms would be those calculated by ordinary wave mechanics, and, for a stationary form of the v wave, the region of singularity incorporated at a point of that wave would be the seat of a wave phenomenon with a frequency equal to the frequency obtained by the usual calculation. In this way, the difficulty disappears.

Another insuperable difficulty of 25 years ago seems to have disappeared in the same way. This difficulty emerges most clearly in attempts to explain Young's well-known interference experiment. I must first of all remind the reader that the appearance of interference or diffraction phenomena on a photographic plate, for instance, is the experimentally verified result of the successive arrival of incident particles (in the case of light, photons). The intensity of the wave (the $|\psi|^2$ of wave mechanics) must therefore be interpreted as a measure of the probability with which the particle can be localized in every point: When the intensity is large, the probability of finding a photon is great; when the intensity is small or zero, the probability of finding the photon is correspondingly low. This new interpretation provides a quite novel justification of the classical view of Young's interference rings. What is important for the purposes of this argument is that the new interpretation uses the methods of classical optics, that is, continuous waves, for the calculation of intensities.

Now to return to my difficulties in interpreting Young's experiment. In it, a beam of light is thrown in the normal direction on a screen having two small openings. In the classical calculation the wave leaving the slits is evaluated on the assumption that the slits are two small coherent sources of equal intensity. Thence it can easily be shown that, in the neighborhood of the axis of symmetry and far from the screen, the equiphase surfaces are ellipsoids and the surfaces of equal amplitude are hyperboloids normal to these ellipsoids. Hence the position of the approximately rectilinear fringes which appear on a plate parallel to the screen in the interference area can be deduced. To describe objective reality by the theory of double solution, the continuous classical wave must be replaced by a u wave with a region of singularity, which must have passed through one of the openings to reach the plate beyond. In that case the slits can no longer be considered the symmetrical sources of classical theory. At the time I thought that the u wave, as it reduced to u_0, was bound to decrease very rapidly in amplitude with distance from the region of singularity, and that it must assume very low values with macroscopic distances from the slit. Hence, it struck me that the two slits could not possibly play the role of two small symmetrical sources, and the entire basis of the classical calculation seemed to me to have broken down. Now, since that calculation gave very accurate results and, moreover, seemed the only method of giving them, I had reached an impasse.

However, the new concept of u waves removes this formidable obstacle in the path of the theory of the double solution. We no longer represent the incident u wave as a highly condensed area around the region of singularity but as the carrier of a region of singularity grafted to a plane monochromatic v wave with the same mathematical form as the classical light wave. In that case, the photon's passage through Young's screen would be tantamount to a region of singularity passing through one of the slits. However, that region has such small dimensions (probably lower than 10^{-13} cm) that even while passing the slit it represents only an insignificant fraction of the slit's (macroscopic) surface. We may therefore assume that, over the entire surface of the two slits, the u wave is practically coincident with the v wave, that is, with the classical light wave, and that the interfering wave is exactly proportional to that considered by the classical theory, the only difference being the addition of a local accident of extraordinarily small dimensions. This is the region of singularity or the particle (here, the photon) which travels inside the wave with the velocity of the guidance formula. As a result, the probability of the particle's arrival at a point of the screen where the interference fringes appear is proportional to the square of the amplitude of the classical wave. Hence, we are back with the traditional calculation of the fringes, despite the localized character of the u wave.*

---

* We may look upon Young's interference experiment as providing direct proof of the nonlinearity of the equation giving the propagation of the u wave. In fact, v is propagated like a classical light wave; if the equation of u were linear, the propagation of u_0, which gives the momentum of the particle, would be *independent* of the propagation of v and could not be affected by the existence of the second Young slit. Only by virtue of the nonlinearity of the equa-

The theory of the double solution was faced with still other difficulties. There were, for instance, a number of problems connected with the dispersion and division of wave trains by a semitransparent mirror or by the collision effects associated by what classical wave mechanics calls "the reduction of the packet of probability."

Let us say a few words about the first of these problems. In the usual (linear) theory of wave propagation, wave trains spread into space with a consequent drop of amplitude. Linear analysis shows that this process is associated with the fact that linear theory considers wave trains as superpositions of plane monochromatic waves. These plane waves are propagated through space independently, whence they are progressively thrown out of phase and consequently dissipated. We may say that the independence of the monochromatic components of the wave train involves its gradual disorganization. In the theory of the double solution, this apparently leads to a rather untenable physical consequence: outside the singular region the u wave must, in fact, reduce to a v wave which, to all intents and purposes, obeys the linear equation of wave mechanics. Hence, if we consider a region of singularity grafted on a train of v waves, the external part v of the u wave must become dissipated as it spreads out, and the u wave would tend to reduce to its needle point. In other words, the particle would lose its wave progressively. Perhaps this conclusion is unavoidable, though I must confess that I find it difficult to fit into a theory striving to present an objective image of the particle, that is, a theory which must take notice of its permanence. Here again nonlinearity may well prove the

---

tion in u, can the propagation of u_0 be related to that of v. My failure to introduce nonlinearity into my 1927 hypothesis was, therefore, the only reason why Young's experiment struck me as being incompatible with my theory of the double solution.

way out of the impasse. If the equation of the u wave is supposed to be nonlinear, nonlinearity should, in principle, hold sway even outside the region of singularity, where the nonlinear terms are generally insignificant. In the region of singularity, on the other hand, nonlinearity predominates, and, as a result, the terms u_0 and v are joined together so strongly that the particle is prevented from losing its wave. Nonlinearity, which is so insignificant in the body of the wave train, can moreover also appear at its edges, where the derivatives of u may assume very large values. Here, too, a special factor may impede the spreading of the wave trains. Hence, a nonlinear theory of u waves may well enable us to obtain "non-dissipating wave groups" representing, for instance, a particle in rectilinear displacement and with a permanent surrounding wave. Other considerations, which we cannot discuss here, indicate that the existence of such wave groups is compatible with Heisenberg's uncertainty relations.

Still greater difficulties are encountered in an analysis of, for instance, the splitting of the wave train by a semi-transparent mirror or by collision. Since the train of u waves splits up, and since the region of singularity must eventually be associated with one of the segments, the consecutive distribution of a number of processes of this kind would necessarily cause the particle to lose its wave gradually. A passage through an absorbing screen would lead to the same difficulty. This, I believe, is one of the gravest objections to my theory. Will nonlinear conceptions enable us to surmount them as well, and to speak of a sort of regeneration of weakened wave trains? I have examined this and other difficult problems connected with the conservation of energy and with the stationary states of quantized systems in a book which I am about to publish. In it, I have expressed the view that such a regeneration is a possibility.

However, I must confess that my conclusions rest on rather weak foundations, and that real proof cannot, at the moment, be adduced. The exact study of the consequences of nonlinearity of the propagation of u waves is impeded by our inability to tell the form of the nonlinear terms of the wave equations. All we do know is that the equations must reduce, almost everywhere in space, to the linear equations of classical wave mechanics. It would appear that only a new theory of "supergeneralized" relativity that would introduce all the categories of u fields into the very structure of space-time can provide us with complete nonlinear equations.

In short, atomic physics strikes me as having failed to explain the true nature of the wave-particle dualism and as having hidden its ignorance under the somewhat vague term of "complementarity." The theory of the double solution developed on purely rational grounds could provide a clear and satisfactory model of this dualism in accordance with all the verified results of current probability concepts. That theory alone could meet Einstein's repeated objection that the current theory, while being statistically exact, is not a *complete* description of physical reality. If, at the price of what is bound to be a long and arduous struggle, we should nevertheless succeed in extending generalized relativity to bring the u waves of various types of particles into the framework of space and time, we should also be able to establish the form of the nonlinear equations satisfied by the u waves and to study events in the region of singularity, and would thus gain a true understanding not only of those spatiotemporal accidents which are the particle but also of the real significance of the quantum of action which we know to be essentially related to the undulatory and corpuscular structure of matter and of radiation. In this way we should obtain (and Rome was not built in one day!) a splendid agreement between the concepts of general relativity and quantum theory.

We have seen that in the theory of u waves, just as in the relativistic interpretation of gravitation, only nonlinear basic equations can explain the intimate relationship between wave and particle. This is how things look at the moment: a train of u waves constituting a particle in the *wider* sense of the word, would be a kind of organized and extended entity, somewhat similar to a biological cell. In essence, it would consist of three parts: (1) a sort of nucleus with a region of singularity—the particle in the narrow sense of the word—as the seat of essentially nonlinear phenomena; (2) a surrounding continuous region, the seat of a perceptibly linear phenomenon; and (3) an envelope constituting the edges of the wave train where nonlinearity may again play an important role. It seems to me that it is the introduction of nonlinear phenomena which would endow this "cell" with its unity, its cohesion, and its permanence.

If nonlinearity were the true key to corpuscular microphysics, we can easily understand why modern quantum physics has been unable to unlock the wave-particle dualism, and why it has been forced to make do with a purely statistical description of atomic phenomena. Based on linear equations and linear analysis alone, the accepted theory erases local accidents due to nonlinearity (such as the regions of singularity and possibly the edges of the wave trains), and thus effaces corpuscular structures. No wonder that, incapable of appreciating the true relation between wave and particle, it is bound to seize on continuous models of a statistical character. To my mind, the reason why the ψ wave has nevertheless led to an adequate statistical model and to exact predictions is mainly the fact that the regular part of the u wave—that is, the part outside the region of singularity—is, by its analytical form, closely related to the hypothetical form of the ψ wave.

One of the advantages of the theory of the double solution would be that it might enable us to give a description and classification of the various types of particles. The constant discovery of new mesons and hyperons renders this task more and more imperative. Now the accepted theory seems unable to give a true description of the particles, simply because it is restricted to the statistical ψ wave and the abstract and statistical formalism of the second quantization and of the quantum theory of fields. One cannot give a full description of individuals by means of purely statistical data.

To conclude: It is quite possible that I am wrong in striving for clearer concepts than those prevailing in theoretical physics today. Nevertheless, there is an urgent need to clear the path which I abandoned 25 years ago because of its difficulties. It might well be that this very path will lead us to the true microphysics of the future.

REFERENCES

1. Louis de Broglie and J. P. Vigier, *La Physique quantique, restera-t-elle indeterministe?* Gauthier-Villars, Paris, 1953.

    Louis de Broglie, *Une tentative d'interpretation causale et non-linéaire de la Mécanique ondulatoire: la théorie de la double solution,* Gauthier-Villars, Paris, 1956.

    ———, *La théorie de la Mesure en Mécanique ondulatoire,* Gauthier-Villars, Paris, 1957.

    ———, "L'interpretation de la Mécanique ondulatoire," *Journal de Physique 20* (1959), p. 963.

2. Einstein and Grommer, *Sitz. preuss. Akad. Wiss. 1* (1927).
    Infeld, Leopold, *Revs. Modern Phys. 24* (1949), p. 408.

3. G. Darmois, *Les equations de la gravitation Einsteinienne* Gauthier-Villars, Paris, 1927.

NINE

The Wave-Particle Dualism
in the Work of Einstein

THE NEWS OF ALBERT EINSTEIN'S DEATH ON APRIL 18, 1955, was received with deep sorrow by scientific circles the world over. The brilliance of his contributions to science, the nobility of mind of an illustrious scholar of whom it could truly be said that he counted nothing human as unimportant, made him a figure both loved and greatly honored. Since he has been a Foreign Fellow of our Academy since 1933, it would be only fitting that I should today render homage to his life and work were it not that I fulfilled this task six years ago, when addressing the Academy on the occasion of our eminent colleague's seventieth birthday.

What I would like to do today instead is to look at only one aspect of his work, an aspect with which the public at large is rather unfamiliar but which bears on one of the most important and puzzling problems of twentieth century physics, the wave-particle dualism.

If I have decided to stress this particular aspect of Einstein's work, it is because I have always been attracted to it. In the course of this lecture, I shall therefore be forced to abandon the impersonal note so characteristic of these annual lectures and to speak of personal matters and remi-

126

niscences instead. I hope that you will forgive me if I thus introduce into what is necessarily a very abstract lecture a somewhat livelier note, the better to throw light on a remarkable contribution to the history of a problem on which hinges the greatest crisis in the physics of our time.

Before discussing Einstein's striking work on the photoelectric effect and on light quanta, I must first give a rapid summary of the reasons why physicists have interpreted the properties of light alternatively by corpuscular and by undulatory theories.

The idea that light consists of grains in rapid movement derives from ancient Greek philosophy, which was greatly attracted by atomic hypotheses. It seemed only natural to consider that a source of light emitted particles in every direction, and that the emitted particles would travel away from the source in straight lines. In this way, the idea of a "ray of light" was born, and could, moreover, be demonstrated by the simplest experiments. Clearly, the reflection of light by a mirror was analogous to the rebounding of a ball, that is, a material object, off an obstacle. Almost intuitively, therefore, the corpuscular nature of light came to be accepted as a physical fact by all those who, for centuries, observed optical phenomena without being able to put them to a truly scientific test.

Only during the seventeenth century, when science as such was given a great impetus, was the study of light first tackled in a really scientific way. Between 1620 and 1670, discoveries followed in rapid succession: the formulation of the quantitative laws of reflection and of refraction by Snell and Descartes; the observation of double refraction in Iceland spar by Bartholin; the first description of diffraction phenomena by Grimaldi; Newton's discovery that white light was split up by prisms; Newton's rings; and countless other discoveries. All these remarkable advances in man's scientific understanding of the nature of light were bound to give rise to a great deal of theoretical speculation. No wonder, therefore, that the next fifty years saw the publication of two fundamental and classical works, Huyghens' *Light* and Newton's *Optics*.

In these two works which, all the advance of science during the last two centuries notwithstanding, continue to fill us with keen interest and the greatest admiration to this day, the undulatory and corpuscular conceptions of light were first contrasted in unequivocal terms. Huyghens, a man of remarkable intellectual clarity to whom we owe so many theoretical and practical discoveries in the field of mechanics, gave geometric expression to the idea that light consists of waves in propagation through a "subtle medium," the ether, which permeates all material bodies and fills the void. By arguments that are used in treatises on physics to this day, he then derived the laws of reflection and refraction, the description of the propagation of light in isotropic media, and the interpretation of double refraction in certain crystals. His remarkable work, which was probably misunderstood by his contemporaries, was, however, incomplete in important respects since it did not, for instance, explain clearly why light in isotropic media should be propagated in rays; even so, it laid the foundation on which, some 150 years later, Fresnel was to base his great contribution.

Newton's *Optics*, which appeared some time after Huyghens' *Light*, was a quite different kind of work. Although it contained a detailed account of its author's experimental discoveries, it made no definite statements on the nature of light. Even so, one gains the impression from it that Newton inclined toward a granular conception of light, and that he considered light rays as the trajectories of particles. Still, Newton's great intellect could not help noticing that the appearance of colored spectra in the rings he had discovered implied the presence of a periodic light phenomenon that could not be explained by the simple hypothesis of independent light particles. To explain this phenomenon, Newton was forced to propound his "theory of fits," according to which light particles, in passing through matter, were acted upon by undulations which caused their motion to undergo periodic fits of alternate preference for transmission and for reflection. The space traversed by the particle between two fits of the same kind was defined by Newton in much the same way that Fresnel later defined the wavelength of monochromatic light. Thus this brilliant scientist who discovered the infinitesimal calculus and universal gravitation had managed to propound a mixed theory of light in which the grains of light on their trajectories were associated with waves which acted upon them. This striking idea, a veritable precursor of wave mechanics but premature in the history of science, was not developed and therefore fell into oblivion.

Although the eighteenth century contributed nothing to the progress of theoretical or experimental optics, the beginning of the nineteenth century was marked by the discovery of a great many new phenomena (interference by Young, polarization by Malus, etc.) and by the triumphant success of the wave theory of light. We all know that this success will always remain coupled with the great name of our compatriot Augustin Fresnel. The scientific career of Fresnel, so studded with great contributions, is too well known for me to describe it again. All I wish to say, therefore, is that Fresnel, who was able to develop Huyghens' ideas with mathematical techniques greatly superior to those available to his Dutch precursor of 150 years earlier, managed to show how an undulatory theory led to an explanation not only of the rectilinear propagation of light but also of the last details of all such phenomena as interference and refraction. Let us also recall that, by introducing the novel hypothesis of the transverse vibration of light to explain polarization, Fresnel was able to develop the theory of propagation of light in anisotropic media much more fully than Huyghens could ever have done, and thus to found the optics of crystals which is described today much as Fresnel propounded it in his time. The growing success of wave theory, its ability to explain the smallest details of optical phenomena, its verification toward 1850 by comparative measurements of the velocity of light in air and in refractive media, all combined to make Fresnel's ideas appear final and definite. Some time later Maxwell, by considering all light as an electromagnetic, undulatory perturbation covering a small wavelength interval, made all optics a subdivision of electromagnetism.

As I cannot enter into the details of all the remarkable developments of nineteenth century theoretical physics, I shall merely try to give you a view of the resulting physical picture. First, the idea of "grains" had given way to that of "fields" in which radiation spread out continuously with time and in which there was no means of distinguishing very small regions of singularity, that is, regions in which the field is strongly concentrated, thus accounting for the presence of granular phenomena. This continuous and undulatory aspect of light was given a very precise form in Maxwell's theory, which considered the luminous field as a special type of electromagnetic field.

Had the antagonism of the particle and wave concepts, which had exercised the minds of earlier generations, finally been resolved by the field theory? Had Newton's desire to synthesize particle and wave finally been superseded? One might well have thought so, had one concentrated on optics and the theory of radiation alone, but the "grains" had meanwhile reappeared with a vengeance in another field. For, at the very moment when continuity and the field concept had banished it from radiation, physicists were forcibly made aware of the atomic character of matter and of electricity in which small grains, electrons, played an unmistakable role. Hence, electromagnetic theory had to be reconstructed to include matter in the form of small "field sources" with a corpuscular aspect. This is precisely what H. A. Lorentz and his successors did when they re-introduced the duality of waves and of particles, of grains and fields, but, as it were, in separate compartments. While continuity was said to govern the electromagnetic field and radiation, granular discontinuity was introduced (rather arbitrarily and quite separately) to account for the estab-lished existence of certain quasipoint sources of the electro-magnetic field associated with electrified matter. This dissymmetry introduced a rather unsatisfactory note into Lorentz' theory, its formal elegance and the remarkable re-sults obtained with it notwithstanding. Though the wave-particle dualism had apparently been expelled from the theory of light in favor of an exclusively undulatory con-ception, it continued to haunt the rest of physical nature.

Moreover, those who were well versed in the history of science had another reason for holding that wave and par-ticle were linked by a hidden factor, generally ignored by the physics of 1900. I am referring to that remarkable the-ory of analytical mechanics developed some 120 years ago by Hamilton and Jacobi which likens all movements of par-ticles in a given field of force to the propagation of a wave in that region of space in an approximation of geometrical optics. By means of this theory the trajectories of particles associated with a wave could be identified with "rays" of that wave, which geometrical optics defined as the curves orthogonal to equiphase surfaces. Hence there appeared to be a very profound, if somewhat limited, correspondence in geometrical optics between the motion of a particle and the propagation of a wave, and I think that the importance of that link cannot be overestimated. But in Hamilton and Jacobi's day and in the years that followed, no precise physical meaning was attached to their model. The wave was considered to be a purely fictitious, mathematical, artifice by means of which all possible trajectories could be represented simultaneously. Thus the real value of Hamilton and Jacobi's theory, *i.e.*, the light it could throw on the true nature of the wave-particle dualism, was not seized upon by nineteenth century scientists, who, as we have seen, were accustomed to place ideas of wave and particle in separate compartments.

Then, in the very theory of radiation, whence it seemed to have been excluded once and for all, this strange dualism was to reappear in a most unexpected and disturbing form.

1905! During that crucial year in the history of physics, Albert Einstein, a 26-year-old clerk in the Berne Patent Office, by a masterstroke unparalleled in all science, introduced, one after the other, two fundamental ideas into theoretical physics that were to change its entire evolutionary course: the theory of the relativity of space and time and that of light quanta. I shall pass over the theory of relativity and its momentous consequences, the better to concentrate on that part of Einstein's work which has direct bearing on the wave-particle dualism.

In 1887, Hertz had discovered the photoelectric effect, a remarkable phenomenon due mainly to the expulsion of an electron by a metal exposed to radiation. The empirical laws describing this phenomenon introduce, significantly and unexpectedly, the frequency of the incident radiation, and this fact could not be explained by the then prevailing ideas about interactions between matter and radiation. For the next 15 years, physicists were forced to take cognizance of this difficulty without apparently being able to do much about it.

But during these 15 years another unexpected event was to absorb most of their attention—the problem of black-body radiation. The experimental law giving the spectral energy distribution of radiation in thermal equilibrium with matter had a form which prevailing theories could not interpret. As a way out of this impasse, Max Planck had suggested a desperate cure in 1900—the introduction into the theory of black-body radiation of an entirely new element, altogether unknown by classical physics, the quantum of action, Planck's constant h. Assuming that electrons could oscillate harmonically about a position of equilibrium with frequency ν, Planck postulated that they can exchange energy only with components of the surrounding radiation (with which they are in resonance) by finite quantities equal to $h\nu$. Conversely, radiation, too, cannot exchange energy with electric oscillations of the same frequency except by grains with the value $h\nu$. With this bold hypothesis, Planck was able to give an accurate account of the empirical law of black-body radiation, the cornerstone of the previous theories. But this brilliant success had a serious drawback. To assume that radiant energy cannot be emitted or absorbed except by grains was surely tantamount to suggesting that the energy in a light wave is not distributed continuously but is concentrated in grains or particles of light. Planck himself recoiled from so revolutionary a consequence of his own ideas, and, afraid that his hypothesis might undermine Maxwell's theory of light, he made do with halfway compromises instead.

Albert Einstein with the enthusiasm of youth was not intimidated by such scruples. In his paper of 1905 he boldly postulated that the energy of all radiation of frequency ν is concentrated locally in the form of grains with energy $h\nu$. He then called these grains "light quanta," his name for what we today describe as "photons." Using this bold hypothesis to give a simple analysis of the energy exchange between light and electrons which is produced in the photoelectric effect, Einstein arrived at a very short proof of a fundamental law, which, despite its simplicity, had eluded all physicists. This remarkable achievement, due only to the introduction of quanta, brought particles back into the structure of light, and once again posed the problem of the wave-particle dualism in particularly sharp form. Since there could be no question of scrapping the wave theory of light, when Fresnel and Maxwell's ideas had proved so successful in interpreting the whole of optics, waves and particles had to be brought into agreement. It seemed that such a synthesis would necessarily have to rest on Newton's theory of fits. Challenging, as it did, the entire picture of optics, Einstein's brilliant paper fell like a bolt from the blue, so much so that the crisis that it ushered in some 50 years ago is not yet passed today. The importance of these revolutionary ideas was at least as great as that of Einstein's theory of relativity, presented a few months later in a memorable paper. Thus the 1922 Nobel Prize was rightly awarded to Albert Einstein for his interpretation of the photoelectric effect and not for the theory of relativity.

During the next ten years (1905–1915), Einstein, though mainly concerned with relativity, Brownian movement, and energy fluctuations, returned time and again, in short but important papers, to the question of light quanta. By investigating the problem of the thermal equilibrium of gaseous molecules and of black-body radiation, he was able to show that photons of energy $h\nu$ must have the momentum $h\nu/c$ (where c is the velocity of light *in vacuo*), and that atoms which emit photons are subject to recoil effects. This analysis and similar considerations, which became the subjects of my own studies a few years later, emphasize the close and important connection between Einstein's two great discoveries, relativity and light quanta. Without the theory of relativity and particularly without the relativistic laws of velocity and their consequences in dynamics, it would be impossible to interpret the properties of light quanta. The photon is inseparably bound up with relativistic physics.

Another strange result of Einstein's work bears on the energy distribution in black-body radiation. By making the empirically verified assumption that the mean energy density is given by Planck's formula and by applying the general formula of statistical thermodynamics to determine fluctuations about this mean density, Einstein was able to show that the expression of the fluctuations introduces two terms giving the corpuscular and undulatory structure of the radiation respectively. By this remarkable result, Einstein had established the wave-particle dualism in radiation, which was to become the object of so many of my own studies.

But though Einstein's ideas on light quanta proved so successful in interpreting the photoelectric effect, and though the great weight of evidence was in their favor, they were challenged by such illustrious scientists as Planck and Lorentz, both of whom were greatly opposed to any changes of the fundamental ideas of the undulatory and electromagnetic theory of light, and hence raised a host of objections. They had little difficulty in showing how impossible it was to reconcile for instance the well-established undulatory explanation of interference and diffraction phenomena with the Einsteinian interpretation of the photoelectric effect. But the difficulties to which they drew attention, though very real, did no more than emphasize a fundamental crisis in light theory without suggesting any solution. For while interference and diffraction were physical facts, so was the photoelectric effect. Had physics, for the first time in its history, arrived at a point where a coherent interpretation of all the known phenomena was no longer possible?

Einstein meanwhile continued to defend his ideas most forcefully and skillfully. While preparing this paper, I have reread his "Survey of Current Ideas on Light Theory," published in the *Physikalische Zeitschrift* in 1909. This remarkable report can still be read with advantage today, and I should like to quote some passages stressing the basic connection between the ideas of light grains and those of the theory of relativity. Having shown that this connection forces one to dismiss the existence of the ether, Einstein continues: "In other words, once we have rejected the ether, the electromagnetic field constituting light is no longer the state of a hypothetical medium, but like *a structure* sui generis *emanating from the source and analogous to an emission.*" * Introducing relativistic considerations, Einstein then shows that all such emissions must be accompanied by a change of mass of the source, and hence concludes: "The theory of relativity has therefore changed our ideas of light, inasmuch as light can no longer be considered the undulation of a medium, but must be looked upon as something which is associated with the very matter of the emissive body, so that we are back with a corpuscular theory of light." Einstein then gives the reasons which strike him as supporting the existence of light quanta. Thus he cites the fact that, when an electron gives rise to the emission of X-rays on striking an anticathode, the X-rays may cause the emission of a secondary electron at some distance from the anticathode, very much as if the energy imparted by the first electron to the radiation were transported *en bloc*, that is,

* Emission in the Newtonian sense. The italics are mine.

like a particle from this first to the second electron. He then makes the following crucial remark: "[In electromagnetic theory] the elementary phenomenon of light emission is said to be irreversible, and this, I believe, is wrong. To my mind, the [corpuscular] theory of Newton is much nearer to the truth, because the energy of a light particle does not vanish into space, but appears in its entirety wherever it is absorbed." After having recalled his work on black-body radiation, Einstein finishes his paper with this far-reaching conclusion: "To my mind, the electromagnetic field of light, like the electrostatic field of the electron, contains singular points and there is no reason why we should not consider the field surrounding these singular points as having the character of a wave, the amplitude of which would depend on the density of these points. In this way, we should arrive at the undulatory and corpuscular theory that the nature of the problem seems to call for."

These profound remarks are, as we have said, still worth pondering today. But while they show the way out of a most perplexing problem, they were a long way from providing a clear interpretation of interference on the basis of grains of light. In the discussion which followed his paper, Einstein suggested that interference might be interpreted as the effect of interactions between the different photons of one and the same wave. Unfortunately this hypothesis was soon disproved by experiment. In 1909, Taylor showed—and the same results were obtained 18 years later by Dempster and Batho—that the same interference fringes could be obtained with weak light and very long exposure as with intense light and short exposure. In other words, interference fringes arise even when the photons arrive on the apparatus one by one, and hence the fringes cannot result from photon interactions. This discovery was a most serious blow to all attempts to establish a physical model in accordance with a wave-particle dualism and was one of the strongest arguments in favor of the subsequent interpretation of waves as purely formal and symbolic constructs, mere representations of probability.

Then around 1920, when the wave-particle problem had become more and more inextricable, wave mechanics, by showing that a wave must be associated with the motion of every kind of particle, made it clear that Einstein's wave-particle dualism had an application far beyond black-body radiation and light quanta.

I must apologize for having to introduce a more personal note at this point. After the end of World War I, I gave a great deal of thought to the theory of quanta and to the wave-particle dualism. After a detailed study of the theory of relativity and Einstein's other contributions, I perceived a direct connection between this dualism and relativistic concepts. I also studied the Hamilton-Jacobi theory, which I mentioned earlier, and, since I preferred to interpret the whole problem by means of intuitive physical images rather than by mathematical abstractions, that theory struck me as pointing not only to a simple mathematical analogy between the dynamics of material points and geometrical optics but also to the existence of a profound physical connection between the propagation of a wave and the movement of a particle. I was also struck by the form of the laws of quantization assumed to govern the possible motions of electrons within atomic systems. The presence of integral numbers in these formulas seemed to indicate that resonance or interference wave phenomena must accompany the motion of every electron.

It was then that I had a sudden inspiration. Einstein's wave-particle dualism was an absolutely general phenomenon extending to all physical nature, and, that being the case, the motion of all particles, photons, electrons, protons, or any others, must be associated with the propagation of a wave. Coupling relativistic considerations, notably of the difference between the frequency of a clock and that of a wave, to the Hamilton-Jacobi theory, I managed to express my ideas in precise mathematical form and to establish between the energy of a particle and the frequency of its associated wave, and hence between the momentum of the particle and the wave length, the fundamental relations $W = h\nu$ and $p = h/\lambda$, which, when applied to the particular case of the photon, reduces to Einstein's formula for light quanta. The new concept also enabled me to attach a physical meaning to Hamilton and Jacobi's mathematical theory and to make an elegant identification of Fermat's principle with Maupertuis' principle of least action. It also gave the first wave interpretation of the conditions of quantizing the momenta of atomic electrons and a first glimpse of a statistical mechanics of the future—Bose-Einstein quantum statistics.

Such were the new ideas which I published in three papers in the *Comptes rendus* of our Academy in 1923. In the months that followed, I did my utmost to develop and extend my ideas still further in preparation of my doctoral thesis. Before doing so, I asked Paul Langevin, who was so well versed in the theory of relativity and in quantum theory, to examine my conclusions, and he saw fit to ask me for a second copy which he proposed to send to Einstein. Einstein quickly realized that my generalization of his theory of light quanta was bound to open entirely new horizons to atomic physics, and wrote back to Langevin saying that I had "lifted a corner of the great veil."* When Langevin communicated this phrase to me, I felt rightly proud of the encouragement by a scientist for whom I had always had the greatest personal admiration.

* "Er hat eine Ecke des grossen Schleiers gelüftet."

My wave mechanics was to receive much further encouragement from that great man. In the summer of 1924 Einstein published an account (in the Proceedings of the Prussian Academy of Science) of a study of the statistics of indistinguishable particles, the basic properties of which had just been described by Bose. Now, unknown to Einstein, I myself had shortly before shown how these particles were related to the concepts of wave mechanics. In the course of his remarkable account, Einstein considered the case of a perfect gas of indistinguishable molecules and hence developed the complete analysis which has since come to be known as Bose-Einstein statistics. By the end of that year, Einstein had received my thesis (which I submitted to the Sorbonne on November 25) through the kind intervention of Langevin. When on January 8, 1925, he published a new paper on the quantum theory of ideal monatomic gases, he not only gave a summary of my own conclusions but also showed how they had helped him to overcome his earlier difficulties and to predict phenomena in which the undulatory nature of particles is manifested.

The scientific world of the time hung on every one of Einstein's words, for he was then at the peak of his fame. By stressing the importance of wave mechanics, the illustrious scientist had done a great deal to hasten its development. Without his paper my thesis might not have been appreciated until very much later.

As it was, Einstein's paper induced many leading theoretical physicists to look at my work more closely. Thus Erwin Schrödinger, then professor at the University of Zurich, published a brilliant series of papers in 1926, which, ignoring the relativistic concepts of my initial attempts, concentrated, much more than I myself had done, on the analogy between my results and the Hamilton-Jacobi theory. Thence he developed the complete formal analysis of wave mechanics, particularly as it applies to energy calculations of the stationary states of quantized systems. He opened the door to innumerable other applications and to many brilliant interpretations, the discussion of which would take us too far afield. This tremendous start of wave mechanics was crowned in 1927 by Davisson and Germer's discovery of electron diffraction in crystals. A host of similar experiments then gave incontrovertible proof that electrons were associated with waves and provided a detailed verification of the concepts and formulas which I had originally enunciated.

While I was quite naturally enthusiastic about these developments, I was not blind to the fact that the wave-particle dualism, the general validity of which became daily more indisputable, still remained shrouded in mystery. All the earlier difficulties in explaining the experimentally certain coexistence of localized light particles (of which the photoelectric effect was one manifestation) and such wave phenomena as interference and diffraction now applied equally to the case of electrons and other material particles. Then, little by little, there sprung up in my mind the idea of a synthetic conception capable of providing an "intelligible" model of the wave-particle dualism. This conception, which I published in the *Comptes rendus* of the Academy between 1924 and 1927, was certainly the more or less unconscious result of Einstein's lifelong ideas on the real significance of the relation between particles and the field concept on which the theory of relativity has always tried to base every description of the physical world.

I shall therefore devote some space to what Einstein has had to say on the subject of particles.

The theory of relativity, both in its general and its original "restricted" form, tries to represent all physical reality by means of "fields," that is, by continuous solutions of characteristic partial differential equations applying throughout space and time. Now, this field theory proves rather difficult to apply to the case of the discontinuous structure of matter and electricity. We have seen that, to introduce discontinuous structures into electromagnetic fields, Lorentz was forced to couple his field equations with extraneous terms representing the densities of the electric charge and current as field sources—an attempt which we have called intellectually unsatisfying. Doubtless Einstein must have had great misgivings when he, similarly, felt obliged to relate his famous theory of gravitation to the framework of general relativity, by putting

$$R_{ik} - \frac{1}{2} g_{ik}R = \chi T_{ik}$$

In this equation, as in Lorentz' formula, the first term is expressed with the help of field components (in this case, the ten components g_{ik} of the metric tensor), while the second term contains the components of the energy-momentum tensor which represents the gravitational field sources.

How dissatisfied Einstein was with this representation of the relation between matter and field is best shown by his remark that "it resembles a building with one wing (the first term) built of resplendent marble, and the other (the second term) built of cheap wood." No doubt Einstein felt much the same way about Lorentz' equations.

What then would Einstein have considered a satisfying method of representing the relation between fields and particles of matter and electricity? He has expressed opinions on the subject which strike me as having grown more and more precise over the years.

His basic idea has always been that all physical reality (including particles) must be described by solutions of field equations. In the ideal theory there would therefore be no terms representing sources of singular solutions reflecting the existence of such sources,* since if field sources and singular solutions are not formally excluded, the differential field equations would not, by themselves, be able to describe the total field completely. Hence Einstein thought that no term of the field equations should refer directly to the existence of particles. This is how he himself put it: "It seems certain to me that the foundations of a coherent field theory need not contain the concept of particles. The entire theory must be based uniquely on partial differential equations, free of any singularities."

Analyzing the Maxwell-Lorentz theory, Einstein wrote: "The combination of the idea of a continuous field with that of discontinuous material points in space strikes me as contradictory. A coherent field theory would consist exclusively of continuous elements not only in time but in every point of space. Hence the material particle cannot possibly be a fundamental concept in any field theory. Thus, quite apart from the fact that it ignores gravitation, Maxwell's theory cannot be considered a complete theory."

This attitude of Einstein's must not be interpreted as implying a denial of the existence of particles. His own contribution to the development of atomic theory was such that he, better than anyone else, knew that the existence of particles was an incontestable fact. But Einstein realized that the particle could not possibly be an extraneous addition to the field—it was bound to be part and parcel of the structure of the field of which it was a kind of local anomaly. For him all the fields in nature (no matter whether electromagnetic, gravitational, or others) must always contain very small re-

---

* Such at least was Einstein's considered opinion at the end of his life, though previously he, too, had thought of representing particles by field singularities.

gions in which the field values are extremely great. These regions, which would correspond to our usual notion of particles, have been given the expressive name of "bunched fields."

This is how Einstein himself put it: "Matter which produces impressions on our senses is really nothing but a great concentration of energy in very small regions. We could therefore regard matter as consisting of regions of space where the field is extremely intense. . . . A stone's throw is, from this point of view, a varying field in which states of maximum field intensity are displaced through space with the velocity of the stone. The new physics will not have to consider fields *and* matter; *its only reality will be the field*. . . . Our final problem, therefore, is so to modify the field laws that they would apply even to those regions of space in which energy is enormously concentrated." Let us note in passing that Einstein must doubtless have been thinking of nonlinear field equations, like those which were introduced automatically into the gravitational field, and which he probably considered indispensable to all field theories.

Einstein knew the difficulties involved and realized clearly that he had failed to construct a bunched field free of singularities and thus capable of interpreting the existence of particles (except perhaps the very strange solution of Einstein and Rosen in the relativistic theory of the static gravitational field), but he added: "Nevertheless, one thing is certain—any field theory capable of representing particles without introducing singularities would describe the behavior of these particles exclusively by differential field equations." And for Einstein, this fact was the essential reason for representing particles by bunched fields.

Einstein's desire to incorporate particles into fields was soon to lead him to an important result in the general theory of relativity. Beyond its field equations, general relativity makes the independent postulate that the motion of a material point in space-time, curved by the presence of other matter, must follow a geodesic of that space-time. Anxious to show that processes in the material world are governed by field equations alone, Einstein tried to prove that, starting with only the equation $R_{ik} - \frac{1}{2} g_{ik} R = 0$ (without the second term T_{ik}), the motion, in time, of a very small region in which the field assumes very high values, should such a small region exist, is necessarily given by a world line representing a geodesic of space-time. He was able to prove this argument in a paper written in collaboration with Grommer in 1927. (A similar proof was presented one year earlier by Georges Darmois.) This theorem, of which fuller and more elegant solutions have been offered since, makes it clear that, if one takes the Einsteinian view that the elements of matter are regions in which the field is strongly concentrated, the motion of elements in a gravitational field is fully determined by field equations alone, that is, the elements follow the geodesics of general relativity. Hence the independent postulate becomes redundant.

I have said earlier that, between 1924 and 1927, I gradually arrived at an interpretation of wave mechanics, a branch of physics then uppermost in the minds of most theoretical physicists, which struck me as providing a clear and intelligible model of the wave-particle dualism, and I have shown to what great extent that model was inspired by Einsteinian ideas.

In his brilliant developments of formal wave mechanics, Schrödinger had started with an extrapolation of Hamilton and Jacobi's opticomechanical theory beyond the limits of geometrical optics. In this way he was able to determine the partial differential equation satisfying the function of the wave associated with an electron (the ψ wave of ortho-dox wave mechanics). He had thus assumed that the ψ wave was a regular solution of the continuous wave equation of classical physics, for example Fresnel and Maxwell's theory. But this suggestive hypothesis had very serious con-sequences. Since all the points in a continuous wave play an equally privileged role, there is no means of defining the position or momentum, and hence the trajectory, of a par-ticle at any given moment. Clearly, therefore, an exclusive consideration of continuous waves must *a priori* preclude a clear and synthetic representation of the wave-particle dualism.

The continuous wave nevertheless enabled Madelung to construct a hydrodynamic model of wave propagation. In it, we consider a fictitious fluid with a density equal, at all points of space and at every instant of time, to the intensity of the continuous wave (*i.e.*, to $|\psi|^2$) and spread-ing out along the streamlines, which can easily be defined analytically. This hydrodynamic image had the advantage of agreeing with a very important proof of Max Born's, namely that the $|\psi|^2$ of wave mechanics represents the probability of locating the particle at every point of space and at every instant of time. Unfortunately, in applying this model to the description of the movement of a *single* particle we find that, since all the streamlines are equally privileged, we cannot consider any one of them as repre-senting the trajectory of the particle. Hence the particle, although unique, must follow *all* the streamlines simulta-neously, but with different probabilities. These considera-tions then led to the paradoxical conclusion that statistics must be used to study the motion of single particles.

This notion, which came to be accepted by most theo-retical physicists, struck me as quite unsatisfactory and as leading to questionable conclusions. To avoid these difficulties, I put forward my theory of the double solution, based on the following argument. Since the streamlines of the continuous wave of wave mechanics give an exact representation of all the possible trajectories of a particle, the wave must necessarily be the correct statistical interpretation of reality. However—and this is a point which Einstein was to emphasize time and again—it is unlikely that this interpretation is a *complete* description of physical reality, since it lacks the singular element needed for locating the particle. Convinced that the true solution of the wave-particle problem must represent the particle as a sort of local accident incorporated in the structure of a wave, I was persuaded that physical reality must be represented by other than regular solutions of the wave equation. These solutions, which I called u solutions (to distinguish them from the regular ψ solutions) contained a (generally mobile) singularity which could be likened to the particle.

I quickly realized that there is a connection (given by the guidance theorem) between the regular and the singular waves which still strikes me as very important. Today I can formulate it in the following general terms: "If it were possible to associate every regular solution of the wave equations with those of a singular solution *having common streamlines*, the mobile singularity would necessarily have to follow one of these streamlines." This conclusion struck me as elucidating the respective roles of the regular and the singular waves. Since the coupled solutions have common streamlines, the regular solution, although fictitious, must give an exact *statistical* picture of the motions, while only the singular solution, which expresses the motion of a singularity along one of the streamlines, can give a *complete* description of the individual phenomenon. From this

I readily concluded that $|\psi|^2$ must give the probability with which the singularity can be located at a point, when we do not know which streamlines the singularity follows.

It might be objected that since my theory introduces a singular solution u of the field equations, it ignores Einstein's legitimate objections to all such solutions. But I have recently come to realize that this objection is without substance: the u wave with a point singularity can easily be replaced with a u wave representing an Einsteinian bunch, that is, a wave containing a very small region where the u field would have very high, but not infinite, values. In that case, the guidance theorem would still apply to the motion of the bunch. We could even assume that, in the interior of the bunch, the u equation will no longer coincide with the linear equation of the ψ wave but will take a more complicated, for example a nonlinear, form, whence it follows that, if the u wave is considered to be a bunched field, the representation of the particle given by the theory of the double solution will coincide with Einstein's model. But since, in my theory, the u field has an undulatory character outside the bunch, the particle appears as a local accident incorporated in a wave, thus explaining the nature of the wave-particle dualism.

I was naturally most enthusiastic about the new perspectives I had helped to open up. Unfortunately my attempts to develop a rigorous and satisfactory basis for the theory of the double solution met with all sorts of mathematical and physical difficulties that I was unable to resolve. Thus when, in May 1927, I gave an account of my results in the *Journal de Physique*, I was filled with misgivings.

In the spring of 1927, when I was concentrating on developing an interpretation of wave mechanics and of the wave-particle dualism in conformity with Einstein's ideas, which had so often guided me, an entirely new viewpoint was presented by Bohr and Born and their brilliant pupils Heisenberg and Dirac. This was, as we have seen, the inevitable consequence of the exclusive use of the regular ψ wave. It was also a consequence of the uncertainty relations that Heisenberg had shown to be a necessary and formal consequence of wave mechanics. Unlike Schrödinger, who had tried to base wave mechanics on the notion of the regular wave alone, to the exclusion of particles, the new interpretation considered both waves and particles, but in a way which relegated both to a sort of phantom existence and without any attempt to connect the two in a clear spatio-temporal model. The particle itself no longer had a fixed position, velocity, or trajectory—it could mark its presence only by revealing a given position, energy, and momentum at the moment of measurement. At any given moment, the particle may therefore be said to have a host of *possible* positions and momenta, each of which has a given probability of being found on measurement. Side by side with this evanescent particle which had ceased to be a definite object in space and time, there now existed a ψ wave that had lost all the physical properties of the classical wave. The wave had become a purely mathematical function representing the probability of obtaining certain results from measurements of the particle.

The new interpretation was very revolutionary. It not only discarded precise descriptions within the framework of space and time but it also abandoned the causality and determinism of physical phenomena. Bohr was soon afterwards to sum it up in his strange and somewhat awkward theory of complementarity, according to which the particle and the wave are complementary aspects of reality—once one aspect was observed the other was excluded. Complementarity was clearly a far cry from Einstein's desire for a synthetic representation of the particle within the framework of space and time.

At the end of October 1927, the Fifth Solvay Congress met in Brussels to discuss wave mechanics and its interpretation. It was here that I gave an account of my work, though in a somewhat abbreviated form, in which I stressed the hydrodynamic aspect of my theory. My account met with rather a cold reception. The very active group of young theoretical physicists around Bohr and Born, including Pauli, Heisenberg, and Dirac, were completely taken with their own purely statistical interpretation. Some raised objections to these new ideas. H. A. Lorentz reiterated his firm belief in the determinism of physical events and in their interpretation by precise spatiotemporal models, but he offered no constructive suggestions. Schrödinger predicted the complete abandonment of the notion of particles in favor of regular waves of the classical type, but I was convinced of the futility of all such attempts.

What was Einstein's contribution to this debate, which might well have led to the solution of the formidable problem that had been uppermost in his mind ever since his brilliant theory of light quanta? To my great disappointment, he said hardly anything beyond presenting a very simple objection to the probability interpretation, which, I believe, has preserved much of its weight to this day. Then he fell back into silence. True, he encouraged my attempts in private conversation, but he refused to take any attitude toward my theory of the double solution, which he apparently had failed to study very closely. He told me that he was convinced that quantum physics was taking the wrong path and that he felt rather discouraged about recent trends. One day he said to me: "These problems of quantum physics are becoming too complex for me. I am getting too old to study such difficult problems." A very strange phrase to come from the mouth of this illustrious scientist then no more than 48 years old!

I left the Solvay Congress very downcast by its reception of my ideas. I saw no way of meeting the objections to my theory. Persuaded that the almost unanimous faith of most leading theoretical physicists in probability theory was justified after all, I, too, decided to rally to it and to change my approach accordingly. The only real (and perhaps the only possible) attempt to resolve the problem of the wave-particle dualism in the sense suggested by Einstein thus came to a premature end.

Einstein nevertheless stuck to his guns. He had meanwhile moved to the United States, from where he continued his outspoken opposition to the purely statistical approach to wave mechanics. This led to a number of sharp controversies, particularly with Bohr in 1935, when Einstein, in collaboration with Rosen, published an article in the *Physical Review* putting forward a new objection to Bohr's approach. Bohr replied in the same issue.

In this controversy Einstein was almost completely alone, having as his associate in the struggle only Schrödinger, who also had raised a number of shrewd objections to the probability approach. But Einstein's attitude remained purely negative. While rejecting the accepted solution to the wave-particle problem, he offered nothing in its place, thus clearly weakening his own position. Einstein then turned his attention to the development of a unified theory which, by extending the scope of general relativity, would lead to the fusion of the gravitational, the electromagnetic, and possibly other fields into a unique structure, on the basis of a suitable development of space-time geometry. This unified theory, which Einstein fashioned and refashioned continually, led to a remarkable conclusion shortly before the end of his life. This conclusion has been the subject of the brilliant studies of Mme. Tonnelat and her colleagues during the past few years.

But no matter what the results of Mme. Tonnelat's research, they cannot possibly lead to an exact representation of physical reality since, at least in their present form, they ignore quanta. Einstein, the discoverer of light quanta, knew this better than anyone else. He was fully aware that he could be reproached with having abandoned all constructive work on quanta, and in his last letter to me on February 15, 1954, he wrote: "I must resemble an ostrich ceaselessly hiding its head in the relativistic sand to avoid having to face the quantum villain."

Nevertheless the controversy slowly died down, and most physicists came to accept probability, some because they found it truly satisfactory, others, more pragmatically, because the formalism of quantum mechanics gave them all the tools they needed for predicting phenomena, and because they were not really interested in the reality hidden behind their curtain of equations.

Time passed, and in 1949 Albert Einstein celebrated his seventieth birthday. On that occasion a jubilee volume was published in the United States, *Albert Einstein: Philosopher and Scientist,* which contained contributions by a great many scientists. As one leafs through this volume, one cannot help being surprised. Where one rightly expects unanimous homage to the brilliant discoverer of relativity and light quanta, one reads in a number of articles spirited and often sharp criticisms. Einstein is attacked for having been unable to appreciate the elegance of the theory of complementarity, etc. These attacks certainly saddened Einstein. When the book appeared he said to his intimates, "This is not a jubilee book for me, but an impeachment."

But when one is accused, one has the right to defend oneself. Einstein used this right. In a signed article at the end of the volume he repeats all the arguments in favor of his point of view. He states quite categorically that, even though contemporary quantum theory may be statistically correct, it utterly fails to give a full description of physical reality. By many examples, he tries to show to what difficulties (no doubt he would have liked to have said to what absurdities) one is led if one mistakes the formalism of that theory for a complete account of reality. This elegant article is one of the most brilliant that came from the pen of Einstein during the last few years of his life.

At the time that this jubilee volume appeared, I was delivering a course of lectures at the *Institut Henri Poincaré*, in which I examined the problem of the interpretation of wave mechanics, a subject that I had not been studying for many years. On this occasion, I discussed Einstein and Schrödinger's objections and Bohr's counter-arguments. While reiterating my adherence to the statistical interpretation, I could not repress my old feelings of uneasiness. The objections struck me as most cogent, and the replies as not always very lucid. Slowly and almost unbeknown to me, my 25-year-old allegiance to the statistical interpretation seemed to vanish into thin air.

It was then, in the summer of 1951, that I became acquainted with the work of David Bohm in the United States. Bohm had re-examined the hydrodynamic model, and had developed some of my 1927 ideas. His paper turned my attention again to my earlier attempts, and a little later, Jean-Pierre Vigier of the *Institut Henri Poincaré* pointed out the similarity between my old guidance theorem and the Einstein-Darmois theorem on the motion of particles in the gravitational field. In both cases, the motion of the particle is completely determined by differential field equations. In 1927, I had unfortunately overlooked this similarity. Had I not done so, I should, no doubt, have been encouraged to persist in my theory of the double solution.

For the past four years [1951–1955], my attention has therefore been increasingly drawn back toward the theory of the double solution, and once again I am engaged in developing that theory, this time with the able help of a num- of young collaborators, Jean-Pierre Vigier in particular. This is not the place to present our results, and I shall merely state that some of the difficulties which I met in 1927 have, in my opinion, been overcome, though others have not.

Einstein, in his Princeton retreat, followed this work with keen interest. Even so, he maintained that reserved attitude, that timidity in the face of quanta, which, since 1925, had prevented him from making, or even from giving open encouragement to, any attempt to solve the problem of the wave-particle dualism. In the special volume devoted to the work of Max Born in 1953, Einstein even raised some objections to my theory, objections which I myself think may be dismissed.

Nevertheless, he was certainly pleased to see the emergence of some opposition to the purely statistical approach of quantum physics to which he himself had never been able to subscribe. He continued to encourage me, in personal letters, and even sent me a photographic portrait of himself.

In one letter* he wrote: "It is true that my Parisian colleagues have, in recent years, been much closer to my approach than American theorists." And, alluding to the fact that the vast majority of physicists adhere to the statistical interpretation, he added ironically: "I find it difficult to understand, particularly in periods of transition and

* Quoted by André Georges in an article in *Synthèses* (May/June 1955).

uncertainty, how much fashion plays a role in science, scarcely inferior to the one it plays in women's dress. Man is truly an animal very sensitive to suggestion in all things and not only in politics."

Albert Einstein died at Princeton on April 18, 1955, in the small house where he had lived, very secluded, for many years. In his youth, the time when he gave proof after proof of his astounding genius, he was the first, in his theory of light quanta, to recognize the wave-particle dualism as a characteristic of all radiation. He at once perceived the difficulty of finding a satisfactory solution to the formidable problem so intimately related to the existence of quanta that this dualism poses. All his life, that problem was to continue uppermost in his mind. In his later years, he witnessed the triumph of a solution that he could never accept, and his opposition to contemporary fashion turned this great scientist, to whom the most important concepts of contemporary physics owe their origin, into a lonely figure, who remained aloof from the scientific developments of his time.

Had he lived longer, would he have seen science moving in the direction indicated by theory of the double solution, and thence toward an interpretation of the wave-particle dualism closer to his own views? While it would be imprudent to affirm the answer too categorically, one thing, at least, seems certain: If such an interpretation could surmount the remaining obstacles in its path, it would provide a model of the wave-particle dualism entirely in agreement with Einstein's own attempts and aspirations. That model would be infinitely clearer and more intelligible than that offered today by the nebulous concept of complementarity.

But the problem is very difficult. Much work must still be done, for nature continues to keep jealous guard of her secrets from man's inquisitive gaze.

The great veil is indeed very difficult to raise!

TEN

The Interpretation
of Wave Mechanics

MODERN AUTHORS OF TEXTBOOKS ON QUANTUM MECHANICS usually ignore the basic idea underlying it. This becomes clear from the very fact that they prefer the term "quantum mechanics" to "wave mechanics," though it is wave mechanics which is the foundation of all the mathematical developments of modern quantum theory. Without it and its wave equations, there might well have been no textbooks at all on quantum mechanics, and by ignoring the insight of the founders of wave mechanics, the authors of books on quantum mechanics are a little like children who disown their parents.

Thus there is good reason for beginning this paper with a historical account.

Wave mechanics was born through the attempt to understand the true nature of the wave-particle dualism, which had emerged in an experimentally certain, but theoretically incomprehensible, way in the photoelectric effect and in Einstein's interpretation of it (theory of light quanta, 1905). Reflecting on this problem, I became convinced that the wave-particle dualism must be a general phenomenon and that it must apply as well to particles other than photons. For this reason, I endeavored to associate the propagation of waves with the motion of every particle and, in the case of the electron, to interpret the quantum conditions which, in Bohr's atomic theory, determine the possible motions of atomic electrons. (These conditions contain integral numbers similar to those contained by the conditions of interference and resonance in wave theory.)

To establish a connection between the motion of a particle and the propagation of a wave, I started from relativistic considerations, and, in applying them, I was struck by the difference between the formulas giving the respective transformations of the frequency of a clock and that of a wave with changes of the Galilean reference system. But I was then trying to interpret the particle as a very small local accident within a wave, and hence to consider it as a small clock in phase with the wave of which it is a part. In studying the difference between the behavior of the frequency of this "clock" and that of its associated wave, I became convinced that their phase agreement necessarily involves the rectilinear and uniform displacement of the particle, which, in the case of plane monochromatic waves which I was then considering, is fully determined. This analysis together with a consideration of Einstein's theory of light quanta enabled me to relate the energy W and the momentum p of an unobstructed particle to the frequency v and the wavelength λ of the plane monochromatic wave by the fundamental equations

$$W = hv \quad \text{and} \quad \lambda = \frac{h}{p}$$

(where h is Planck's constant), which, when applied to the special case of photons, become the light-quanta equations.

To my eyes, these ideas went deeply into the nature

of wave-particle dualism—they showed that the particle must be part and parcel of an associated wave.

The Hamilton-Jacobi theory and the work of Schrödinger

As I realized from the start, results similar to mine could be obtained by a well-known theory of classical analytical mechanics, the Hamilton-Jacobi theory. This apparent coincidence did not really surprise me, since if my ideas on the wave-particle dualism were correct, they must have been implicit in classical mechanics, in so far as the dualism must have applied within its framework.

In this theory developed 120 years ago, first by Hamilton and later by Jacobi, all possible movements of a particle in a given field were related to the propagation of a wave in it, as an approximation of geometrical optics. All possible trajectories of the particles associated with a wave were identified with "rays" of that wave, that is, with curves orthogonal to equiphase surfaces. In this way, the theory drew attention to the very basic, though limited, correspondence, as a first approximation of geometrical optics, between the momentum of a corpuscle and the propagation of a wave. But the real nature of this correspondence was misunderstood until the advent of quantum theory—not surprisingly when we consider that its full significance could only be brought out through the quantum of action.

Let us look more closely at the Hamilton-Jacobi wave model. The theory is based on a first-order partial differential equation identical with the equation of geometrical optics. Every complete integral of that equation $S(x,y,z,t)$ is shown to represent the phase of a wave whose propagation obeys the conditions of geometrical optics, and which corresponds with an infinite number of rays, the possible trajectories of the particle. This is illustrated in Figure 1, the broken lines of which enclose equiphase surfaces $S =$ const., while the unbroken lines represent some of the curves normal to them, that is, the rays (possible trajectories of the particle).

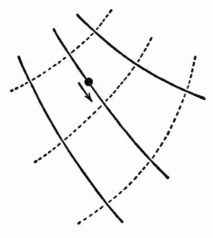

Figure 1

Here we must notice an essential point. The Hamilton-Jacobi theory, being a dynamic theory of material points, makes the *implicit* assumption that the particle must describe *one* of its possible trajectories, that is, the theory combines the propagation of waves and their rays with a small local accident (the black dot in Figure 1), which is intimately related to the wave and follows one of its rays.

Clearly, therefore, by introducing the supplementary hypothesis of the quantum of action and its role as mediator between energy and frequency, the Hamilton-Jacobi theory can be reduced to the fundamental equation of wave mechanics. However, since that theory applies to geometrical optics alone, and since from the point of view of wave mechanics, geometrical optics is an approximation valid only under certain conditions, it follows that classical mechanics, too, are only valid under certain conditions. In my thesis (1923–1924) I suggested that mechanics reflecting the wave-particle dualism must be wave mechanics related to classical mechanics much as undulatory wave theories are related to geometrical optics. In particular, wave mechanics would have to explain the interference and diffraction phenomena which eluded the descriptions of classical mechanics, for example Davisson and Germer's discovery in 1927 of the diffraction of electrons by crystals.

At that time I was absorbed in another problem, the precise amplitude of the wave associated with a particle. It was tempting to assume, by analogy with the waves of classical physics, that the amplitude must vary continuously throughout space without marked local accidents. But I realized that, in that case, the wave would be devoid of any local singularity and hence would be unable to represent the particle. Only the phase of the wave, of which Jacobi's S function was a first approximation of geometrical optics, struck me as having a physically certain significance. I therefore preferred not to commit myself on the possible form of the amplitude, though I felt strongly that, far from being regular, it must have some sort of local singularity.

Early in 1926, Erwin Schrödinger developed a very important generalization of my earlier work in a series of (now) famous papers. Keeping within a nonrelativistic framework, he naturally ignored my original, relativistic considerations. Instead, he consolidated the link between my approach and the Hamilton-Jacobi theory and, in particular, tried to discover a wave equation of which the Jacobi equation was the expression in geometrical optics. Thus he arrived at the (nonrelativistic) wave equation for particles without spin which bears his name. By establishing a formal analogy between his and the Hamilton-Jacobi theories, Schrödinger showed that, in every system of particles, the motion of the system could be related to the propagation of a wave in generalized space of n dimensions, defined by all the coordinates of the particles of the system, and hence gave the equations governing wave propagation in that space.

We know how successful Schrödinger's equations have proved, and need not dwell on this point. But despite this success, despite the formal elegance and the practical results, Schrödinger may rightly be said to have made two dangerous assumptions, which, though quite natural at the time, can nevertheless be said to have turned wave mechanics in a bad direction. The first of these assumptions is that *all* the solutions of wave equations must be waves of continuous amplitude in which there is no local accident to define the position of the particle; the second assumption is that the propagation of the waves of a system in generalized space is equivalent to the propagation of the wave of a particle in physical space.

Let us consider a single particle and the equation of its associated wave in physical space, and let us suppose that the propagation of that wave is governed by the approximations of geometrical optics. In that case, we must return to the wave model of Hamilton-Jacobi, in which the function S is proportional to the phase in such a way that the surfaces $S = $ const. are equiphase surfaces, and that the rays of the wave, curves normal to the equiphase surfaces, represent the possible trajectories of the particle. Now, the systematic and exclusive consideration of waves of continuous amplitude cannot possibly lead to the identification of the motion of the material point which is implicit in Hamilton-Jacobi's wave model, that is, the black dot of Figure 1. As a consequence, all the trajectories normal to $S = $ const.

must be considered all at once and on the same footing so that, instead of the picture of an individual particle describing a trajectory, we have no more than the fictitious and statistical picture of an infinity of particles describing all the trajectories, and hence comparable with a fluid of molecular structure. It can easily be shown that the density of this fictitious fluid is equal to the square of the amplitude of the continuous wave,* so that this quantity must give the probability of finding the particle at a given point and instant.

So far, we have assumed the propagation of a wave to obey the approximation of geometrical optics, and hence the Hamilton-Jacobi equations. If, instead, we apply wave mechanics to the case where the wave propagations no longer obey the approximation of geometrical optics, we can still define the streamlines associated with the propagation of waves, and consider them as possible trajectories of the particle, but, since we are using a continuous wave, all these trajectories are equally privileged and we have no means to define any one as *the* trajectory of the particle. All we can do is to consider the square of the amplitude of the wave as giving the probability with which the particles may be present at a given point, since this magnitude may be considered as giving the density of a fictitious fluid consisting of an infinity of particles describing all the streamlines simultaneously.

In any case, the exclusive use of regular solutions of wave equations necessarily eliminates the model in which the particle is localized and describes a definite trajectory in time. The only physical reality in Schrödinger's model is the wave, and hence the particle, too, is a pure wave phe-

---

* If the continuous Schrödinger wave is designated by ψ, and if we put $\psi = ae^{(2\pi i/h)\varphi}$, a and e being real, the square of the amplitude a^2 can be written in the classical form of $|\psi|^2$.

nomenon. This hypothesis strikes me as incompatible with the experimentally verified existence of localized manifestations of the particle. Alternatively, we can take Bohr and Heisenberg's view in which both wave and corpuscle lead a sort of phantom existence, and in which the particle is "distributed" statistically over all the possible trajectories and states of motion, while the wave has become a purely subjective representation of probability (even though, in case of need, a shadow of objective reality may be assigned to it from time to time). It is this latter view, which, despite its obscurities, has been the orthodox interpretation of wave mechanics for the past 25 years.

Let us add that, by equating the propagation of the wave of a system in generalized space with that of the wave of a particle in physical space, Schrödinger has robbed his continuous wave of the last shred of objective reality, simply because the propagation of a wave in abstract generalized space is bound to be purely fictitious. Once this assumption was made, the wave of wave mechanics had willy-nilly been turned into an abstraction.

The interpretation of wave mechanics by the theory of the double solution

During the period 1925 to 1927, it occurred to me to give an altogether different interpretation of wave mechanics by means of the theory of the double solution which I first enunciated in the *Journal de Physique* in May 1927.

Anxious to retain, side by side with the wave notion, that of a localized particle, I considered the particle as a sort of local accident in the structure of the wave so that physical reality was not exclusively reflected in Schrödinger's continuous solutions of wave equations but in other solutions with very small, generally mobile, regions, in which the solutions assumed very high values.* To my mind, the great advantage of considering the particle as being "incorporated" in a continuous wave phenomenon was that, while it enabled one to speak of a localized particle, one could also assume that its motion was influenced by the presence of obstacles at some distance from its trajectory, and thus interpret interference and diffraction by local effects.

However, I felt that the statistical interpretation of the continuous wave had to be retained, for, while the wave with a singularity would reflect physical reality, the continuous wave, though fictitious, would give a statistical picture of the position and possible motions of the particle, provided only that it was somehow related to the wave with a singular region. Now I have already mentioned the essential role in my original work of the phase of the wave. It was mainly the persistent phase agreement between the particle, considered as a clock, and the surrounding wave that had led me to the fundamental relations of wave mechanics. Hence, I assumed that only if the same phase were attributed to the real and the fictitious continuous waves, could the fictitious wave provide an exact statistical description of the motions of the particle. On the other hand, the amplitude of that wave struck me as not reflecting any objective reality and as having the purely statistical significance that its square gives the probability of finding the particle at a given point and instant.

All real phenomena must be describable within the framework of space and time, and hence I felt that Schrö-

---

* At the time, I assumed that the wave function contained a mathematical singularity of infinite value at the center of the small region. Since then, I have dropped this hypothesis in deference to Einsteinian concepts.

dinger was wrong to think that the problem of n particles in interaction could be solved only by considering the propagation of a fictitious wave in generalized space. To my mind, the problem had to be posed and resolved by considering the interactions of n waves with regions of singularity in three-dimensional, physical space. Hence, one would have to show that the statistical result of these interactions coincides with the result of Schrödinger's abstract considerations for generalized space.

In 1927, my attempts to develop this idea culminated in what I have since called my "guidance theorem" which I felt was of great importance. It can be summarized as follows: If the solution of a wave equation contains a very small region of singularity in which it assumes very high values, this region will describe a definite trajectory, that is, a curve normal to the equiphase surfaces. Now, if we assume that the fictitious continuous wave is in phase with the real wave, we may conclude that the particle's trajectory will also be normal to the equiphase surfaces of the continuous wave. The guidance theorem, therefore, applies to the general case where the propagation of a wave is not necessarily governed by the approximation of geometrical optics. For greater clarity, we shall consider the special case in which the approximation of geometrical optics applies, the Hamilton-Jacobi theory (Figure 1). Here, the wave with a singular region has equiphase surfaces $S =$ const., and the small region of singularity follows a determined path, the unbroken line of Figure 1. The figure is then a complete representation of physical reality, the propagation of a wave in which the dot marks the local accident, the particle as a part of the wave. On the other hand, the continuous wave whose equiphase surfaces are the same but whose amplitude is devoid of any region of singularity corresponds to Figure 1 *without* the black dot, and does not fully reflect physical reality. It is fictitious and contrived and by virtue of the relation between the "rays" and the possible trajectories of the particle leads to accurate statistical predictions; for instance, the square of its amplitude will give the probability of locating the particle.

My original guidance theorem applied to the only forms of wave equations then known (Schrödinger's equation and its relativistic generalization, the Klein-Gordon equation). More recently (1) I have given a new proof based exclusively on the classical method of integrating first-order partial differential equations, which has the advantage of applying to all the wave equations used by modern wave mechanics and, in particular, to the equations of Dirac's electron theory. In all these wave equations, the propagation of a wave can be likened to the flow of a fictitious fluid with definite lines of current. In this way I was able to prove the general theorem that covers the special case we have discussed: If two solutions of a wave equation of wave mechanics, one regular and the other with a mobile region of singularity, have common lines of current, the singular region of the second solution will follow one of the streamlines.

After Bohm's publication in 1951–1952 of some of my early ideas, I enlisted the active collaboration of Jean-Pierre Vigier to re-examine the interpretation of wave mechanics by the theory of the double solution, which I had abandoned in 1928 because of the great difficulties involved. Vigier and I have been able to bring the theory of the double solution into closer accord with the Einsteinian interpretation of particles as very small regions in which the field (gravitational, electromagnetic, or any other) assumes very high values. This agreement with Einsteinian ideas, to which I shall return later, has persuaded us that the true equations of the propagation of waves with singular regions must be nonlinear if they are to reflect physical reality. However, their nonlinear terms would only become significant in the singular region—outside it the values of the wave function would be so small that the equation would assume an approximately linear form and coincide with the form of the usual equation of wave mechanics governing the motion of the particle.

I shall now explain the advantage of the nonlinear approach. Vigier and I realized that the wave with a singular region (which I called the u wave to distinguish it from the continuous ψ wave of the usual wave mechanics) must resolve $u = u_0 + v$, where u_0 is negligible with respect to v outside the immediate neighborhood of the singular region, but assumes large values near and within it, while v is a regular solution of the linear wave equation whose general mathematical form must be that of the usual continuous wave equation of the problem under consideration. Thus the functions u_0 and v are two solutions, one regular, the other singular, of the usual linear wave equation, the complete u wave appearing as a v wave of the same mathematical form as the usual ψ wave together with a localized needle point in it (see Figure 2). I have shown that this form of the u wave is absolutely essential if the theory of the double solution is to take cognizance of the success of usual wave mechanics in calculating proper values and in explaining interference phenomena, for example, Young's slits.

The guidance theorem enables us to show that the very small region in which the large values of u are concentrated, follows a clearly defined path along the streamlines of the v wave. It is in this small region, also, that the equation satisfied by u became nonlinear, for if that equation could *everywhere* be reduced to the usual linear equation of wave mechanics, u_0 and v would be completely independent, and we should have no ground for assuming that they would follow the same streamlines, or that the motion of the needle point u_0 is determined by the streamlines of v. If, on the other hand, the equation of the u wave is nonlinear in the singular region in which that wave assumes very large values, u_0 and v are united because of nonlinearity of the wave equation in the singular region, and this doubtless is the reason why the particle is guided by the wave.

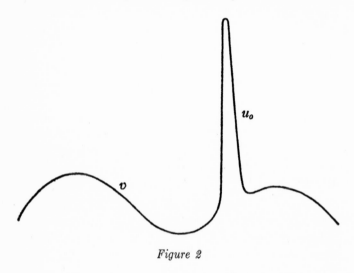

Figure 2

It is important to bring out the relation between the function v, the part of the wave outside the singular region, and the ψ wave usually employed in wave mechanics. Since the u wave of the theory of the double solution is an objective reality, independent of observational data, the v wave, which is a part of u and which coincides with u outside the singular region, must be an objective reality as well. In particular, the v wave must have a clearly defined amplitude which the observer cannot "normalize" at will. What he can do is to form a mental picture of a ψ wave that would everywhere be proportional to v, and hence normalized by an arbitrarily chosen coefficient of proportionality. Even if the v wave were to occupy a great many regions of space, an observer can, according to the information he has on the state of the particle, choose different values of the constant of proportionality for these different regions. It is this possibility that strikes me as providing an intelligible interpretation of what Heisenberg has called the "reduction of the probability packet."

Our conception of the ψ wave explains why the adherents of the statistical interpretation of wave mechanics have apparently been oscillating between the notion of a purely subjective wave function, a simply mathematical representation of probability, and the notion of a wave function with a measure of physical reality. In our conception, though ψ is a purely subjective mental structure depending on observational knowledge, it is nevertheless built on the basis of the v wave, which is an objective reality. In this way alone can the ψ wave lead to precise statistical predictions despite its subjective character. Thus we have drawn a clear distinction between subjective and objective reality, a distinction which seems to have gone by the wayside in the usual statistical interpretation of wave mechanics.

We cannot go into all the very complex details of the problems involved in attempts to interpret *all* the phenomena of microphysics by means of the theory of the double solution while, at the same time, bearing in mind the success of statistical wave mechanics and quantum field theory. A great many of these problems are still unsolved, and their future solution, if any, will undoubtedly involve a great deal of painstaking research. All we can do is to show why the reintroduction of the concept of localized particles in space, assumed in the theory of the double solution, strikes us as an urgent and important task.

The need for re-establishing the concept of localized particles

If we reflect on the means of making experimental measurements of a particle on the microphysical scale, we at once realize that all such measurements must be based on observable macroscopic phenomena released by this or by another particle (cascades of chemical phenomena producing a photographic impression due to the action of a photon or an electron; condensation of droplets of water or passage of an electric discharge due to the arrival of a particle in a Wilson cloud chamber or in a Geiger counter; etc.). In his analysis of measuring techniques, von Neumann and his successors (2) have not, to my mind, paid sufficient attention to these macroscopic phenomena; instead they have paid exaggerated attention to the role of the measuring instrument, which, when all is said and done, does no more than measure the macroscopic phenomena once they have been released.

While there is no end of measurement techniques that we could study,* I shall restrict my remarks to only one method of measuring energy and momentum, the better to show by one simple example how, if we fail to postulate the permanent localization of particles, we are forced into quite inadmissible conclusions, as Einstein and Schrödinger realized only too well.

Let us consider the collision of two particles whose initial energies and momenta are known precisely. After these particles have collided, exchanges of energy and momentum will cause them to move off in different directions. The

* I have given a more detailed account of various sorts of measuurement techniques in the course of lectures which I delivered to the *Institut Henri Poincaré* during the winter of 1955–1956.

analysis of this process by the usual methods of wave mechanics shows that the two particles, which were initially associated with two monochromatic wave trains A_0 and B_0, must, after the collision, be associated with series of wave trains A_1, A_2, $\cdots$ for the first, and B_1, B_2, $\cdots$ for the second particle.

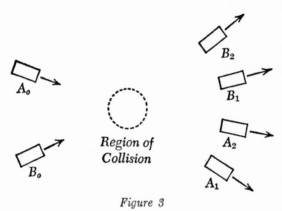

Figure 3

These wave trains are distributed in correlated couples A_1–B_1, A_2–B_2, $\cdots$, two of which are shown in Figure 3. For each of these couples the sum of the final energy and momentum of the two particles is equal to the sum of the initial energy and momentum. The orthodox (and statistically accurate) interpretation of wave mechanics establishes a correlation between the probability of finding the two particles in the wave trains of each couple. In other words, it assumes that, if the first particle is found in the wave train A_i, the second particle will necessarily be found in the wave train B_i, and not in any other wave train B_k. If, then, we place an instrument, say a counter, in the path of one of the wave trains, say A_1, so that the particle can release a macroscopic observable phenomenon in it, the observation of this phenomenon would show that the second particle is in the correlated wave train B_1, and hence that the second particle has the final energy and momentum corresponding to B_1. We have thus "measured" the energy and momentum of the second corpuscle by observing a macroscopic phenomenon released by the first.

How can this result be reconciled with the orthodox interpretation of wave mechanics which asserts that the particle is not localized in the wave? It seems that we would have to concur with von Neumann's view that the observer's perception of the observable macroscopic phenomenon (in the Geiger counter) results in localizing the particle which was previously distributed statistically between $B_1, B_2, \cdots$, in B_1. This interpretation strikes me as inadmissible: the observer's conscious processes cannot possibly have an effect on the localization of the second particle at a distance from the observer. How can the observer's opening and shutting his eyes possibly affect the distant particle?

Another, hardly more reasonable, interpretation might be the following. The act of observation of A_1 in the Geiger counter localizes the second particle, previously distributed statistically between all the wave trains B_i, in B_1. But this interpretation is no more admissible than the first—a phenomenon observed in A_1 cannot possibly cause the localization of the second particle in B_1, particularly since A_1 and B_1 may, at the moment of measurement, be at a great distance from each other. According to Schrödinger, only magic could explain this phenomenon, and "magic" is, in fact, the only word to describe it.

With further research, it became quite obvious that a theory in which particles are not localized in a wave cannot lead to a reasonable interpretation of the correlation of wave trains and the resulting measurements. These difficulties disappear automatically in a theory which, like that of the double solution, re-establishes the permanent localization of particles in space. According to the (unknown) initial positions occupied by the two particles at the interior of A_0 and B_0 respectively, these two particles would, during the collision, describe a trajectory completely determined by the guidance theorem, which would eventually lead them into one of the wave-train couples, for example the first particle into A_1 and the second into B_1. If an observable phenomenon is released by the first particle in A_1, it is only because the first particle is, in fact, in A_1, and hence the second particle must necessarily be in B_1. There is thus no inadmissible action at a distance from the observable phenomenon—there is no more magic. The act of perceiving the first particle, by which the observer can ascribe a given energy and momentum to the second particle, has then become no more than a discovery of a fact, independent of the observation, and hence in accordance with the concepts of classical physics.

Quite apart from emphasizing the need of localizing the particle in the wave, this analysis of measuring processes has a great many other important consequences. Quantum physics has shown that every act of measurement must necessarily and inevitably be considered as a disturbing intervention into physical events, and that any precise measurement of, say, the position of a particle generally precludes the precise measurement of its momentum. In the theory of the double solution this fact is explained in the following way. All such measurements necessarily involve either the passage of the u wave associated with the particle through an instrument which alters its path or an interaction of that wave with the wave of another particle (as in Figure 3). Hence the measurement must lead to a modification of the u wave and usually to its fragmentation into wave trains separating out into space. Moreover, the modification of the wave needed for measuring one of its magnitudes is not generally the same modification needed for the measurement of another magnitude, and it cannot therefore be established by the same measuring instrument. Clearly, all these facts are the direct result of the connection between the particle and the wave in which it is incorporated, which was postulated in the guidance theorem.*

The study of these questions shows clearly that the probability distributions of the different measurable magnitudes considered by wave mechanics apply only after the particle has been subjected to a process of measurement of a given magnitude, and before the results of that measurement are known. As measurement techniques must differ according to the nature of the magnitude to be measured, and since it is thus impossible to measure all the magnitudes simultaneously by one method, all the probability distributions deduced by wave mechanics from the form of the ψ wave before measurement cannot apply simultaneously. In the language of statistics, they do not correspond to one and the same aggregate, and it is false to consider them all as referring to the state which existed before any measurement was made. Thus von Neumann was able to prove very rigorously that the introduction of hidden variables (which would lead to attributing a fully determined position and momentum to the particle at every instant) cannot possibly enable us to attribute all the probability distributions of wave mechanics to one and the same original aggregate. But, contrary to von Neumann's belief, this conclusion does not by any means imply that the introduction of hidden variables precludes us from attributing a determinate position and momentum to the particle at any instant. The theory of the double solution, by introducing such variables,

* Bohr says that these facts are the result of the quantum of action, but, since the quantum of action governs the relation between the particle and its wave, his view can easily be reconciled with ours.

associates every form of the wave with the possible positions and momenta of the particles—only one of these possibilities is realized, but we do not know which. The totality of these possibilities corresponds to an aggregate with easily defined probability distributions, but these (unobservable) distributions are not those postulated by orthodox wave mechanics. The moment we measure any of the particle's magnitudes, the associated undulatory state is altered by the process of measurement, so that, after measurement, it corresponds to a new aggregate for which the probability distribution of *the measured magnitude* is that of orthodox wave mechanics. Bearing all these points in mind, we see that the theory of the double solution leads to statistical models of the classical type, in which the paradoxes of the orthodox point of view have disappeared. Clearly a causal interpretation by means of waves with regions of singularity is much more satisfactory than the customary interpretation.

Let us now say a word about the Heisenberg uncertainty relations, according to which we may measure either the coordinate x of a particle or the corresponding component p_x of its momentum. We can never make these two measurements simultaneously because they involve using different instruments. Nevertheless, the knowledge of the probability distributions given by the usual equations of wave mechanics enables us, before measurement, to calculate the *a priori* uncertainty introduced into either measurement. The Heisenberg relations show that the product of the two uncertainties is always of the order of Planck's constant.* Clearly, therefore, the Heisenberg uncertainties are the uncertainties introduced into the possible results of two incompatible measurements (that of the position and that of the momentum), but they are only *predictive uncertain-*

---

* This is the well-known relation $\delta x \cdot \delta p_x \approx h$.

ties and do not necessarily imply any real *indeterminism* of the position and momentum of the particle.

The possible consequences of the theory of waves with singular regions

We have just seen the advantages of considering the particle as a permanent localization inside a wave, and as having its momentum defined by the guidance theorem. It is quite possible to arrive at the same result more simply by adopting the somewhat naïve point of view which, in 1927, I called the theory of the pilot wave. In it, particle and wave are taken as given, and the particle, placed inside the wave, is assumed to follow one of the streamlines of the wave with the momentum defined by the guidance theorem. In this theory, the particle is a kind of foreigner in the wave, and is "piloted" by it, much as a cork is carried along by a current.

In adopting this point of view, I was always disturbed by the fact that the continuous wave of orthodox wave mechanics has a purely subjective character and is only a probability representation. This character emerges clearly when we consider that the probability packet is reduced whenever the observer obtains new information about the particle —a reduction that is incompatible with the existence of an objective wave. Hence, a satisfactory theory of the particle cannot possibly be based on the assumption that the particle is piloted by a purely subjective phenomenon. However, we have already distinguished two continuous waves, the subjective ψ wave of orthodox wave mechanics and the objective v wave (the external part of the u wave in the theory of the double solution). We may therefore assume that it is the v wave which pilots the particle; in other words, starting with a u wave with a singular region, we suppress this region (by reducing u to v) and replace it with a particle, the foreign body piloted by the v wave. This concept might strike one as simpler than that provided by the wave with the singular region, but I believe it to be less profound. I shall try to show that the theory of the double solution opens up perspectives that completely escape the pilot wave theory.

First of all, one of the most important subjects which theoretical physics will have to study is that of the constitution and the properties of particles on the microscopic scale. We know today that these particles are much more numerous than physicists believed only a few years ago, and that new mesons and hyperons are still being discovered almost daily. We know that these particles differ in the values of their electric charge and their spins, and that the values of their mass form a discrete spectrum, but we have no knowledge of the real nature of these phenomena nor have we a theory of the structure and properties of particles. Now, the pilot wave theory, by fitting the particle into the wave as a foreign body, cannot possibly lead us to a solution of this problem. More recently, attempts to describe particles by the statistical concepts of wave mechanics have involved analyses of the form of the wave equations associated with different particles on the basis of group theory and symmetry. While these attempts are valid, because the wave equations and their solutions necessarily reflect the structure and symmetry of the particles, they are all based on purely statistical wave function and cannot therefore lead to a *complete* description of individual physical entities. The theory of the double solution, on the other hand, could lead to just that result, because an exact calculation of the value of u in its singular region should give a complete description of the structure of the particle and explain all its properties. True, we are still a long way from being able to make this calculation, particularly since we do not know the nonlinear form of the u equation in the singular region, but the theory of the double solution does show a way out of the difficulties and points to the path which may one day lead to a true theory of particles on the microphysical scale.

The theory of the double solution has other important consequences as well, since it alone can lead to a fusion of quantum physics and general relativity, a much-needed alliance which most theorists apparently chose to ignore. In his penetrating reflections on the basic concept of generalized relativity, Einstein concluded that physical reality must be described exclusively by fields (gravitational, electromagnetic, or others), that is, by clearly defined magnitudes at every point of space and time. To his mind, the particle must be defined not as a field source (the usual way of defining it in electron or gravitational theory) but as a very small region of space in which the field assumes very high, though finite, values. The properties and the motions of particles would then be completely given by field equations. "There will be no place in the new physics," Einstein wrote, "for both fields and matter, that is, particles, *because fields will be its only reality.*" If we assume the u waves of the theory of the double solution to exist side by side with other fields (gravitational, electromagnetic, etc., which themselves would be the u waves of gravitons, photons, etc.), we see at once that the theory of the double solution falls in completely with Einstein's program and, moreover, that it has the additional advantage that, since its u fields are undulatory, it provides a complete picture of the wave-particle dualism. The motion of the particles is thus completely determined by the conditions of the propagation of the u field, and Einstein's conditions are satisfied by the guidance theorem.

It is therefore not unreasonable to hope, and these are the great perspectives I have mentioned, that we may one day combine within one vast unified theory all the many known types of field, including the u field of the theory of the double solution. All these fields will contain singular regions with very high values containing the various types of particle (photons, gravitons, electrons, protons, mesons, etc.). Only the equations of the total field, consisting of all these individual fields, can determine the motions of all the singular regions, and *consequently give a complete account of all their interactions.* True, this is still no more than a program the realization of which will be most long and difficult but, I repeat, this objective holds great promise, far beyond that of statistical wave mechanics or the truncated concept of the pilot wave.

And, on reflection, it strikes me that the guidance theorem is the cornerstone on which we must build the future edifice of a theoretical physics that would unite in the best possible way what are now two isolated branches of physics, quantum theory, and relativistic field theory.

REFERENCES

1. L. de Broglie, *Comptes rendus de l'Académie des Sciences* *239* (1954), p. 737; *241* (1955), p. 345.
2. London and Bauer, *La théorie de l'observation en Mécanique quantique.* Actualités scientifiques, Hermann, Paris, 1939.

ELEVEN

My Meeting with Einstein at the Solvay Conference

EVER SINCE I BEGAN MY STUDIES OF THEORETICAL PHYSICS AT the age of 19, I have been an ardent admirer of both the person and the work of Albert Einstein. I knew that at the age of 25 this illustrious scholar had introduced ideas into physics that were so revolutionary as to make him the Newton of modern science, and I studied intensely and painstakingly, for I was then merely a beginner, that elegant theory of relativity which bore his name. I also knew (and since I was immersed in the study of quantum theory, that part of his work interested me most keenly) that Einstein had offered a bold hypothesis on the subject of light, his theory of light quanta, in which he had reformulated the old corpuscular concept of radiation, abandoned since Fresnel, the better to interpret the photoelectric effect and to analyze the problem of energy fluctuations in black-body radiation. In short, in all my studies I was constantly brought face to face with the work of this lofty thinker.

When, after a long absence, I returned to my studies with greater maturity at the end of World War I, it was once again the ideas of Einstein, this time on the wave-

Essay written in 1952.

particle dualism in light theory, that guided me in my attempts to extend this dualism to cover the case of matter and led me to propound the basic concepts of wave mechanics in the *Comptes rendus de l'Académie des Sciences* at the end of the summer of 1923. During that period of my life I caught a glimpse of Einstein, though only from afar, while he was on a visit to Paris. He was then on an international lecture tour to present his ideas on the theory of relativity and in particular on generalized relativity, which had crowned his previous achievements in 1916. While attending his lectures at the Sorbonne and the *Collège de France*, I was struck by his charm and by his facial expressions which could vary from meditative aloofness to vivid, or even playful, animation.

In November 1924, I had submitted my doctoral thesis, in which I had put forward my new ideas on wave mechanics. Paul Langevin had sent my thesis to Einstein, who immediately evinced interest in it. A little later, in January 1925, the illustrious scientist presented a paper to the Berlin Academy of Science in which he stressed the importance of the ideas underlying my thesis and deduced a number of its consequences. That paper of Einstein's drew the attention of scientists to my work, and for that reason alone I have always felt that I owe him a great personal debt.

By 1927, the basic concepts of wave mechanics were widely acclaimed, thanks largely to the brilliant papers published by Schrödinger in 1926 and the remarkable experiments of Davisson and Germer and of M. G. P. Thompson on electron diffraction. In June, H. A. Lorentz invited me to participate in the Fifth Solvay Congress, to be held in Brussels during October, which was to be devoted to the study of recent developments in quantum physics. I was charged with presenting a report on wave mechanics to that meeting, and though clearly conscious of the great honor bestowed on me and full of intellectual pleasure at being invited to address so august a body of scientists, I was mainly looking forward to my probable meeting with Albert Einstein at the Congress and to our exchange of ideas on that occasion.

My hopes were not disappointed and I did, in fact, meet the idol of my youth. During a fairly long talk, he made a profound impression on me and fully confirmed my faith in him. I was particularly won over by his sweet disposition, by his general kindness, by his simplicity, and by his friendliness. Occasionally, gaiety would gain the upper hand and he would strike a more personal note and even disclose some detail of his day-to-day life. Then again, reverting to his characteristic mood of reflection and meditation, he would launch into a profound and original discussion of a variety of scientific and other problems. I shall always remember the enchantment of all those meetings, from which I carried away an indelible impression of Einstein's great human qualities.

But here I must rather mention the scientific controversy in which both of us were involved during what were often the very lively arguments of an assembly of eminent physicists.

Though the concepts introduced by wave mechanics were generally accepted at the time, the details of the physical interpretation of the wave-particle dualism were not, and while some of the physicists who had directly contributed to the rapid development of new forms of quantum physics, like Schrödinger and myself, tried to present a concrete and causal interpretation, by and large in agreement with the traditional concepts of physics, others, like Born, Bohr, Heisenberg, Pauli, and Dirac, presented a novel, purely statistical, interpretation based on Heisenberg's recently discovered uncertainty relations.

For the previous eighteen months I had been constructing my "theory of the double solution," which had struck me as providing a quasi-classical interpretation of the main experimental results of wave mechanics. In my report to the Solvay Congress I presented this theory in a somewhat simplified form, and I waited anxiously to see what reception the illustrious assembly before whom I developed my ideas would accord to them. As it turned out, the indeterminist school, whose adherents were mainly young and intransigent, met my theory with cold disapproval. On the other hand, Schrödinger was somewhat less equivocal, and Lorentz, who presided over the meeting, spoke out as a convinced partisan of determinism and of the concrete images of classical physics. He did not commit himself on my theory, which, moreover, he had had little occasion to study, but presented a picture, magnificent in its precision, of what he thought a satisfactory physical theory ought to be.

But what would Einstein say? Although he had never expressed the opinion that I had found a definite solution of the problem, he had always encouraged me in private conversations to persevere on my path, and I was most anxious about the stand he would take. But all he did do, in a very short address, was to criticize the purely statistical interpretation and to muster up telling examples to show why he thought it incomplete.

On the return trip from Brussels to Paris with him for the centenary of the death of the great French physicist Augustin Fresnel, we had a final conversation on the arrival platform of the *Gare du Nord*. Einstein told me again that he had very little confidence in the indeterminist interpretation, and that he was worried about the exaggerated turn toward formalism which quantum physics was taking. Then, possibly going farther than he might normally have liked to go, he told me that all physical theories, their mathematical expression apart, ought to lend themselves to so simple a description "that even a child could understand them." And what could be less simple than the purely statistical interpretation of wave mechanics! Outside the station he left me by saying: "Carry on! You are on the right road!"

I was never to see him again except for a brief meeting at a lecture he gave two years later at the *Institut Henri Poincaré*, where I had meanwhile been appointed professor. Then there came that cruel period of trials and tribulations of the Hitler regime in Germany. Forced to leave his country, Einstein left for the United States, where he was received with open arms. He never returned to Europe, and my only subsequent contact with him was by letter—always cordial but rather infrequent.

As for the controversy about the interpretation of quantum physics, it was soon settled in favor of Bohr and Heisenberg's indeterminist thesis. Discouraged by the difficulties which I had met in trying to develop my theory of the double solution, I, too, adopted the almost unanimous view of quantum physicists in 1928, and I have ever since been teaching and expounding it. Einstein, however, stuck to his guns and continued to insist that the purely statistical interpretation of wave mechanics could not possibly be complete.

In recent times, there have been renewed efforts (by Bohm in America and by Vigier and myself in France) to present my old ideas of 1926–1927 in new form. I must admit that so far my old difficulties have not yet been completely overcome by these recent attempts. The future alone will tell if the purely statistical interpretation of quantum physics is the only possible one, or if the views of the great discoverer of relativity and light quanta have been more perceptive than those of his opponents.

PART THREE

Some Questions of General Interest

TWELVE

Scientists and the Problem
of Popularizing Science

THE PROBLEM OF POPULARIZING SCIENCE, THAT IS, OF BRINGING it within the layman's reach, is now of vital importance, since it is essential that public opinion at large be kept in touch with the latest scientific advances and their tremendous repercussions on our thoughts, life, and future. The problem is also a very delicate one, because, as scientific knowledge grows from day to day, it tends to become increasingly complex and hence increasingly difficult to put into simple words. Thus there is a conflict between the legitimate and irrepressible desire to make known the discoveries of science and the scientist's conscientious scruples lest he obscure the truth or make claims which are not absolutely borne out by his scientific research.

The modern scientist cannot very well ignore these problems, which, on the one hand, have become of increasing public interest, and, on the other hand, cause a good deal of conflict as he struggles to overcome his habitual reserve. Scientists would much rather make direct contributions to the progress of science than give simplified accounts

Inaugural lecture to the Association of Scientific Writers, January 1951.

189

of their own or their colleagues' achievements. This attitude is quite understandable, since it is by specialized research and not by popularization that science has attained its present stature. Moreover, many eminent scientists lack the special gift of putting their ideas across to the lay public, with the resulting danger that scientific popularization is left in the hands of people who may be unfamiliar with the latest achievements of science or, worse still, are more concerned with how many books they can sell than with serious instruction. Such people are bound to sacrifice what little knowledge they may have to popular appeal.

Hence the true scientist, conscious of his role in modern society, cannot afford to ignore popular science, by which alone the man in the street can be persuaded of the intellectual grandeur of science and the immense practical consequences springing from it. Even if the scientist feels disinclined to become a popularizer himself, he should nevertheless try to exercise some sort of control over popular scientific writing, if only to help the defenseless reader to sort the wheat from the chaff.

True, this would not always be an easy task, because popular science can assume various guises, each of which must be judged on its own merits. There are, first of all, the popular books written by qualified scientists and mainly addressed to an educated audience: teachers, lecturers, engineers, or scientists in other fields. These books, though extremely valuable, do not really reach the public at large, and they cannot replace the somewhat less rigorous works that pay less strict attention to detail. Among these simpler works are a great many which merit our fullest praise, though it is over them that scientists might well begin to exercise some control, lest their authors be tempted to sugar the pill too much. Finally, there are those popular works that concentrate exclusively on "spectacular" aspects of science or draw spectacular conclusions from unspectacular facts. True, they may serve to fire public enthusiasm, particularly the enthusiasm of young and uninformed readers, for the achievements of science, and thus perhaps persuade them to devote themselves to pure or applied science. But there is no doubt that this kind of writing is often very dangerous. Although certain imaginative writers of genius, for instance Jules Verne, deserve to be admired for their uncanny predictions of future developments, it is nevertheless necessary to say that prophecy is full of pitfalls, and that a large dose of prudence is needed to avoid them.

Scientists must therefore make a sustained effort to keep popular science from degenerating into myth. Our country, so rightly famed for its love of intellectual rigor and precision, has every reason to feel satisfied with its achievements in this, as in other, spheres. Thus I was delighted when, in a book review in the *Journal of Applied Physics*, I read that no country had made a greater effort toward its postwar scientific rehabilitation than France, and that it (the book under review) was the most convincing proof that French research workers had not only overcome their wartime handicap but also were once again making the most original contributions to science. If France merits this praise in the important field of scientific research proper, she would enhance her international reputation further if she could take justified pride in her popular scientific writing as well. And I think that the elegance and precision of our language, together with the clarity of the French mind, do, in fact, entitle us to claim that in this field, too, France could take pride of place.

That is the importance of the new organization which M. Lionnais and his colleagues have had the foresight to found. By bringing together scientists and qualified scientific writers, the Association is bound to enhance popular scientific writing, which through the competence of its authors will instruct without distortion and raise the intellectual level of the reader. The Association must be careful to encourage only works of unquestionable merit, works that will draw people to admire science for the right reasons. If it succeeds in doing that, it will have rendered a great service both to science and to French thought.

THIRTEEN

Is Scientific
Education Enough?

SCIENCE AND ITS APPLICATIONS PLAY AN INCREASINGLY IMPOR-
tant part in the life of modern society. The new ideas introduced by science and the unexpected horizons which it opens
cannot fail to leave a profound impression on an increasing
number of young minds. At the same time, innumerable
scientific discoveries that have transformed and will continue to transform the conditions of our day-to-day existence cannot fail to stimulate growing interest of the younger
generation in the ideas that prompted the discoveries.

It therefore seems inevitable that science will play an
ever increasing part in the mental make-up and the education of our children. Not only will scientific knowledge be
needed for a greater number of careers, but a well-rounded
education will be incomplete without a knowledge of the
history of science and of scientific achievements. Hence the
very basis of our educational system, on which the culture
of centuries has rested, will have to undergo a revolutionary
change: science will increasingly take the leading position
formerly held by the humanities, that is, the study of classical and post-classical literature and thought. No one could
wish to deny the paramount role of classical thought in the

intellectual development of mankind. The depth of the philosophical concepts which it has bequeathed to us, the beauty of its sculpture, and the brilliance of its analysis of human emotions have more than justified the agelong reliance of mankind on the classics as their educational ideals. But we are moving farther and farther away from the past, and as our knowledge broadens, there has been an inevitable decline of the educational scope of classicism. Hence a new cultural ideal must take its place, an ideal in which scientific advances that have transformed our mental horizon and are turning more and more young people into technicians will play an ever increasing part.

Since this educational trend is inevitable and is a direct consequence of the progress of civilization, some radical reformers have suggested that our entire intellectual outlook should now be fashioned exclusively by scientific precepts, and that the teaching of science should be pursued to the exclusion of all classical learning. Needless to say, I hold science in the highest esteem, and admire its precise methods, the boldness of its theories, its fresh outlook, and the great benefits it bestows on us in illness and in health. Still, I am convinced that a purely scientific education cannot provide a nation with all the knowledge which, today more than ever before, has become a vital need.

Science has a very important part to play in education, not only because scientific studies prepare young people for various careers, but also mainly because its general ideas, its original ways of thinking, and the mastery of its accurate and often difficult methods have an undeniable educational value. True, not all our children have an equal ability to benefit from the study of science, particularly since many of them have a clear aversion to the abstractions of mathematics, which are required in an increasing number of scientific disciplines. Still, there is no reason why even these

young people should not be taught the practical consequences of scientific progress or shown what new light science has thrown on the riddle of nature and on other
problems which have always challenged man's intelligence.
There is no reason why the history and the philosophy of
science should not be taught in such a way as to bring home
to all pupils the grandeur of science and the scope of its discoveries.

Some people have therefore argued that, by using new
teaching techniques if need be, we should set up a new kind
of humanism which owes nothing to Greece or Rome but
is based exclusively on the scientific study of natural phenomena. They point out that it was precisely in this way
that the great schools of Greek philosophy were born. They,
too, owed nothing or little to an earlier tradition; they
looked at nature with fresh eyes and tried to understand it
by reflecting on what they saw. Only in that way were they
able to pose problems and to develop those intellectual
concepts that continue to hold our admiration to this day.
Today, with the help of accurate experimental methods and
much greater knowledge and much more highly refined techniques, modern man, too, should develop new intellectual
paths and move toward a new humanism, greater and more
scientific than that of the ancients. But even if this new
humanity were ever to become a reality, I for one cannot
believe that a purely scientific culture can completely meet
all mankind's intellectual needs.

Man is not constituted of intelligence and reason alone;
he also has feelings and volition. Thought and desire play
an equal part in his destiny. No matter how noble our
thoughts, they are not enough by themselves. If priority had
to be accorded to one of the three integral parts of our being
—thought, feeling, and action—feeling would unquestionably outweigh the other two, since in the final analysis our

emotions are the mainsprings of all our thoughts and actions. Science itself, no matter whether it is the search for truth or merely the need to gain control over the external world, to alleviate suffering, or to prolong life, is ultimately a matter of feeling, or rather, of desire—the desire to know or the desire to realize.

It is not enough to know nature experimentally or to be skilled in analyzing it mathematically; above all, we must know ourselves. A general education truly worthy of the name must combine love of scientific knowledge and a deep concern for the human personality in all its complex aspects with respect for the art of living—of feeling and of wishing. This is the essence of every humanistic trend and the true meaning of humanism, no matter whether it is based on classical elements or not. For that very reason humanism must always reserve an important place for the study of literature.

The study of literature helps us to develop skill in handling our own language or eventually foreign languages, and hence to appreciate its scope and fine points. Such skill is quite indispensable in so complicated an age as ours, when subtle shades of meaning must be given precise definition. This linguistic need is felt even by the sciences, in which language has to express all the subtleties of the complex thoughts of modern scientists. Nor is that precision the sole aim of literary studies, for, quite apart from training us to express ourselves lucidly, literature helps to develop our emotions, teaches us to analyze our feelings, and brings us close to the hidden resources of the human soul. Here literary studies join forces with historical learning, with the study of philosophy, with the fine arts, and with music. Geography, a science in its own right, also has human aspects directly related to the study of literature. Physical training, by strengthening our will, contributes to the formation of total personality. Clearly, therefore, there is a host of disciplines whose educational value perhaps is as important as that of scientific instruction proper, and without which no training of our combined intelligence, heart, and will can be complete.

Let us briefly summarize: Ultimately the essential object of any education worthy of the name will always be the complete study of the human personality in its natural setting. Hence it rightly may be said that the sole object of all knowledge is our inner life. All our knowledge passes through it and is reflected by it—our thoughts, sensations, feelings, desires, decisions, even our science. This is why I feel that a complete education must be based on respect for all the aspects of the human personality. Purely scientific instruction, which by its very nature abstracts the deep sources of our desire and our will, is therefore not enough. Classical studies may continue to decline, but we must make certain that we replace them with nothing short of a fuller culture, to which nothing human is foreign. For this very reason such a culture cannot be built on a basis too narrowly scientific and technical.

FOURTEEN

The Varied Aims of Scientific Research

SCIENCE ADVANCES BY THE JOINT EFFORTS OF A VAST NUMBER
of individual scientists who, although pursuing a common
goal, nevertheless differ in their approach, ability, turn of
mind, and methods.

First of all, there is a clear distinction between theorists
and research workers, between those who try to arrive at
what are often bold and unexpected generalizations and
those who battle patiently and ceaselessly to force nature
to reveal her secrets one by one. While the theorist is generally given to reflection and meditation, while his usual
theatre of operations is his study, and while his thought
is inclined toward mathematical abstractions, the research
worker is usually confined to his laboratory, and, even when
forced to work outside, he always carries his measuring and
other instruments and, hence, the laboratory atmosphere
with him. In permanent contact with physical reality, fully
aware of the technical problems involved in applying his
techniques, and always anxious to avoid errors of measurement and false interpretations, the experimental scientist
proceeds with extreme prudence. He is generally disinclined
to place too much trust in theoretical views, and merely ex-

pects mathematics to serve him as a useful tool. If he draws
on theoretical concepts at all, he often does so rather
naïvely. Thus Faraday's excursion into the theoretical field
filled theorists with amusement. Conversely, research workers often look upon theoretical pursuits as being rather oversimplified and as ignoring the full complexity of observable
events.

Nevertheless there have always been scientists who
were both skillful experimenters and good theorists and who
knew how to combine two essentially distinct approaches to
the investigation of natural phenomena. However, the difficulties and complexities of modern theories, on the one hand,
and the great skill involved in handling apparatus to probe
an ever growing number of phenomena, on the other, have
made it increasingly difficult for modern scientists to play
the role of laboratory worker and theorist successfully. This
trend has the rather unfortunate consequence that many research workers take a number of contemporary theories as
fully proven simply because they do not realize on what
shaky foundations these theories rest, while theorists often
take the results of measurements for granted because they
are in no position to criticize the experimental methods involved or to appreciate what errors could have crept into
them.

So much for the first distinction between the two kinds
of researchers, a distinction that is often so clear-cut that
the two groups seem as poles apart. Thus it is hard to see
any similarity between two men as different as Albert Einstein and Victor Regnault: Einstein, preoccupied by philosophical ideas, flying with the fearlessness of genius from
one theory to an even bolder one; Regnault, meticulous in
his strict concern for established facts, consecrating his life
to the satisfaction of being able, after long experiments and
scrupulous examination of possible errors, to add a decimal

or two to the value of some physical constant. Yet individuals as different as these two have, despite all their differences, contributed to the single task of scientific progress, a task in which a variety of approaches can be combined with the greatest advantage.

Further reflection will reveal still other differences between scientists. Thus theorists themselves can be subdivided into logicians and intuitionists. Logicians attach great importance to developing their arguments with extreme rigor. They start from a minimum of simple principles and endeavor to arrive at what strict logical consequences they can, which are then verified by experiment. In this way they arrive at their austere theories in which imagination plays no part, and which rest on the combination of a logical, theoretical core and careful experimental verification. There has been no period in the history of science in which great minds have not been attracted by this cold approach. In France, Pierre Duhem has been one of its most eloquent advocates; it has been the guiding principle of the energeticists who waged so long and so bitter a rearguard action against the atomic theory of matter. More recently the same formal approach has been adopted by the upholders of the statistical interpretation of quantum mechanics.

Intuitive theorists, on the other hand, have a need for conceptual models; they have an aversion to all over-abstract arguments and, being perhaps more certain than the pure theorists of the real existence of the external world, they feel that a measure of intuitive divination is often as useful as, and sometimes more fruitful than, the dry rigor of their rivals' axiomatic method. Intuitionists, too, have played a leading role in the history of theoretical science. Thus modern physics owes the introduction of the atomic hypothesis and the development of corpuscular theories to them. If the current state of quantum physics seems to lend weight to the arguments of logicians rather than to those of intuitionists, there is no reason for holding that things will always be so, and that imagination may not one day re-invigorate theories which, for the moment, strike one as having become lost in abstraction. Also, the experimenter is generally much closer to the intuitive theoretician than to the logician: having to handle instruments that take up so many square feet of his laboratory, he has a natural pref-erence for clear-cut spatial intuitions, and is generally dis-inclined to assume that, as one modern physicist puts it, the atom or the electron is simply "a system of equations."

There is, then, a strong possibility that in the future as in the past both abstract logic and intuitive imagination will continue to play an important part in the development of science, the former to build a solid structure without flaws, the latter contributing new ideas that will "raise the dough." Moreover, since human nature is extremely complex, all men's intellects contain both logic and intuition, though in varied proportions. An intuitionist who dismisses logic com-pletely will inevitably become the victim of an exaggerated imagination, while the logician who has no tinge of intuition in his make-up will soon fall victim to the most sterile form of scholasticism. No wonder then that scientists represent an immense variety of tendencies, ranging from extreme rigidity to almost complete reliance on intuition, for exam-ple Henri Poincaré. Our remarks do not refer to theorists alone, since experimenters, too, can be divided into similar categories. Thus men like Jean Perrin can be called "strate-gists," since, taking in a situation at a glance, they imme-diately design a crucial experiment that will decide a basic question, while others, whom we might call "tacticians," are more adept at perfecting experimental techniques. Still others, including many theorists, may excel at performing long and exacting tasks involving incredible patience, for instance the compilation of long numerical tables. Today their work is made very much easier by calculating machines.

In applied science, too, theorists and experimenters exist side by side. Thus technicians and engineers may be specialists with rather narrow horizons or men of wide interests who fully merit the name of scientist. Any complete analysis of all their differences would necessarily involve a full examination of their psychological motives, which cannot be given here. We shall therefore be content to end this rapid survey with the following conclusion. Science and its applications are the work of human beings and reflect all the differences that go into man's own make-up. This is true not only of science but also of all other human achievements, and even of man's evolution. This diversity of tendencies and opinions, far from paralyzing progress, is its very mainspring, since conflict alone can overcome inertia and routine, and continuously poses old problems in a new light or poses new ones. Like life itself, science is indebted to diversity and instability—without them it would have stood still.

FIFTEEN

Deduction and Induction
in Scientific Research

THOSE INTERESTED IN THE NATURE OF SCIENTIFIC THEORIES must have noted that in his research the scientist has always followed one of two almost opposite paths, deduction and induction. Deductive reasoning starts from *a priori* concepts and postulates, tries to derive their logical consequences, and then tests these consequences by experiment. The most exact tool of deduction is mathematics, since mathematics offers the quickest and safest route from premises to conclusions. Representing abstract arguments or hypotheses about physical magnitudes by symbols, the deductive scientist constructs his equations according to the rules of logic and then arrives at final, verifiable relations. At this point, he must replace his symbols with numerical values by which alone reality can be tested—reasoning has given way to calculation. Such, by and large, is the deductive procedure of all strict scientific disciplines. By virtue of its clarity and rigor, deductive reasoning appears at first as *the* essential instrument of scientific progress. We shall give our objections to this view later.

Inductive reasoning is less easy to define or to analyze. Based as it is on analogy and intuition and on subtle distinctions rather than geometric precision, induction attempts to *divine* unknown relations, and thus to establish new principles from which deductions may then be made. Clearly, inductive reasoning is much bolder and much more adventurous than deductive reasoning. Deduction is certainty, at least in appearance; induction is risk. But risk is the price paid for all great achievements, and that is why induction, because it disdains established truths to venture forth into unexplored fields, may be said to be the true source of all great scientific advances.

Although rigorous deduction enables us to go forward with almost absolute certainty and precision, it also has a great weakness—starting from a set of certain postulates it can never deduce any fact not contained in them. In a perfect science with a set of firmly established basic principles, deduction would, in fact, be the only correct method, but in an imperfect science still in the process of being shaped (which branch of science can be said to be otherwise?), deduction cannot provide anything but verifications or applications, which, though often very important, cannot lead to really new truths. Great discoveries and leaps of scientific thought are always the result of induction, an adventurous but the only truly creative method.

Naturally this does not mean that the rigor of deductive reasoning has no merit. It is thanks to deduction that our imagination is prevented from getting out of hand and that the consequences of inductive discoveries can be checked against the facts. Deduction endows scientific theories with their indispensable precision and provides an invaluable antidote against flights of fancy. But shackled as it always has been by its own rigor, deduction alone can never hope to be more than just that.

Hence the reader will understand why the axiomatic method, although most satisfying intellectually, is least fruitful in practice. Many brilliant minds, attracted by the elegance of logic, have made great efforts to develop established physical theories in an axiomatic and, hence, a rigorous way. I do not dismiss their efforts as useless. They enable us to clarify basic concepts and postulates, to reveal the formal skeleton of an established hypothesis, to determine its precise scope, and to predict all its consequences. Unfortunately, hardly has this long and often laborious work been completed, when the theory often proves to be inadequate in interpreting the experimental facts, and thus forces the theorist to modify or even to reject all his previous labors. Thus theoretical physicists produced a rigorous interpretation of classical thermodynamics just when the discovery of the atomic structure of matter, of energy fluctuations, and of the true nature of Brownian movement proved their abstractions to be irrelevant.

Although rigorous axiomatic theories cannot be called useless, they do not generally make any great contributions to important scientific advances simply because they ignore intuition, which alone can reveal previously unknown facts.

The reader knows that, mainly during the past few years, scientists have developed remarkable calculating machines capable of performing the most complicated calculations with much greater rapidity and accuracy than those of even the quickest mind. In fact, a recent branch of science, cybernetics, which embraces a number of apparently unrelated scientific disciplines, has tried to liken these calculating machines and similar instruments to the human brain. Certainly these similarities exist and may be useful in determining the functions of the nervous system. But we must not forget that calculation, or more generally deductive reasoning, constitutes the most "mechanical" part of our cerebral activity. This is the reason why, once the correct data have been fed into it, an appropriate machine can perform a given calculation at least as surely as the human brain. But could we imagine a machine capable of giving inductive arguments with all the subtle analogies and brilliant strokes of genius they involve? For my part, I think not, for, when all is said and done, inductive reasoning is a manifestation of our creative faculties. Surely so complex an activity as scientific thought cannot be likened to the automatic functioning of a calculating machine (and the human mind with all its complexity has other aspects!). Such comparisons ignore all that is spontaneous and creative in our scientific discoveries, and creativity, after all, is what most matters in them. The subtle and almost emotional quality of the inductive discoveries of men of genius can have little in common with the automatic workings of a machine.

SIXTEEN

The Role of the Engineer in the Age of Science

ADVANCES OF SCIENCE ALWAYS LEAD TO A BETTER UNDERSTAND-
ing of the laws of nature—science provides us with new
means of acting on the external world and thus controlling
an increasing number of phenomena. In this way, man has
accumulated more and more knowledge and more and more
accurate techniques which have enabled him to build all the
industries that have brought about a veritable revolution
in modern civilization.

In this new phase of human history, the engineer has
come into prominence, and thus it is only fitting that, on the
occasion of the fiftieth anniversary of the foundation of a
leading engineering college, I should say something about
his specific contributions to modern society.

A full appraisal of this contribution would take us too
far afield because it would involve examining the social and
human role of the engineer, his place in urban life, his function as an employer of labor, his personal relations with
his subordinates, in short a psychological survey quite beyond the scope of this brief address and also beyond my

Lecture on the fiftieth anniversary of the founding of the Ecole
Charliat, *May 5, 1951.*

competence. Instead, I shall restrict what few remarks I shall make to his relationship with the pure scientist.

The engineer is, by way of definition, one who has specialized in certain applications of science. This definition shows that he is a man of specific scientific knowledge—of industrial techniques, equipment, which has grown more complex, and scientific developments. All these have driven the engineer ever more closely into the arms of science. As a consequence, engineering colleges have had to raise the level of their instruction and to take a far wider view of science than they used to. Under these conditions it is not surprising that engineers, while fulfilling their practical tasks, or rather the better to fulfill these tasks, are frequently led into purely scientific research. I think that this is true of all branches of engineering, but I shall cite only one example best known to me. In the important fields of electronics and radio electricity, engineers have made almost as great a contribution as professional scientists, and hence have contributed to important technical advances, many of which are based on complicated mathematical theories.

Nevertheless, the role of the engineer is inherently different from that of the scientist. The scientist in his laboratory or in his study is mainly concerned with pure research. His searches for possible applications of his discovery are not his principal preoccupation. Doubtless he may be interested in them momentarily, and there have been notable cases of such interest. In antiquity, Archimedes, the discoverer of the principle of the lever and of the laws of hydrostatics, was a brilliant theorist who had no objection to devoting himself to the application of his discoveries. In particular, it is said that by perfecting a converging mirror, he was able to concentrate the heat of the sun on the Roman ships which were laying siege to Syracuse, and thus to set them on fire. More recently, Christian Huyghens, one of the

founders of modern mechanics and the precursor of the wave
theory of light, developed a clock driven by a spiral spring.
At the beginning of the nineteenth century, Ampère, whose
brilliant contribution to electrodynamics laid the foundation
for the modern science of electricity, was the first to tackle
the construction of an electric telegraph. We could multiply
these examples and thus make it quite clear that the pure
scientist, who like every human being has many sides to
his character, may well take time off to apply his scientific
principles and to develop or at least suggest suitable instruments. But these applications and these instruments generally serve him as means rather than ends, and he usually is
quite content to leave the details in the hands of more practical people. Moreover, the scientist is rarely worried about
the fact that the instruments which he has designed are
fragile or clumsy and hence not suitable for general use. He
himself does not mind working with makeshift apparatus,
nor does he usually mind that his instrument cannot be
mass-produced profitably—a vital concern for the engineer.
Similarly, if a scientist is a mathematician or a theorist, he
will develop his ideas or calculations for the simple pleasure
of opening new vistas on the abstract world of numbers and
functions or on the hidden harmonies of nature. In either
case, his activity is purely disinterested and is directed exclusively toward the pursuit of human knowledge.

The engineer's point of view is radically different. His
aim is always practical, and even if he is given to theoretical
speculation or abstract calculation, he always keeps the
possible technical applications at the back of his mind. Undoubtedly there are engineers who for a time ignore all applications and allow themselves to be carried away by the fas-
cinations of pure science. But in so doing they have ceased
to be engineers, if only momentarily, and have begun to
think and feel like scientists. The true engineer cannot for

long ignore his final aim of producing strong and easy-to-handle machines. Pure research and disinterested observation no longer suffice where mechanical and economic considerations must be coupled with accurate technical knowledge. Although accuracy plays an undeniable role also in the work of the scientist, notably in his measurements, the engineer has a particular attitude to precision: the art of "fitting" the parts to the whole. The various pieces of machinery must be studied individually and severally, free play must be reduced to the minimum, weak links and manufacturing flaws must be eliminated, and any possible future contingencies must be provided for so that the machine may continue to function without constant supervision by specialists.

As a result, the engineer sets about his work with quite a different attitude to, and in quite a distinct atmosphere from, the scientist. The engineer can do his job efficiently only if he can draw upon the services of a competent team of draftsmen, if he has a well-stocked machine shop and a fully equipped drawing office, the essential tools of his trade with which the scientist can generally dispense.

Another significant distinction, to which we have alluded earlier, is the question of spare parts. For the scientist, who generally works with a simple prototype, this question does not even arise, but when a machine or an instrument, for example a car or a radio, is used constantly by great numbers of people, identical spare parts must be made available, and these spare parts must, moreover, be so designed that they can be installed by any workshop or even in the home. This is a typical example of what engrosses the engineer but does not concern the scientist at all.

Despite these important distinctions between the attitudes of scientist and engineer, it is nevertheless a fact that increasing contact is tending to wipe out the dividing line between them, so much so that one and the same individual will be able to combine the faculties of the true engineer with those of the true scientist. Not only are engineers increasingly being compelled to follow closely all the advances of science in their own chosen field and hence to engage in scientific research of their own, but scientists, too, because of the growing complexity and centralization of laboratory research are increasingly brought into contact with a multitude of instruments. This contact necessarily involves familiarity with engineering problems and with the engineers who manufacture the apparatus. Today even research laboratories have their own workshops in which improvised instruments can be designed and repaired. This symbiosis of scientific research and technical problems has become an accomplished fact, especially in the United States, where the relations between scientists and engineers are particularly close. A typical example of this collaboration is American atomic research. Among the armies of scientists and engineers working in square miles of specially constructed laboratory-factories, it would be very difficult to say where science ends and where technology begins.

Moreover, if laboratories have their workshops, industrial plants often have their busy and well-equipped research laboratories. Even in France, where the collaboration between science and industry may not yet be as close as it could be, there are a number of remarkable examples of this symbiosis, in both the private and also the public sectors of industry.

By and large, therefore, the engineer is being brought into ever closer contact with the scientist. This is true even of the theoretical field. Modern engineers are constantly faced with difficult problems which only theoretical scientists can resolve, and theoretical scientists have often benefited from solutions of engineering problems, notably in the field of electronics. Thus the Heaviside "rational" unit of electric charge was the theoretical solution to practical engineering difficulties.

Another important aspect of this symbiosis is its growing influence on teaching methods. Long ago, the education of engineers was somewhat eclectic. Engineering colleges taught a smattering of scientific concepts, while technical schools ignored pure science altogether or treated it like a stepchild. It was due to private initiative alone that French engineering colleges were pulled out of this rut, and it is the result of that initiative, 50 years ago, that we are celebrating today. Since that time, and particularly during the past few years, the education of French engineers has been considerably broadened while its practical tasks have still been borne in mind. All that is to the good, for if higher technical training is to be true to its aims, it must combine direct contact with reality with a love for education. And education can no longer be identified with a knowledge of ancient languages or a critical appreciation of classical literature. However valuable these aspects of man's achievement, they are not the primary concerns of those who will make up the future élite of our country. What is essential for the general cultural framework, to free the engineer from the restrictions of routine and excessive specialization, is a taste for general ideas and a desire to extend his horizon beyond immediate necessity—in a word, that curiosity which, united with practical aims, is the basis of all the inventions and advances of civilization. In this form, broader than the old one, modern culture must enter into even our technical teaching.

In addressing you on the role of the engineer in the modern world, I have stressed only the indispensable and growing collaboration between science and technology. Nevertheless it would be wrong to think that science and technology, the concerns of the scientist and the cares of the engineer, will not remain separate and directed toward different aims. The pursuit of knowledge and the desire for practical results will continue to be opposed in many ways. Here we have one aspect of the latent conflict between thought and action, between the contemplative desire for knowledge and the active joy of implementation—an ancient opposition that has its roots in the very depths of human nature. Even so, thought and action cannot be separated and can never function independently. Pure theorists are in danger of becoming lost in the vanity of ideologies or in the rigidity of scholasticism, while action without the guide of reason cannot but stray into futile fantasy. Hence the need for, and the fruitfulness of, a permanent union between scientific research and engineering know-how.

If we wish to give philosophic expression to the profound connection between thought and action in all fields of human endeavor, particularly in science, we shall undoubtedly have to seek its sources in the unfathomable depths of the human soul. Perhaps philosophers might call it "love" in a very general sense—that force which directs all our actions, which is the source of all our delights and all our pursuits. Indissolubly linked with thought and with action, love is their common mainspring and, hence, their common bond. The engineers of the future have an essential part to play in cementing this bond.

SEVENTEEN

Contemporary Science and Traditional Values

THE LAST FEW CENTURIES HAVE WITNESSED A FASTER AND faster rate of accumulation of scientific knowledge and its applications. The very way of thinking and acting of those generations who have helped this acceleration has become so modified by science that we cannot as yet appreciate the full extent of the repercussions. Instead of looking at this process in detail, I should merely like to show briefly how modern scientists have nevertheless held fast to some of the traditional moral and spiritual values of the past.

The better to appreciate this fact, we shall look at two aspects of a scientist's life—his work and his attitude to science as such.

A scientist, like any other human being, can achieve worthwhile tasks only at the cost of painstaking effort. Thus the scientist must spend long hours in his laboratory or study to design delicate instruments, master difficult techniques, and meditate on challenging problems. Neither talent nor even genius is a substitute for genuine effort and discipline, and since the scientist generally pursues disinterested aims and has no royal road to nature's secrets, the discipline of work is even more inflexible for him than for others.

To resolve the delicate problems he meets constantly and unexpectedly, or even to keep in touch with the discoveries of other scientists at home and abroad, the scientist cannot afford to relax his concentration for any length of time. His life must be consecrated to science, often to the exclusion of many other delights, and this implies a sort of asceticism. He must be scrupulously conscientious, honest in all his intellectual efforts. Vulnerable, like all men, to the temptations of arrogance, of which intellectual pride is the worst, he must nevertheless remain sincere and modest, if only because his studies constantly bring home to him that, compared with the gigantic aims of science, his own contribution, no matter how important, is only a drop in the ocean of truth.

Hence the scientist cannot but practice the most ancient virtues, and would therefore do well to appreciate their full worth. True, scientists, simply because they are human, have their faults and weaknesses, but their work usually follows traditional precepts, and these in turn can supply them with solace and encouragement.

Having looked at the scientist bent on his task, let us now consider the aims and aspirations of science as such.

Even ignoring all metaphysical speculation, we cannot deny that science has great spiritual value. Man's intelligence is unquestionably the greatest milestone in the long evolution of living forms. Thanks to his intelligence, man is capable of plumbing the laws of nature, of associating them with the laws of his own thought, and even of putting them to such use that the entire future of our planet may be modified. Scientists have faith in the value of the human spirit and in scientific achievements. They believe that all the difficulties impeding the progress of science will always be surmounted, that man will be granted an ever fuller vision of the harmonies of nature and an ever greater control of her phenomena. The true scientist, no matter what his other philosophic or religious attitudes, is always a believer, a man who believes in the value of science and the power of man's spirit to resolve the problems that observation of the external world and the constant increase of our knowledge ceaselessly pose.

To that faith he joins a hope, the hope that scientific progress, while consolidating the power of our minds over matter, will be accompanied by a progressive appreciation of spiritual values, bound to a spiritual evolution reflecting the very tendencies of life itself. This attitude toward progress can take many different forms, and according to their personal inclinations scientists may range from mystics to positivists. Even so, all scientists have a common ground for their hopes and faith. True, the pronouncement by the Catholic savant, Professor Rémy Collin, that "God Himself has inscribed the idea of order into the mind of scientists the better to help them appreciate God's thought in nature," is a far cry from Jean Perrin's, "It is thanks to the evolution of more and more differentiated living beings, in which it organizes its substance, that the universe has advanced toward thought, and hence to volition that directs its own destiny." Although these two points of view may strike one as dissimilar, it is nevertheless easy to see that they have a common denominator—faith in spiritual evolution.

Still, the effects of science are not purely intellectual; they also involve a continuous increase in our power of action. It is because of this increase that the last two centuries have seen the birth of so many new industries, of so many great practical achievements, and of so many victories over illness and death. A new figure has entered the arena of science. Bent on overcoming the difficulties of daily life and the miseries of our human condition, he strives to help men, to provide them with new means of action, to ameliorate their existence, to succor and to heal them. Thus science has assumed the great mantle of charity. Many great scientists are particularly sensitive to that social, human, and beneficial aspect of science, which has done so much to assure the regard of the masses for scientific effort.

Unfortunately, the achievements of science are not always used for the good of mankind. Science also provides those formidable weapons that we use against one another. The danger to the future of humanity in this deplorable use of science has become evident in the invention of the atomic bomb. We need not stress the moral and international repercussions of this discovery, and we can only hope that human beings will be wise enough not to abuse the tools with which science has provided them, but will put them to peaceful uses instead. This, indeed, is a hope shared by all scientists.

Because it believes, because it hopes, because it sympathizes, modern science is a great source of ideals. Not wedded to any particular metaphysical school, science embraces all the great moral values that, in the course of centuries, have recommended themselves to the spirits and hearts of all men of good will.

EIGHTEEN

Reflections of
an Elder Scientist

TOWARD THE END OF ONE'S LIFETIME (AND WHO AMONG US can be certain that it is not at hand?), it is only natural that he tries to assess the meaning of his life and pass judgment on all his past activities. Those of us who have devoted the greatest part of our lives to scientific research will be particularly concerned about the material and spiritual values of science and its rightful place in civilization and the general evolution of the human race, and about the destiny of the universe and human thought. Let us therefore suppose that our last hour has struck, and let us meditate on these grave problems.

Some hundreds of millions of years ago, when life first appeared on the surface of the earth, it was undoubtedly so lowly that it could barely be distinguished from inert matter. Then, in the course of centuries or millenia, a mysterious force, which we are still far from understanding, helped life to spread out in the oceans, in the air, and on land, producing more and more complicated organisms, better and better adapted to the diverse conditions of life. Palaeontological findings make it very probable that all species go back to a common source, although we do not know by which con-

218

tinuous processes (gradual evolution or sudden mutations) the different living forms, past or present, first came into being. In the course of this long and astonishing evolution of life on our planet, of this gradiose epic which Jean Rostand has justly called "the adventure of protoplasm," living organisms have adapted to environmental conditions with incredible subtlety, to arrive at the measure of prodigious complexity and the wealth of forms that we observe in all species, particularly in the higher vertebrates. The astonishing physicochemical mechanism that has ensured the life of individuals and its perpetuation over successive generations, together with the function of the sense organs by which living beings keep in contact with their environment, cannot but fill us with wonder and admiration. It is the ability to discriminate between advantageous and dangerous environmental factors that makes the structure and unparalleled sensitivity of such organs as the eye and the ear in higher animals as perfect as they seem to be, and it strikes one as incredible that such organs could have been produced by the effects of pure chance, even over eons. Living structures seem to be the products of some kind of organizing force which does not appear in inert matter, and whose true nature completely eludes us.

Side by side with the grandeur of living beings and with their faculty of perception, there arose one of the most astonishing phenomena in nature—consciousness. The most highly developed animal, man, is conscious of his individuality and autonomy in the physical world; that is, he consciously interprets the messages that the external world transmits to him by way of his sense organs, so that they become reflected within him. A profoundly mysterious faculty! We can explain, for instance, how light enters the eye, falls on the retina, and causes the optic nerve to transmit an electric impulse which stimulates certain nervous cells of our brain, but we cannot possibly explain the transformation of these purely physical phenomena into their conscious perception.

The appearance of thought marked another milestone in the history of life on earth. Bound up with the existence of consciousness, which is its necessary condition, thought is superior to it. Its higher forms, which tend by abstraction and generalization to assimilate the necessarily limited and specific data of perception, are infinitely superior to simple consciousness. Although elementary consciousness is found in relatively inferior species, thought, in even its simplest forms, can be found only in the most intelligent vertebrates, and it reaches its full measure in man alone. It has often been said that thought constitutes man's dignity and ensures his exceptional place in nature.

The appearance of man on earth and his development of reason, thanks to the prodigious complexity of his cerebral mechanisms, have so changed the course of evolution that each new chapter of history has reflected the growth of human intelligence. Man has tried to understand what he observes, to classify phenomena, and to detect their inner cohesion. He has grown in understanding as he has interpreted nature, and as he has communicated his newly won knowledge, first by word of mouth and then by symbol and paper. In looking for laws and causes, the human mind asks a series of "hows" and "whys," and thus poses those scientific and metaphysical problems which are its torment while redounding to its credit.

Clearly, the gradual appearance of consciousness and thought in the physical world is the more astonishing and incomprehensible, as there is no reason we know why nature should not have remained eternally unconscious and inert. What a strange fate that the small bits of animated matter that we are should, by sheer dint of effort over generations.

have managed to refashion some element of that nature from which we have sprung. Our body consists of atoms made up of countless electrons, protons, and other elementary particles in which quantum transitions occur ceaselessly. Our nervous system, the main instrument of all our activities, is the seat of innumerable electrical phenomena. Our inner balance and the processes which ensure the continuity of our existence depend on the action of hormones, vitamins, and an immense number of complicated organic substances. These, though inside us, would have eluded us completely had not modern science revealed their existence. Science is therefore a strange sort of penetration into a world which through human consciousness and reason has learned to become aware of itself. Who would have expected this astonishing conclusion to the adventure of protoplasm?

Hence the eminent value of human thought in general and of scientific thought in particular. Through it man has become the consciousness of the universe, and every scientific advance marks an advance of that consciousness.

Here is the real grandeur of disinterested science. But there is another way of looking at things, the active viewpoint. We have said that the appearance on earth of more and more complex conscious organisms has set life on a new path. Rooted in inert matter and under constant inner pressure, living matter, as it broke up into entities conscious of their autonomy, began to have a direct effect on the environment and to modify evolution itself. This is particularly true of man who, unlike other organisms which reacted to their environment by evolving sense organs and by responding to sense impressions by anatomical and physiological actions, has learned to extend the evolution of his sense organs by making use of scientific instruments. The telephone and the radio enable him to hear over incredible distances, and optical instruments allow his eyes to probe the mysteries of the heavens and the heart of the matter. While science improves and refines our powers of perception, it also gives us unexpected means of action—the railway, the steamship, the submarine, the automobile, and the airplane enable us to move across the earth, the sea, and the air with ever increasing speed. The steam engine, the internal combustion engine, and the power station supply us with energy where and when we need it. Chemistry with its ever greater number of compounds offers to industry unlimited possibilities of extension. Rapid advances in medicine and surgery have led to a reduction of illness and fatal diseases, and biology has begun to throw some light on the mystery of life itself, particularly on the mechanism of heredity. Biology does, in fact, provide the best illustration of how life has become conscious of itself.

And thus thanks to science and its technical applications, man rules over the earth and transforms its history. He knows its entire surface, he plows it with skill, he gains increasing control over its flora and fauna. By means of atomic energy and other discoveries still to be made, man will extend his mastery ever farther. No one can tell the limits of this expansion, or whether some accidental or deliberately induced mutation will not give birth to a superman with a much vaster intelligence than our own, one who will use unsuspected resources to further the work which we have begun.

Fired by these prospects, the man of science can justly be proud that he, more than anyone else, has a share in this progressive evolution. He might well be tempted to exclaim with Jean Perrin that "it is thanks to the evolution of more and more differentiated living beings in which it organizes its substance that the universe advances toward thought and hence to volition which directs its own destiny."

Nevertheless some of us take a rather pessimistic view

of things. Life, thought, and will are only known to exist on the surface of the earth, that small planet of a modest solar system. Man's activity is restricted to that planet, and even to limited regions of its surface. Clearly, other solar systems may well have planets where life can manifest itself, where thinking beings similar to ourselves may perform tasks similar to ours. While we might think that man may one day manage to leave the earth and extend his influence in the universe, that influence must always remain miserably insignificant when compared with the immensity of the heavens, the gigantic dimensions of a universe in which the galaxies float like so many giant islands separated by hundreds of millions of light years. The gradual evolution of life on earth, the achievements of our intelligence and our will—everything that makes us so proud and confident—are as nothing in the face of the immensity of space and the immensity of time. The inevitable death of the earth and the solar system, the sole theatre of all our present or future activities, oppresses us with morbid thoughts and may fill us with despair.

Perhaps we are the victims of an illusion and attach too much importance to space and time, the simple framework of our perceptions. Perhaps we are wrong to assume that the true value of a phenomenon can be assessed by the volume of space or the interval of time it occupies. Perhaps the entire perceptible universe from the atom to the spiral nebula is nothing but a small slice of a very much vaster reality which some superman may one day come to know, if only partially. In that greater reality, our efforts which must strike an observer on, say, Sirius, as so localized and so impermanent might yet prove valuable and rewarding. As we stitch away at a small corner of the tapestry of life, we are unable to appreciate our own contribution to the final masterpiece which we rightly hope to admire one day. Similarly, human thought of the future may well be able to look beyond the confines of space and time to behold the veritable meaning of the work which man, extending and crowning the efforts of life, has striven ceaselessly to accomplish. This is the greatest comfort to all scientists who have arrived at the end of their task.

PART FOUR

On the History
of Science

NINETEEN

The Value of
the History of Science

THE HISTORY OF SCIENTIFIC THOUGHT IS ONE OF THE MOST curious and most instructive branches of the history of civilization. It presents us with the epic spectacle of man's powerful and uninterrupted effort to wrest nature's secrets from her and his gradual mastery of her forces as he extended his dominion over his environment, over the dangers and maladies that assailed him, and—alas!—over his fellow men. The history of science helps us to evaluate to what extent scientific discoveries have influenced man's mentality and outlook and the development of civilization itself. Laplace rightly said of man's scientific efforts that "progress in this field distinguishes nations and centuries from one another and constitutes their true glory."

The history of science can tell us a great deal about the way men think when faced with external problems. It tells us how man's innate curiosity drove him first to observe phenomena, then to classify or relate them according to the observed similarities, and later still to fit his new-found knowledge into sweeping theories and to invent instruments to measure and harness nature's forces. Clearly, no single man could have performed all these tasks unaided. There is a division of labor in science as in the factory, and each scientist may be said to be primarily an experimenter, a theorist, or a technologist. Here the history of science can teach psychology many important facts about the nature of human intelligence.

The history of science is also an excellent means of teaching science in schools and colleges. Science can be taught in one of two main ways, or in a combination of both. The first way is to present science in its contemporary state and to present all its known laws. This is the logical and deductive approach, in which historical developments are ignored. The second way is to follow the march of scientific thought and of its advances in historical perspective, thus showing how experimental discoveries and theoretical views grew up and succeeded one another. For practical purposes, the first method has the advantage of being quicker, since it goes straight to the point and ignores any erudite discussions about the past. But how much more instructive is the second method, which alone can demonstrate by what often strange, often tortuous, routes the human spirit must advance if it is to arrive at the truth! In resurrecting the knowledge and theoretical concepts of the past, this method makes us privy to the very basis of science and enables us to see it in perspective. Some people have argued that by concentrating on the deductive method of teaching we eliminate all the accidental factors that have beset scientists in the past. This is a false view, since modern science, willy-nilly, bears the marks of previous achievements. No study of electromagnetism would be complete without reference to electricity produced by friction or permanent magnets, not because these phenomena are simple (they are, in fact, so complicated that even modern physics finds it difficult to explain them), but simply because they have been known since antiquity and have therefore become familiar to all of us. Would optics be taught in the customary way, had the photo-electric effect been discovered before interference, or electron diffraction by crystals before those phenomena which lead us to think of the electron as a particle? In principle, there is no reason why the granular aspect of light should have been discovered before the wave aspect, or the wave aspect of the electron before its granular aspect, in which case our teaching of physics would have been quite different. One could find similar examples in other branches of science, and we may therefore say that the sciences advance by a process of historical accretion, which is bound to be reflected in scientific education. At every period, any given branch of science bears the unmistakable stamp of that series of steps, often accidental, which have gone into its making. Like the individual, every science carries the permanent traces of a long heredity, and this is one of the main reasons why the history of science, which studies these "hereditary" factors, gives us a true insight into the value and the limits of our knowledge.

Thus the history of science brings out the close connection between the reasoned attempts of successive generations to gain a better understanding of natural phenomena. It brings home to us how much tenacity, talent, and sometimes genius were needed to formulate the principles underlying all our current knowledge, principles which strike us as obvious only because we have been taught to take them for granted. Who can help being moved, for instance, by the painful, prolonged, and often vain efforts of those great men who, toward the end of the Middle Ages or at the beginning of modern times, laid the foundations of mechanics in the face of the then reigning misconceptions of Aristotelian dynamics, and at a time when mathematics provided physicists with only the most rudimentary tools? Theirs was an uphill struggle, and we, who from adolescence onward have been provided with so much more precise and more extended knowledge and with powerful mathematical tools, must render homage to those who, ignorant and ill-equipped, nevertheless managed to lay the foundations of our own vast knowledge.

By combining the efforts of generations of scientists, science, despite its errors, failures, and innumerable deviations, has managed to construct that immense body of modern knowledge which daily becomes greater and wider. Without necessarily being aware of it, scientists have combined to perform a great common task, and this is perhaps the best lesson we can learn from the history of science.

TWENTY

Pascal and the Dawn
of Modern Science

ON FEBRUARY 11, 1650, RENÉ DESCARTES SUCCUMBED TO THE
unfriendly climate of Stockholm, where he had taught
mathematics to that very strange woman, Queen Christina
of Sweden. With his death, there passed away a great genius
whose philosophical ideas and scientific discoveries will long
be remembered. But a new star of incomparable brightness
already shone in the brilliant firmament of French thought
—Blaise Pascal.

Pascal was born in 1623. His father, Etienne Pascal,
was a very learned man who, after serving as President of
the Court of Aids at Clermont-Ferrand, retired to Paris to
pursue his studies and give his children a good education.
Subsequently he was appointed Administrator of Normandy.
Etienne Pascal was keenly interested in mathematics and
a member of a small group of scientists who met regularly
at Père Mersenne's. Brought up in a scholarly atmosphere,
young Blaise soon proved an infant prodigy who, not content with studying ancient literature, is said to have redis-
covered the first 32 propositions of Euclid by himself. At
the age of 16 he wrote a work on geometry, his "Essay on
Conics," in which he discovered new properties of conic

sections and propounded a theorem which continues to be known by his name. He also wrote other books on geometry, which unfortunately have been lost.

Joining his father in Rouen, Pascal tried to simplify his father's laborious tax calculations by inventing the first calculating machine, so ingenious an instrument that even Descartes, who was not greatly given to admiring the work of others, could not hide his admiration. In constructing this machine, Pascal showed rare inventive qualities, not usually found in theorists and philosophers of his rank. The same combination of qualities also enabled him to launch and organize the first commercial omnibus service in Paris.

At the time when Pascal reached the age of 20, physicists were particularly interested in the hydrostatic problems presented by vacuums. It was said that nature abhors a vacuum, and this vague phrase had been used to explain the action of pumps. But in 1638, after consultations with a Florentine fountainmaster, Galileo had shown that water cannot rise beyond eighteen spans (a little more than 10 meters) inside a vacuum. Nature's abhorrence of a vacuum was therefore not unlimited—a very troubling discovery. Then, in 1644, Torricelli invented the mercury barometer and thus raised the problem of vacuums again.

Young Pascal was passionately interested in this problem. He repeated Torricelli's experiment and explained that the height of the mercury in the barometer was the result of air pressure on the mercury in the open arm of the U tube. Nature, according to Pascal, knew pressure effects but no abhorrence. When he tried to prove this contention by ingenious variations of his original experiment, the whole problem became the subject of keen scientific controversy.

Clearly a crucial experiment was needed to silence his critics. Pascal realized that, if he was correct, the barometric column must fall with altitude—that is, with reduced air pressure—and that a demonstration of this effect would in fact be proof positive of his theory. Possibly other scientists, such as Mersenne and Descartes, had similar ideas, but certainly they did not formulate them clearly or try to verify them experimentally. However, Pascal wrote to his brother-in-law Florin Périer in Clermont-Ferrand and asked him to repeat Torricelli's experiment, first at the foot and then at the peak of the Puy de Dôme. Périer was busy with other things and put off the experiment, but finally, on September 19, 1648, with the help of some local scientists, he made a series of precise barometric measurements in the center of Clermont-Ferrand, at the peak of the Puy de Dôme, and halfway up the mountain. The results fully confirmed Pascal's predictions. Pascal was delighted with the news, and he immediately repeated Périer's experiments in a building in Paris and on the St. Jacques tower with equal success.

The Puy de Dôme experiment was a memorable event in the history of science. Périer's carefully controlled measurements may be said to have ushered in the era of experimental physics, and for the first time a theoretically predicted physical phenomenon was confirmed by accurate experiment.

Pascal called this experiment the "experiment of the equilibrium of fluids," for he fully appreciated its connection with the general principles of hydrostatics which he was then in the process of developing. Shortly afterwards, in 1653 and 1654, he published his *Treatise on the Equilibrium of Fluids,* and his *Treatise on the Weight of Air,* which have remained classics.

In 1654 this astonishing man of genius also laid the basis of the probability calculus during his work on the "geometry of chance." In particular, he described the arithmetical triangle, from which he quickly deduced the many formulas which are still part and parcel of arithmetic and algebra.

But his extraordinary destiny suddenly drove him into an entirely new path. During the night of November 23, 1654, Pascal had a mystical vision which changed his whole outlook. From that night onward, metaphysical and religious problems were to occupy the center of his thoughts, and though he would occasionally return to mathematics, for instance to study the "roulette" (or cycloid as we call it today), he never again published anything except isolated papers, generally under a pseudonym. In the course of his later work he came very close to discovering the infinitesimal calculus, but the honor fell to Newton and Leibnitz.

In 1662, Blaise Pascal died at the age of 39, bequeathing to the world, quite apart from his great scientific work, the imperishable heritage of his moving *Pensées*.

In 1666 Colbert reorganized the small group of scientists whom Père Mersenne had previously gathered around him into the Royal Academy of Science. The Paris Observatory, which will always be associated with the brilliant names of Cassini, Picard, and Roemer, was built in 1667. While Boyle, Mariotte, and Hooke developed different branches of physics, and while Christian Huyghens was about to launch his great work on mechanics and optics, a taciturn young man, Isaac Newton, was making ready to propound the main principles of the infinitesimal calculus, of Newtonian mechanics, and of universal gravitation. These men and their brilliant ideas ushered in the dawn of modern science.

TWENTY-ONE

Science in the
Century of Genius

FROM THE SCIENTIFIC POINT OF VIEW, THE EIGHTEENTH CEN-
tury was a continuation of the seventeenth, which had seen
extremely rapid advances in scientific knowledge due to the
work of brilliant men. In mathematics, Descartes had invented analytical geometry; Fermat had made his tremendous contribution to the theory of numbers; Pascal had laid
the bases of his probability calculus; and Newton and Leibnitz had introduced infinitesimal analysis. Galileo, Huyghens, and Newton had founded mechanics; Kepler, Galileo,
and Newton had helped celestial mechanics to its feet. Snell,
Descartes, Fermat, Huyghens, and Newton once again had
turned optics into a precise quantitative science, while Gil-
bert, Hook, Boyle, and Mariotte had developed other
branches of physics. Physiology and biology, then still in
their infancy, owed a great deal to the work of Harvey,
Malpighi, Leuwenhoek, and others, while men like Tournefort had helped to infuse new life into botany.

Heir to so brilliant an epoch, the eighteenth century
began its work with enthusiasm. True, by 1750 it had not
made nearly as great a contribution as that of its forerunner
and had rather concentrated on developing and clarifying

235

earlier findings. It had nevertheless good reason to be proud
of having witnessed the great work of Newton and Leibnitz'
heirs—Euler, Clairaut, and d'Alembert. It saw the *Académie
des Sciences* become the leader of the scientific movement
of the time and send out two expeditions to Lapland and to
equatorial America with instructions to measure the length
of a degree of the local meridian accurately. While d'Alembert did much to develop mechanics, Maupertuis introduced
his principle of least action, in a somewhat questionable
form, it is true. A new branch of physics, electricity, was
born, thanks to the work of Gray, Du Fay, the Abbé Nollet,
and Benjamin Franklin. The achievements of Linnaeus in
botany and those of Réaumur, Charles Bonnet, Maupertuis,
and Buffon in natural history were as substantial as they
were brilliant. While Bouguer created photometry, chemistry, still in its infancy, received from Stahl its fallacious but
nevertheless remarkable phlogiston theory.

Clearly, scientists in the middle of the eighteenth century had every reason to be enthusiastic about all these advances. Adopting strict scientific methods of inquiry, they,
more than their great seventeenth century predecessors,
managed to rid themselves of traditional prejudices, and they
looked forward to a new age of reason in which science would
go from strength to strength. Dazzled by these prospects, they
had no hesitation in calling theirs the "Age of Enlightenment," and while subsequent events may not have borne out
their hopes, the nobility of their aspirations cannot be
denied.

In those days scientists were still amateurs, and the
universities concentrated on classical learning. Hence scientists were not yet tied to academic disciplines and were freer
to follow their inclinations. Many, like Maupertuis, Bouguer,
and La Condamine, who participated in the work of measuring meridians, were explorers in their own right, and it is

partly to La Condamine that we owe the discovery of India rubber. D'Alembert, the first permanent secretary of the *Académie française,* and Maupertuis, the president of the Prussian Academy founded by Frederick II, were men of letters as well as scientists. Still, physicists often looked like so many jugglers and were given to entertaining gaping audiences. Even the more serious scientists, such as the Abbé Nollet and Benjamin Franklin, could not restrain the satisfaction of dazzling their contemporaries—an activity which nowadays strikes us as being incompatible with the dignity of the true scientist.

We must not be astonished to learn that, side by side with serious scientists, there existed a host of charlatans who tried to exploit the credulity of a gullible public. No wonder that the hoaxes of Mesmer and Cagliostro took in even the best educated people, and that, as Bachelard has stressed, serious scientific works continued to exist side by side with a host of pseudo-scientific nonsense, full of flights of fancy and traditional misconceptions. But, when all is said and done, are we very much better off today?

All these shortcomings of the eighteenth century must not blind us to its great achievements. On the one hand, it produced some of the greatest masterpieces of all time, and on the other hand, although unquestionably frivolous in many respects, it was the backdrop for the activities of many curious and keen scientific spirits, who tried with sympathy and enthusiasm to keep abreast of human advances. Writers like Voltaire and noble women like his friend the Marquise du Châtelet, read, translated, or expounded the work of Newton, while the Empress Catherine II invited d'Alembert to become her son's tutor. Never before or since have the highest and the most refined forms of human intelligence been held in greater honor.

We have been left with one great monument to the

noble age, the French *Encyclopaedia*. That survey of the sum of all human knowledge, an immense work by its very nature, was compiled by a group of distinguished scientists and eminent scholars headed by d'Alembert, the editor of its Preface. D'Alembert, to whom mathematics, mechanics, and physics all owe an everlasting debt, was an almost universal genius, and his countenance, as portrayed magnificently by La Tour, reflects his intellectual stature. The *Encyclopaedia* was finally completed in the face of great difficulties and opposition, some of it justified, for it must be admitted that its sentiments were not always as impartial as they could have been and, hence, challenged not only prejudices but also honest and respectable convictions. Despite its imperfections and flaws, the French *Encyclopaedia* remains a remarkable document. From the scientific point of view, a number of its articles make interesting reading to this day because, edited by scientists of repute, they give us an accurate idea of the scientific knowledge of the time. The modern reader cannot help being infected by its enthusiasm and hope, enthusiasm for scientific research and hope that science may contribute to the common weal. Ultimately, these sentiments, despite the many exaggerations and illusions which have gone into them, redound to the credit and honor of the "Age of Enlightenment."

TWENTY-TWO

D'Alembert: Mathematician
and Man of Letters

ONE DAY IN NOVEMBER 1717, AN INFANT WAS FOUND ABAN-
doned on the steps of the Church of St. Jean Lerond, hard
by Notre Dame in Paris. The child was subsequently discovered to have been the result of a lapse on the part of a
noble but irresponsible canoness, Mlle. Tencin, with a dash-
ing officer, the Chevalier Destouches. Destouches later found
the child, devoted himself to the boy's education, and left
him an income of 1,200 pounds per year. When the police
picked up the baby, they named him Jean-Baptiste Lerond,
after the church in front of which he was found, and handed
him over to the wife of a poor Parisian glazier, Mme. Rousseau, who became his foster mother. It was in her house that
the Chevalier Destouches eventually found the boy and
then charged himself with his education.

After his father's death, Jean Lerond, then twelve years
old, entered the *Collège des Quatre-Nations*. He proved a
brilliant pupil, matriculated, and then attended lectures at
the School of Law. It was at that stage that, for unknown
reasons, he changed his name first to d'Arembert and later
to d'Alembert—the name under which he was to become
so famous. At the age of 20 he had an insatiable thirst for

knowledge but, like so many promising youngsters, little taste for hard work. Thus he refused to be called to the bar, although his studies qualified him for it. Instead he turned to medicine, only to abandon his medical studies soon afterward. Meanwhile he became more and more interested in mathematics, and in 1739, at the age of 22, he read a paper to the *Académie des Sciences*. While this paper was not remarkable, subsequent ones attracted the attention of the mathematicians of the Academy.

Today the gates of the Academy are closed to all but mature men, but in 1742 science had not yet reached its modern sedateness. Thus d'Alembert was appointed Fellow in Astronomy at the tender age of 24, and Associate in Geometry four years later. The remainder of his academic career was less brilliant. Though he was made a supernumerary pensionary in 1756, it was not until 1765, when he was 47 years old, that this mathematician of world renown was appointed a full pensionary, that is, a full member of the Academy. The reason for this strange delay was that d'Alembert had meanwhile become one of the founders of the *Encyclopaedia* and thus incurred the displeasure of what we should nowadays call the "powers that be."

But let us return to the work which from 1742 to 1755 had gone to make up d'Alembert's mathematical reputation. Above all, d'Alembert applied mathematics to mechanics and to astronomy; quite apart from that, he also developed important results in algebra, particularly the fundamental theorem that bears his name—the theorem that every algebraic equation has at least one real or imaginary solution. But his earliest claim to fame rests on his publication in 1743, at the age of 26, of his famous *Treatise on Dynamics*, which in the history of mechanics marks a halfway stage between the work of Newton and that of Lagrange. While Newton had propounded the principles of this new science with magnificent clarity, neither he nor his immediate successors had the time to develop the powerful synthetic methods by which a host of mechanical problems could be expressed by equations—methods which Lagrange was to develop rigorously at the end of the eighteenth century in his immortal *Treatise on Analytical Mechanics*. It can reasonably be claimed that it was d'Alembert who first opened the path that Lagrange so triumphantly followed. In fact, the famous d'Alembert principle, first propounded in the *Treatise on Dynamics,* continues to be the basis of analytical mechanics to this day.

In this treatise d'Alembert considered the general case of a mechanical system in motion under internal constraints. He showed that, for the internal forces to be balanced, there must be an equality, one could say equilibrium, between the actual forces that imposed motion on the system and the forces that would be necessary to give it this motion if the internal forces did not exist. In this way he showed how the laws of dynamics could be reduced to considerations of static equilibrium. By treating dynamic problems as instances of the "principle of virtual velocities" (our principle of virtual work), he laid the foundations for Lagrange's subsequent magnificent generalization of analytical mechanics.

D'Alembert's *Treatise on Dynamics* alone would have ensured him lasting fame, but with youthful enthusiasm he continued his work. He wrote a book on winds and atmospheric currents, containing a wealth of brilliant ideas and a number of errors, which we cannot really hold against him, meteorology being a difficult and uncertain science. In 1749 he also published a remarkable paper on the precession of the equinoxes. This cosmic phenomenon, with a period of roughly 26,000 years, was already known to Hipparchus. Newton had rightly attributed it to the action of gravitational forces on the earth as an imperfect sphere, but d'Alembert produced a quantitative interpretation of all the observations. He also tackled other problems of mathematical astronomy with equal success, in particular, the difficult problem of the apparently capricious motion of our own satellite, the moon. If we may call d'Alembert the precursor of Lagrange in mechanics, we may also call him the precursor of Laplace in celestial mechanics, to which he contributed some of its most important concepts.

Another problem investigated by d'Alembert at about that period was that of the vibration of strings, previously studied by Taylor. D'Alembert managed to show that these vibrations could be expressed by a partial differential equation, and he even suggested the general solution to that equation. We may say that, in so doing, the great mathematician became one of the founders of mathematical physics, since he formulated the first of those wave equations which now play so great a part in all branches of theoretical physics—in acoustics, optics, electromagnetism, right up to wave mechanics. It is only fitting that the operator by which wave equations can be expressed in shortened form is generally known as the d'Alembertian. D'Alembert's work on vibrating strings is sufficient to make his name immortal, the more so because it gave rise to a most fruitful discussion with Euler, who had given a trigonometrical solution to the problem which seemed to differ radically from d'Alembert's. A comparison of the two solutions and the explanation why Euler's trigonometrical solution can be applied to all initial states of the string, together with Fourier's brilliant contribution to heat theory, have led to the formulation of that essential theory of modern physics, the theory of values and characteristic functions.

We shall pass over d'Alembert's work on probability, which Daniel Bernoulli was later to develop so successfully. By a strange paradox, which shows how difficult the basis of probability theory really is, d'Alembert's keen intellect never came to grips with it, and his studies of the famous St. Petersburg problem led him to propound contradictions which no modern statistician would overlook. Probability was d'Alembert's only mathematical weakness.

On the other hand, d'Alembert continued to develop his equilibrium theory and extended it to the movement of fluids and their resistance to the movement of immersed bodies. We know that hydrodynamics is a particularly difficult branch of mechanics and that many of its problems are unsolved to this day. It is to d'Alembert that we owe the famous paradox according to which it can be proved from simple hydrodynamical principles that a body must move through a liquid without resistance or, what comes to the same thing, that a pylon plunged into a swirling river should not experience any upthrust. This result is clearly contrary both to our intuition and to experiment, and the paradox was solved only very recently when modern hydrokinetic theory replaced the simple and continuous solutions of hydrodynamics by solutions containing discontinuous layers and turbulent flow.

A little later, in 1750, d'Alembert, who was then 35 years old, changed the direction of his work. From then on, he published important scientific papers more and more rarely, for example his 1771 contribution on the eastward deflection of projectiles. The reason was simple. He had turned writer and become a keen partisan in the raging polemics of his time. He became a close friend of Voltaire and an associate of Diderot, one of the chief founders of the encyclopaedic movement; he had joined the French Academy in 1755, and became its permanent secretary in 1772. In short, his time was devoted to matters other than science.

It would take us too far afield to give a detailed account of this aspect of d'Alembert's activity, which falls

into the province of literature and philosophy rather than
that of the history of science. We must nevertheless mention that the French *Encyclopaedia,* this gigantic work, was
intended to tabulate the sum total of human knowledge in
the middle of the eighteenth century. Conceived by a group
of liberal intellects (or "libertarians" as they were then
called) the *Encyclopaedia* was suffused with a critical and
anticlerical spirit, and its outlook was based on the rational-
ist philosophy then in great vogue. Diderot, the dynamic
force behind it, recruited a great number of distinguished
and famous men as his collaborators. Among these d'Alembert was one of the most active, and the honor of presenting
the work to the public fell to him. The *Discours prélimi-
naire* which he contributed to the first volume of the *Encyclopaedia,* published in 1751, was received with mixed
judgment, for while some were astonished by the wide learning of its author, by the loftiness of his views, and by the
elegance of his style, others called him a sectarian, a systematic purveyor of false philosophic and literary opinions,
and accused him of a lack of respect or feeling for the
masterpieces of thought and art. There is no doubt that
praises and attacks were equally justified. D'Alembert was
a most erudite scholar, but he was also inclined to let his
sharp tongue run away with him. This, combined with his
dogmatism, tended to spoil some of his work. This is true of
many of the articles in the *Encyclopaedia* which he edited.
Then his work as an Encyclopaedist was cut short. Influen-
tial circles, notably those shocked by the *Encyclopaedia*'s
irreligious tendencies, made every effort to suspend a publication which they hated, and despite the sympathy of even
the royal government, a special decree was passed against
its publication. D'Alembert, who had no taste for martyr-
dom, retired from the enterprise and left Diderot and his

friends to pursue and finish the task when conditions should prove more favorable.

Without stressing d'Alembert's quarrels with his contemporaries, and his great polemics in defense of freedom of thought and against clericalism, we shall conclude this rapid sketch of the life and work of d'Alembert with a brief reference to his association with Mlle. de Lespinasse. Around 1750 d'Alembert, already famous and loved for his amiable disposition, was in the habit of frequenting a number of salons where he met the leading figures of his time. It was at one of these gatherings in the house of Mme. du Deffand that he first met Mlle. de Lespinasse, who worked there as a tutor. The intelligence and charm of this young society lady quickly captivated him and, when Julie de Lespinasse left Mme. Deffand after a quarrel and installed herself in modest lodgings, d'Alembert left the home of Rousseau, where he had lived up to then, and went to live with his new friend. His well-known lack of romantic sentiment soon gave way to great passion, which was the greater because it had so long been kept in check. Paraphrasing Tasso, he wrote: "All these years I have spent without love were so many wasted years"—a strange cry from a man who had achieved so much.

D'Alembert was not happy in his love. Mademoiselle de Lespinasse was capricious, frivolous, and unfaithful, and she caused him constant anguish. Even so, he never ceased to love her; when she died in 1776 he was so grief-stricken that he spent the rest of his life in gloomy solitude. D'Alembert died at the age of 66 on October 29, 1783—old before his time and deeply discouraged.

D'Alembert was a simple, easy-going man whose heart was in the right place. The love he bore the Rousseaus, his foster parents, never flagged, and even after he had become famous he continued to share their humble existence. Nevertheless, his caustic tongue often belied his natural kindness. Thus he had the bad taste to write of a respected fellow-academician, Fontaine, that "society has gained more by his death than geometry has lost by it."

D'Alembert was not given to ostentation and loved his independence above all things. He preferred to live humbly on his modest income rather than accept the most tempting offers of King Frederick II of Prussia and Czarina Catherine II, who were anxious to become his protectors. Faithful to his friends and to his country, whose ingratitude he often deplored, he preferred his familiar environment to a brilliant, though servile, life at court. His love of independence was such that he has been called "the slave of his own liberty."

D'Alembert has often been judged severely. That severity was only to be expected from clerics and conservatives who must have hated his dissolute talk. Even a writer like Gustave Lanson who had no such prejudices treated him harshly in his *History of French Literature:* "D'Alembert, the illustrious mathematician, the man who loved independence more than ambition and personal interest, cultivated his peace of mind to the point of egotism and of refusing to take a public stand, while inciting others to compromise themselves. He was a narrow-minded critic whose spirit was shut to art and to poetry, an intolerant philosopher who hated religion and priests, a clumsy and tactless writer with an innate lack of elegance and a dryness that was only too thinly disguised as eloquence or nobility. His literary contribution seems slender, and will decrease in value with the passage of time."

No doubt Lanson was right to say that D'Alembert had many personal faults and that his style sometimes lacked grace, but we must also remember the breadth of his intelligence, and the great value of his scientific work. D'Alembert was the indispensable link between the great "initiators" of modern science—Newton, Huyghens, and Leibnitz—and the great "codifiers"—Laplace and Lagrange.

As for his role as polemicist and philosopher, we may fairly say that d'Alembert and those of his contemporaries who went along with him and who appreciated that their epoch marked a turning point in the history of civilization were intoxicated by the remarkable advances of the science of their time. Like adolescents, they allowed themselves to be carried away by their newly acquired powers, and were convinced of the rejuvenating mission of the Age of Enlightenment. Their hopes were not free of naïve illusions or sectarian attitudes, but they nevertheless were noble men who valued liberty highly. Because they had faith in human progress based on thought and reason, they may be forgiven much that we might rightly hold against lesser men.

TWENTY-THREE

The Life and Work
of Pierre Duhem

PIERRE DUHEM, WHO WAS BORN IN PARIS ON JUNE 10, 1861, and died in his home at Cabrespine on December 14, 1916, at the age of 55, was one of the most original French theoretical physicists of his time. Apart from his brilliant scientific work on thermodynamics, he is known for his great contribution to the history and philosophy of science.

Endowed with a great aptitude for mathematics and physics, Pierre Duhem entered the *Ecole Normale Supérieure* at the age of 22, and in this great seat of learning, which provided France with so many brilliant men of letters and science, he immediately proved his worth. It was at the Ecole that he first concentrated on thermodynamics, a subject to which he was to devote the rest of his life.

Studying the work of Thomson, Clausius, de Massieu, Gibbs, and the other great founders of thermodynamic theory, Duhem was struck by the similarity between the methods of Lagrangian analytical mechanics and those of thermodynamics. This similarity led him, at the age of 23, to introduce the general concept of thermodynamic potential and then to publish his *Thermodynamic Potential and Its Application to Chemical Mechanics*.

248

Two years after taking his degree in 1885, Duhem, whose name was by then well known in scientific circles, was appointed senior lecturer to the Faculty of Science at Lille, where he became a brilliant teacher of hydrodynamics, elasticity, and acoustics. He was married at Lille, but his wife died soon afterward, and for the rest of his life he lived with his only daughter. At the age of 32 he was appointed to a chair in the Faculty of Science in Bordeaux and retained this post until his death.

During his entire life, Pierre Duhem preserved his original scientific approach. From the theoretical point of view, this approach meant the construction of a general dynamics containing analytical classical mechanics and abstract thermodynamics as particular cases. Having a systematic mind, Duhem was always attracted to axiomatic methods with precise postulates from which he could derive logically unimpeachable conclusions, however abstract. He was utterly opposed to any suggestion that the abstractions of dynamics be discarded in favor of the doubtful models provided by atomic theories, nor was he in the least inclined to support Maxwell, Clausius, and Boltzmann's attempts to give a concrete interpretation of the abstract concepts of thermodynamics by means of kinetic theory. If he admired Willard Gibbs for the rigor of his thermodynamic arguments and for the algebraic elegance of phase rule, he certainly did not agree with the great American's attempt to base the atomic interpretation of thermodynamics on general statistical mechanics. From his *Commentaires sur la Thermodynamique,* the work of his youth, up to his great *Traité d'Energétique générale,* his crowning work on matter, Duhem persevered in his efforts to develop axiomatic principles. He carefully sifted all the basic notions of thermodynamics, and managed, for instance, to give a purely mathematical definition of the quantity of heat and thus to rid that concept of any intuitive content and of any hint of begging the question. This marked preference for abstraction makes Duhem's theoretical work appear extremely dry so that, despite his great achievements, his books did not appeal to all.

It must, however, be remembered that Duhem, no matter how much he concentrated on setting up his axiomatic system, never lost sight of the practical consequences of his theories. Thus in chemical mechanics, with which he was familiar from early youth, he made a thorough investigation of, and subsequently developed, all the practical consequences of Willard Gibbs's complicated ideas.

Duhem also contributed to hydrodynamics and to the theory of elasticity, two branches of science which he regarded as particular aspects of "general energetics." His work on the propagation of waves through liquids, particularly shock waves, is as relevant today as it was then. He was apparently less successful in his efforts to axiomatize electromagnetic theory, largely because he was always opposed to Maxwell's laws and preferred to adopt instead Helmholtz' now forgotten principles. Moreover, his deep antipathy toward all concrete models prevented his acceptance of Lorentz' electron theory and his appreciating the full significance of the new atomic approach.

Despite these flaws, which were no doubt the result of his oversystematic approach, Pierre Duhem bequeathed to theoretical physics much that modern scientists can still study to advantage.

Pierre Duhem was also a great historian, particularly in the familiar field of mechanics, astronomy, and physics. Fully aware that science was constantly evolving, and rightly convinced that all great scientists had their precursors, Duhem gave clear proof that the great upswing of mechanics, astronomy, and physics during the Renaissance and at the beginning of modern times was rooted in the scientific thought of the late medieval period, a period whose contribution to science has too often been misunderstood. In many of his writings, and particularly in his important *Leonardo da Vinci,* a work in three volumes, he stressed the important role played by the scientists of medieval universities during the thirteenth and fourteenth centuries, especially those attached to the University of Paris. He showed that after the death of St. Thomas Aquinas a reaction set in against Aristotelian ideas, and that this reaction was the main reason why Greek conceptions of motion were discarded in favor of principles of inertia, the work of Galileo, and modern mechanics. He established that Jean Buridan, Rector of the Sorbonne about 1327, was the first to have considered inertia and to have introduced, under the name of *impetus,* a rather badly defined quantity related to what we would call kinetic energy and momentum. Duhem also analyzed the important contributions to science of Albert of Saxony and of Nicole Oresme. Oresme's work, in particular, was of considerable importance, since his ideas on the solar system and on analytical geometry made him the precursor of Copernicus and Descartes respectively. By his discussion of uniform acceleration, Oresme even foreshadowed the work of Newton. Duhem also threw much light on the work of Leonardo da Vinci, that universal genius who launched mechanics on the course which Galileo and his successors were eventually to pursue. By these writings, particularly by his contribution to the history of mechanics, Pierre Duhem, who was also an expert on seventeenth century science and a leading commentator on the misunderstood work of Père Mersenne and Malebranche, justified his place among the foremost scientific historians of his time. In his later life he tackled a gigantic task, a history of cosmogonic theories from antiquity to modern times. At his death he had finished eight

volumes of this work, the last three of which are held by
the *Académie des Sciences* in manuscript, never having been
published because of financial difficulties. The whole work
is a monument to its author's erudition, as well as a mine
of valuable documents covering the history of science from
antiquity to the Middle Ages. We can only hope that, financial difficulties notwithstanding, we shall one day be allowed
to read this work in its entirety.*

Great theoretical physicist and erudite historian that
he was, Pierre Duhem quite naturally turned his attention
toward the philosophy of science. Having a systematic mind,
he held definite views on the meaning of physical theories
which he put forward in a number of his writings. The most
important of these is his *Physical Theory, Its Object and
Structure,* which was very successful in France. This important book reflects the clarity and conviction of the author's
own personality. We shall not give a complete analysis of
this profound work, but we shall outline some of its essential
points.

Pierre Duhem insisted on separating physics from metaphysics. His reading of the history of physical theories, no
matter whether based on continuous or discontinuous models
or on field or atomic principles, had convinced him that they
were inherently incapable of containing all reality. Not that
Pierre Duhem, the convinced Catholic that he was, rejected
all attempts to probe reality out of hand; he merely wished
to establish metaphysics as a separate discipline based on
revealed religion. This separation made him the unwilling
bedfellow of the positivist, at least with regard to the interpretation of physical theories. In his own words: "A physical
theory is not an explanation. It is a system of mathematical

* The sixth volume has meanwhile been published by Hermann's,
who intend to complete the edition as rapidly as possible.

propositions with the object of representing as simply, as completely, and as exactly as possible the totality of experimental laws."

Physical theories were therefore no more than methods of classifying physical phenomena which prevented scientists from getting lost in their complexity. And thus Duhem, whose positivist and pragmatic outlook brought him very close to Henri Poincaré's eclectic views, was at one with the positivist Mach in proclaiming that every physical theory is above all an "economy of thought." For him, the hypotheses underlying all physical models were transitory and impermanent—only the algebraic relations which good theories have established between phenomena have any lasting value. Such, by and large, was Duhem's basic approach to theoretical physics. Much of it greatly pleased the physicists of his day, and continues to please a great many modern quantum physicists, but others have reproached him, and will continue to reproach him, for minimizing the knowledge of reality which physics can provide.

To be fair to Duhem, we must stress that he did not carry his views to excess. Like most physicists, he instinctively believed in the existence of external reality, and therefore he cannot be called a physical idealist. Adopting a characteristic personal attitude, quite different from that of phenomenalism, he asserted that the mathematical laws of theoretical physics, although not revealing the deep reality of nature, nevertheless exhibit certain aspects of an ontological harmony. In their development physical theories assume the character of a "natural" classification of phenomena, where "natural" has, according to Duhem, a very specific meaning: "The more perfect a theory, the more the logical order in which it arranges its experimental laws reflects an ontological order." In this way, he was able to temper his scientific positivism, realizing as he did that "if physical theories fail to provide useful and logical classification of observable phenomena, they cannot possibly anticipate experiment and predict the existence of unknown phenomena." Hence he concluded that physical theories were more than mere methodical classifications of known facts. In particular, his writings show that he fully appreciated that the similarity between the mathematical symbols of physical theories covering different phenomena generally reflected more than a purely formal similarity—it was evidence of a profound relationship between the different aspects of reality.

Such, in brief, was Duhem's notion of the meaning of physical theories. It might be argued that, despite the "softening" of his doctrine by the introduction of the concept of natural classification, Duhem took too intransigent and rigid a view of the purpose of science, that his horror of any conceptual models made him reject atomic theory, and that his faith in energetics prevented his correct evaluation of the contribution (during his lifetime) of statistical mechanics to the abstract conceptions of classical thermodynamics. Thus he neither appreciated the immense impetus which modern atomic theories gave to physics or foresaw the tremendous role it would play some 50 years later. Those passages of his books in which he derides the notion of the electron and deplores its introduction into science have since then been more than disproved by the extraordinary advances of microphysics.

Nevertheless, Duhem's opinions fully deserve our respect, since, even where we disagree with him, we cannot but benefit from his many keen judgments and interesting examples. I need only mention Duhem's profound remarks on Bacon's crucial experiment. According to Duhem, no experiment can ever be crucial, since experiment can confirm only one aspect of a given theory. There is no reason why other consequences of that theory should not be contradicted by experiment or why some other (future) theory might not interpret the observed facts equally well. As an instance, Duhem mentions Foucault's famous experiment to prove that light travels faster in water than in air. In choosing that example Duhem proved extremely perspicacious, for, in his day, that experiment was, in fact, considered a crucial proof that light was undulatory and not corpuscular. Very rightly, Duhem objected that Foucauld's experiment could not be crucial, since, although it upheld Fresnel's wave theory and ran counter to Newton's corpuscular theory, there was no good reason why another corpuscular theory based on new postulates should not interpret the results equally well. How right Duhem was and how shrewd in choosing just that example were shown by subsequent developments, which he could not possibly have foreseen. For in the same year that Duhem was writing his book (1905), Einstein presented science with his notion of light quanta (photons) whose existence has since been established beyond all doubt. Hence, no matter what our interpretation of the wave-particle dualism, the final theory will have to reconcile Foucauld's experiment to the existence of photons. What better illustration could there be of the profundity of Duhem's criticism of "crucial experiments" or of his great insight?

Duhem, though a kind and affable man, was also given to intransigent views, and did not always treat his opponents with the respect they deserved. While everyone valued his integrity, many of his contemporaries resented his rudeness. No wonder that he had many enemies and that this eminent scientist, thinker, philosopher, and historian was not accorded what every Frenchman of his rank has the right to expect, a chair at one of the great universities of Paris. True, he did nothing to encourage such an appointment and, one day when he was pressed to teach the history of science at the *Collège de France,* he replied that he was a physicist and could teach no other subject. Still, three years before his death he had the satisfaction of being appointed Visiting Member to the *Académie des Sciences.*

When Pierre Duhem died at the age of 55, he had made a vast contribution to physics, philosophy, and history. The value of his purely scientific writings, the depth of his thought, and his incredible erudition make him one of the most remarkable French physicists at the turn of the century.

TWENTY-FOUR

Mechanics in the Seventeenth Century

RENÉ DUGAS, TO WHOM WE OWE AN AUTHORITATIVE *History of Mechanics* (Dunod, Paris, 1950), in which, combining historical erudition with great scientific knowledge, he has examined mechanical concepts from antiquity to the twentieth century, has recently done more detailed work on one period covered by this magnificent study and published the *History of Mechanics in the Seventeenth Century* (Dunod, Paris, 1954).

His new work is not a mere development of his previous findings; it examines the seventeenth century from an entirely different viewpoint. Rightly convinced that all great scientists, their declared opinions to the contrary notwithstanding, always have an underlying metaphysical approach, Dugas demonstrates the influence of philosophic notions on mechanics at a time when the list of its great exponents contained such famous names as Descartes, Pascal, and Leibnitz. He stresses the fact that his book is meant to be neither a pure history nor a pure philosophy of science, but a general attempt to look at scientific thought in all its complexity, covering both its technical and also its philosophical ideas.

257

Scientific research has always alternated between two tendencies: on the one hand, the careful observation and accurate mathematical expression of experimental facts; on the other, the deduction of natural laws from *a priori* and, hence, necessarily metaphysical, assumptions. All advances of science have resulted from continuous compromises between these two tendencies, which were particularly opposed to each other during the seventeenth century when some of the best scientists may rightly have been accused of adhering to an arid scholasticism. Yet the seventeenth century, mainly under the aegis of Bacon, also recognized the value of experiment, and it is not surprising that its science was rent in two by bitter controversies. What makes this conflict so poignant and highly instructive is that its protagonists were some of the greatest scientists of all time. For that reason, Dugas' book is able to reconstruct for us some of the most remarkable and moving episodes in the history of human endeavor to interpret nature in the face of recurring difficulties.

In a book as well documented as Dugas', a discussion of the great precursors of seventeenth century science is, of course, only to be expected. But here we shall merely give an account of Dugas' central theme, the work of Descartes, Pascal, Huyghens, Newton, and Leibnitz.

Descartes is treated in a special chapter, and, since Dugas realizes that he cannot do full justice to the work of this great genius in other fields, he concentrates on his contribution to mechanics alone. He points out the great influence of Beeckman on Descartes' early studies, discusses Descartes' analysis and critique of Galileo's work, and recalls his many bitter polemics with other scientists, particularly with Roberval. Having a much too systematic mind, and being overconfident of the superiority of his own ideas, Descartes failed to make as great a contribution to modern

science as he could have made. True, he supplied the basic
concepts of analytical geometry, the precise formulation of
Snell's laws of reflection and refraction, and an elegant rain-
bow theory, but in mechanics itself he may rightly be said
to have been wrong most of the time. Thus he was utterly
mistaken in the formulation of his principle of the conservation of momentum, and it was this mistake which was to
haunt mechanics for many years to come. Similarly, his misconceptions about vortices were an inauspicious influence in
the evolution of physics at that time. Nevertheless Descartes' work as a whole was of utmost significance because,
by breaking with scholastic explanations, Descartes set science on its modern path of developing the consequences of a
set of basic principles in clear mathematical terms. Dugas'
profound analysis makes it clear that Descartes, despite his
many errors and character faults, made a great contribution to the advance of modern science and is worthy of our
respect.

Though Blaise Pascal is known mainly for his literary
and philosophical work, he was also a great mathematician and physicist, particularly during his youth. Naturally,
Dugas concentrates on Pascal the scientist rather than on
Pascal the philosopher. He devotes much space to Pascal's
great discovery that air has weight, and analyzes the development of his ideas on this subject and the influences to
which he was exposed in designing this and other experiments. Though Pascal, too, had his precursors, it is nevertheless to him that we owe the conclusive demonstration of
the vacuum and also the precise and correct interpretation
of the existence of atmospheric pressure and its effects on
the mercury in barometric tubes. Pascal also made a fundamental contribution to hydrostatics. Paradoxically enough,
the very man whose *Pensées* are suffused with mysticism
was a positivist in his scientific pursuits—no scientist of his

time had fewer metaphysical prejudices or was more careful not to be swayed by anything but experimental evidence. Nor is that the least curious aspect of the intellectual mold of this great thinker.

Huyghens, a Cartesian by training, was a consistently original and independent thinker who often criticized his master's errors. In mechanics, he went much further than Descartes, and never went wrong. He formulated the laws of conservation of momentum, which Descartes had completely misunderstood; in the course of his profound studies of circular motion, he introduced into dynamics the notion of a centrifugal force; and he enunciated the theories of the cycloidal and compound pendulums. His scientific work was always meticulous and worthy of our greatest admiration. Huyghens was a virtuoso when it came to handling even the most subtle mathematical arguments; he was the perfect physicist who, while heeding experimental results, never lost sight of the fact that these results must be fitted into a synthetic theory, based on solid mathematical deductions. Huyghens, it must be remembered, was the first to present a scientific wave theory of light. Thus he was the precursor of Fresnel, and this alone ensures his lasting fame.

The long chapter which Dugas devotes to Newton is as thrilling as it is remarkable. In it Dugas attempts to present an analysis of genius, and that is never a simple task. Newton's work was altogether prodigious and magnificent. He advanced optics by brilliant experiments; he shares with Leibnitz the honor of having created the infinitesimal calculus; he gave mechanics its modern form; and he discovered universal gravitation. And yet Newton, the man, has remained a complete mystery, and strikes us as a mass of contradictions. Wild and lonely in his youth, he later hankered after honors, and became the prototype of the "official" scientist. No doubt under the influence of doctrinaire

TWENTY-FIVE

The Fiftieth Anniversary of the Discovery of Radioactivity

TOWARD THE END OF THE NINETEENTH CENTURY, THE REMARK-able discovery of radioactivity opened a new chapter in the history of physics.

Radioactivity was first discovered in March 1896 by Henri Becquerel who had been asked by Poincaré to investigate whether fluorescent uranium salts made an X-ray impression on photographic plates. Becquerel noticed that uranium salts, which had been left, quite unintentionally, in a dark drawer containing the photographic plates, had produced an impression on them. Thus he hit upon the great discovery that uranium salts emitted radiation even when they had not previously been exposed to sunlight, and that this radiation could penetrate through paper and cardboard. Hence he was able to show that radioactive phenomena were quite distinct from X-ray phenomena, and also that radioactivity was a property of the uranium atom itself and not the result of its chemical combinations. Becquerel then demonstrated that this new radiation caused an electroscope to become discharged, and could therefore be detected with that instrument.

It is at this point that we must introduce the brilliant

work of Pierre and Marie Curie. Pierre Curie, born in Paris in 1859, was by 1896 a most distinguished physicist whose research had attracted the attention of the entire scientific world. The son of a doctor, he, together with his brother Jacques, had launched upon a scientific career at an early age. In 1880 they jointly published a paper on the measurement of the wavelength of infra-red radiation down to seven microns, a considerable advance in the spectral technique of his time.

Starting from theoretical ideas about the symmetry of crystals, the two Curies soon afterwards discovered the piezoelectric effect, that is, the production of electricity by mechanical actions on asymmetrical crystals. Jacques and Pierre Curie then investigated the relations between the piezoelectric and the known pyroelectric effects, and, in conformity with the theoretical ideas of Gabriel Lippmann, they showed the existence of an inverse piezoelectric effect by which a piezoelectric crystal can be deformed under the action of an external source of electricity. They also produced the first piezoelectric quartz crystal, the applications of which, particularly in the fields of radio electricity and ultrasonics, are too numerous to be listed here.

In his work on the piezoelectric effect, Pierre Curie was always guided by his belief in the symmetry of physical phenomena, a belief which he expressed in a great many papers starting in 1885. Influenced by the ideas of Bravais and other crystallographers and those of Pasteur, he developed a general theory of symmetry and showed that the symmetry of natural phenomena had a tendency to increase, that is, that there must always be at least as much asymmetry in a given cause as is in its effect. These ideas are so important that all their consequences have not yet been fully exhausted.

In 1892 he began a research project which in 1895 resulted in his doctoral thesis on the *Magnetic Properties of Bodies at Different Temperatures.* In it, he once again displayed his exceptional qualities, and, in particular, he showed that for a paramagnetic substance the magnetic susceptibility per unit mass is inversely proportional to the absolute temperature—Curie's law—while the magnetic susceptibility of a diamagnetic substance is independent of the temperature. As for ferromagnetic substances, Pierre Curie showed that at a given temperature, the Curie point, their strong magnetic properties give way to weak paramagnetic behavior.

After these brilliant contributions, Pierre Curie was rightly considered to be a physicist of the first rank. In 1896 he was made Professor of General Electricity at the *Ecole de Physique et Chimie industrielles,* where he met and married the young Polish student Marie Sklodowska. It was at this point that Henri Becquerel had just made the important discoveries which we mentioned earlier. Madame Curie then suggested to her husband that he investigate whether substances other than uranium also had radioactive properties, and he followed her advice. Drawing on his great knowledge of piezoelectric phenomena, Pierre Curie soon developed an electric method of measuring the radiation emitted by uranium. Madame Curie had meanwhile discovered—independently of Schmidt, who had come to the same conclusion—that thorium, like uranium, was radioactive, and together with her husband she established that some thorium and uranium compounds were more radioactive than their elements. It therefore seemed likely that their intense radioactivity was derived from a substance much more radioactive than uranium or thorium. A great discovery was about to be made.

Pierre and Marie Curie then turned their attention to the properties of Joachimsthal pitchblende, a very complex mineral containing oxides of uranium. From it they managed to extract a product four hundred times as radioactive as the pitchblende itself, and Madame Curie called this new product polonium, in honor of the country of her birth. Then the two young scientists, with the help of Bémont, isolated a substance more than a million times more radioactive still —radium. Radium was shown to be a chemical element whose properties resembled those of barium, but which had a much higher atomic weight. Demarçay's spectral analysis of radium lines then led to the accurate identification of that element, and when Pierre and Marie Curie had isolated radium chlorides and bromides, they were able to fix the atomic weight of radium at about 226. While Debierne, working with them, went on to discover actinium, the Curies studied the effects of radium and demonstrated its property of inducing phosphorescence in a great many substances, of discharging an electroscope instantly, and of producing noxious effects on living organisms. French scientists had thus demonstrated the existence of an entirely new phenomenon, induced radioactivity, that is, the ability of radium to communicate its radioactivity to substances in its neighborhood. This mysterious phenomenon was subsequently explained by the assumption that the radium atom disintegrates to give rise to an atom of a new radioactive element, radon, which acts on surrounding bodies.

Pierre and Marie Curie's work earned them universal acclaim. They shared with Henri Becquerel the Nobel Prize in physics, and Pierre Curie, who had meanwhile become a professor at the Sorbonne, was called to the *Académie des Sciences* in 1905. Then, in 1906, a ghastly accident put a sudden end to his life and to the career of one of the greatest names in French science—Pierre Curie was run over by a truck. Marie Curie carried on his work nobly. She was appointed professor at the Sorbonne in his stead, and continued there for nearly 30 years, while at the same time doing important research at the Radium Institute, a center of learning and research created for her and today directed by her daughter Irène Joliot-Curie.

In so short a lecture it is impossible to discuss all the extraordinary developments of the Curies' momentous discovery. All I can hope to do is to give a summary of its main stages.

For 15 years after the discovery of radioactivity, scientists concentrated on listing and classifying spontaneously radioactive substances and on the general laws governing their behavior. In this work the Curies and Becquerel were joined by the great English physicist Lord Rutherford and by other eminent scientists, including Soddy and Fajans. Together they discovered a host of radioactive substances, all of large atomic weight. All these elements could be arranged in series whose decay-chain links bore a parent-daughter relationship, with lead as their common end product. Hence it could be shown that a radioactive atom will undergo spontaneous disintegration with a given probability in unit time. Here, physics was first introduced to those statistical laws whose real nature and deep significance quantum and wave mechanics were to bring out later on. Moreover, all radiation emitted during radioactive transmutations could be shown to fall into one of three distinct groups, alpha rays, beta rays, and gamma rays.

Although all these findings did much to clarify a number of previously obscure points, they also raised a host of new problems. Radioactivity was obviously the result of intra-atomic processes, yet physicists had no means of penetrating the atom. They were also puzzled by the continuous and often considerable liberation of heat which accompanied radioactive transformations. Pierre and Marie Curie had shown that one gram of radium liberates 80 calories per hour, that is, enough heat to melt one gram of ice. Whence came this continuous energy? Had the law of the conservation of energy broken down or was there an undetected radiation which, when absorbed by radioactive substances, caused these substances to disintegrate and to release heat?

It was only about 1910 that these questions began to be answered. His theory of relativity had enabled Einstein to enunciate his law of inertial energy according to which mass is merely one possible form of energy and can therefore be transformed into radiation or into kinetic energy, and hence into heat. The energy liberated in the course of a radioactive transformation was thus shown to be the result of the change of atomic mass caused by atomic disintegration. A very small change of mass could lead to the liberation of a large amount of energy—the principle of the conservation of energy was obeyed and there was no need to introduce any unknown radiation into the theory. Paul Langevin seems to have been the first to have drawn this conclusion, which has since become the basis of all energy-exchange calculations of nuclear physics.

We have said that physicists had the impression that radioactive disintegrations must take place in the very heart of the atom. This somewhat vague idea was greatly clarified by the famous work of Rutherford and Bohr, from which we know that the atom is formed of a central positive nucleus and its surrounding negative electrons. Those atomic phenomena which we can easily produce in our laboratories, namely the emission of light or molecular transformations, have their seat in the peripheral part of the atom, that is, the electron, while radioactivity, which physicists could not materially affect, took place in the central "fortress" of the atom, the nucleus.

In 1919, Rutherford made his first successful attempt

to penetrate this fortress when he managed to split the nitrogen nuclei by bombardment with alpha particles. His achievement marked a milestone in the history of contemporary physics. By producing nuclear disintegrations experimentally, Rutherford had finally done what Henri Becquerel and the Curies had predicted 20 years earlier. Scientists were now able to launch a large-scale investigation of nuclear phenomena.

From then on there was no going back, and particularly from 1930 progress was almost continuous. The disintegration of nuclei under the action of a host of projectiles revealed the existence of an ever growing number of isotopes, and made nuclear chemistry a science in its own right. The discoveries of the neutron, the positive electron, and the meson (or rather of mesons, for more than one type of meson is now known to exist), the new conception of the structure of the nucleus resulting from the work of Heisenberg and Bohr, and the demonstration of uranium fission which followed in quick succession marked the main stages in the development of nuclear physics between 1930 and 1940. Here I would only like to mention the contribution to these magnificent advances, particularly to the discovery of the neutron, to the production of artificial radioactive elements, and to the study of fission effects, by the Curies' daughter Irène and her husband Frédéric Joliot-Curie. Continuing the Curies' great work, they, in turn, were awarded the Nobel Prize in 1935.

I need not tell you about the recent developments of all these remarkable scientific advances, which have enabled mankind to harness the enormous reserves of energy concentrated within the atomic nucleus—they are common knowledge. It has been claimed that the conquest of atomic energy has opened a new era in the history of humanity, and that claim is no exaggeration if we remember what gigantic stores of energy have thus been placed within the reach of all of us. To arrive at this point, man had to traverse the long but exceedingly rapid route which led from the discovery of radioactivity 50 years ago to the liberation of atomic energy in recent times. No matter how great the contribution of others, it is to the Curies and to Henri Becquerel that we owe the fact that these discoveries could have been made in the first place. Today we can fully appreciate the importance of their work, not only at the theoretical level, but also in the practical terms of the incredible power we have derived from it. It is therefore only right that, on the occasion of the fiftieth anniversary of the discovery of radium, we render homage to those who, by their skill and devotion, provided mankind with one of its greatest achievements.

TWENTY-SIX

Artificial Radioelements

THE GREAT SCIENTIFIC EVENT WHOSE TWENTIETH ANNIVER-
sary we celebrate today, the discovery in 1934 of artificial
radioactive elements (radioactive nuclides) by M. and Mme.
Joliot-Curie, marked one of the most important stages in
the development of contemporary physics.

We may say that nuclear physics was born in 1896
when Henri Becquerel discovered the radioactive properties
of uranium. A little later, Pierre and Marie Curie identified
the new element, radium, and demonstrated its intense
radioactivity. These splendid discoveries, of which our country can justly be proud, became the basis of a new and particularly important branch of physics.

Although not wishing to enter into the historical details
of the development of this new science and the great contribution of the Cambridge school and particularly of Rutherford, I shall give a brief account of what, after 50 years
of intensive research, was the interpretation of the phenomena involved. Simple atoms came to be looked upon as
consisting of a central positive nucleus surrounded by moving electrons. The nucleus of all elements other than hydrogen is a complex particle whose weight and electric charge

increases with the atom's position in the Mendeleev scale.
Now, naturally radioactive chemical elements represent the
end of that scale—their nuclei are therefore the heaviest and
most highly charged of all, and hence their radioactivity,
that is, their instability, must be the direct result of their
great internal complexity. It has, in fact, since been demonstrated that radioactive atoms degenerate spontaneously
into atoms of elements lower in the Mendeleev scale with
an associated emission of radiation (alpha, beta, and gamma
rays). The newly formed atoms are generally radioactive
as well, and as they degenerate in turn, they set up the three
distinct decay chains which we call the radioactive series,
all of which have a stable atom of lead as their end product.

One of the apparent characteristics of all radioactive
transformations was that they completely eluded observational techniques so that no method seemed capable of in-
fluencing their behavior—high temperatures or pressures and
electromagnetic fields had no apparent effects on natural
radioactivity. It was a great day, indeed, in the history of
physics when Rutherford in 1919 managed to transform an
atomic nucleus, thus realizing the ancient dream of the
medieval alchemists. After bombarding nitrogen with alpha
rays emitted by radioactive polonium, Rutherford was able
to show that the nitrogen nuclei absorbed the radiation to
release a hydrogen nucleus—a proton—with appreciable
liberation of kinetic energy.

Rutherford's famous experiment, quickly confirmed and
developed by other scientists, had opened an entirely new
path to nuclear physics. Today we know that even some
light nuclei of atoms low on the Mendeleev scale can be
transformed by bombardment with suitable particles. However, we must not anticipate events. Shortly after Rutherford's first experiment, J. J. Thomson and Aston introduced
the notion of isotopes to explain the fact that one and the

same chemical element, all of whose atomic nuclei have the same electric charge and hence the same atomic number, may yet have nuclei of different *mass*. Now, artificial transmutations of the elements often produce isotopic nuclei rarely found in nature, and hence greatly enlarge the scope of nuclear physics.

Nevertheless, it was not until 1930 that this new discovery could begin to be put to further use. It was then that physicists managed to perfect their "atomic artillery," that is, to invent ingenious techniques whereby very great velocities could be imparted to the particles used for bombarding atomic nuclei. Of these new projectiles, the neutron deserves special mention. Its discovery, in which M. and Mme. Joliot-Curie were instrumental, dates back to 1932. This electrically neutral particle is particularly suited to enter into nuclei, since their electrostatic fields cannot protect them against it.

By means of these new techniques, physicists between 1930 and 1934 managed to produce a great number of new transmutations and hence a great many new types of nuclei, particles, and radiation. These transmutations could be grouped into distinct categories, and the application of the principle of the inertia of energy, an important consequence of the theory of relativity, enabled physicists to establish energy exchanges corresponding to these transmutations. In this way they set up nuclear chemistry with its own formulas and specific reactions.

Now, at first, all these "manufactured" nuclei were found to be comparable with the nuclei of the stable, non-radioactive atoms. Nevertheless it seemed clear that artificial transmutations ought also to produce radioactive nuclei. In effect, the violent disorganization of the structure of the bombarded nucleus must necessarily result in an unstable product emitting radiation spontaneously. Somehow

physicists failed to appreciate this fact, and they were therefore taken by surprise when in January 1934 they learned
that M. and Mme. Joliot-Curie had managed to produce
artificial radioactive nuclei, a discovery which was to earn
them the Nobel Prize.

At that time, physicists had just discovered a new unstable particle in cosmic rays, the positive electron, or positron, which is the electrical counterpart of the usual negative
electron. Now, while natural radioactive nuclear disintegration was known to be capable of emitting negative electrons, no emission of positive electrons had ever been observed. However, as the study of artificial radioactivity was
proceeding apace it became clear that, apart from electrons,
positive particles, the so-called transmutation positrons,
could also be emitted during transmutations. While investigating the minimum energy of alpha rays needed for transforming aluminum with the emission of positrons, M. and
Mme. Joliot observed that this emission was not instantane-
ous but that it began only some time after the radiation phenomenon had set in, and continued for some time after the
radiation had ceased. The bombardment of aluminum nuclei
with helium nuclei (alpha rays) resulted in the production
of an unstable and radioactive phosphorus nucleus which
has a mean life of two minutes fifteen seconds and which
emits positrons. The Joliot-Curies then reported to the
Académie des Sciences (*Comptes rendus*, January 15, 1934)
that "for the first time it has been possible to create radioactivity in atomic nuclei."

These new radioactive nuclei, which we distinguish from
naturally radioactive nuclei by placing an asterisk behind
their atomic symbol (for example P* denotes radioactive
phosphorus), are known as radioactive nuclides, and a great
many of them have been produced since 1934. All in all, we
now know more than three hundred different types with dis-

tinct half-lives and radioactive emissions. Thus, for every element of the Mendeleev series, we now know a number of radioactive isotopes, and that fact alone is enough to show the tremendous scope of the Joliots' discovery.

Other lecturers will soon be able to tell you of all the many technical applications of these discoveries during the past twenty years both in physics itself, where their appearance and decay can be used in a host of experiments and measurements, and also in biology and in medicine, where they have led to the diagnostic use of tracer elements. Even history has benefited greatly from them since the decay of radioactive carbon-14 enables historians to determine the age of mummies and to date events in the distant past. But, to keep to my own subject, I shall merely relate the importance of the Joliots' discovery to the development of physics.

Scientists have known for the past 20 years or so that nuclei consist of protons and of neutrons, particles of similar mass but electrically positive and neutral, respectively. Today the proton and the neutron are looked upon as two different states of one and the same nuclear particle, the nucleon. Nucleons can change from the neutron state to the proton state with the creation of a negative electron, or from the proton state to the neutron state with the emission of a positive electron. Now, for a nucleus to be stable, the number of its constituent protons and neutrons must be in a given proportion. In the case of the light elements, there must be roughly as many protons as there are neutrons, whereas heavier elements are stable only if there is an excess of neutrons over protons. This excess must be the greater the higher we go up in the Mendeleev series. Very heavy nuclei are highly complex structures with a tendency toward spontaneous instability, that is, toward natural radioactivity. Their excess neutrons frequently become transformed into protons by spontaneous disintegration, which explains their emission of beta rays consisting of negative electrons. On the other hand, radioactive nuclides may as often as not have an excess of protons over neutrons, which explains why they can emit electrons as well as positrons, the latter not emitted by naturally radioactive nuclei. This is one of the first and most important consequences of the discovery of radioactive nuclides.

Thanks mainly to the development of our "atomic artillery" we now know hundreds of radioactive nuclides covering all regions of the Mendeleev scale and with characteristic masses and half-lives. We also know the nature of their respective disintegrations and the kind of particles they emit. We know that every element in the Mendeleev series contains, side by side with a small or even a single number of stable nuclei, a host of unstable nuclei, some with an excess of protons and hence emitting positrons, others with an excess of neutrons and hence emitting electrons. The wealth of data which physicists have thus acquired has enabled them to gain a fair idea of the laws governing the behavior of nuclei. Radioactive phenomena raise countless problems of the utmost importance to nuclear physics, for example the capture of peripheral electrons by nuclei, the existence of nuclear isomers, and the properties of the transuranic elements and of plutonium in particular. Here we have an almost inexhaustible source of future information about the most intimate structure of matter. And all the new knowledge springing from it is the direct consequence of the discovery of radioactive nuclides and the subsequent discovery of nuclear fission, to both of which M. and Mme. Joliot-Curie made so momentous a contribution.

Looking back over 20 years of constant and often sensational advances in nuclear physics, we can only marvel at the incredible consequences of these discoveries. Continuing along the path opened up, some 50 years ago, by the

Curies' discovery of natural radioactivity, M. and Mme. Joliot-Curie helped nuclear physics to its present eminent position. In rendering homage to them, we are doubly thankful that, by their contribution, they enabled French physics to play a leading role in modern science.

Index

steamlines, common, 147, 167-
169
Stueckelberg, E. G. G., 29, 46
subtractive field, theory of, 43-
50
Szilard, Leo, 60

Tasso, Torquato, 245
tau meson, 28
Taylor, Sir Geoffrey, 137, 242
technology, 222
telecommunication, 53; mathematical study of, 55-56
telegraph, electric, 209
theorists, vs. logicians, 200
theory of numbers, 235
thermal noise, 65
*Thermodynamic Potential and
Its Application to Chemi-
cal Mechanics* (Duhem),
248
thermodynamics, 248, 254; biology and, 68-69; laws of,
59-60; neg-entropy and,
58; and statistical mechanics, 249
Thomas Aquinas, St., 251
Thompson, M. G. P., 181
Thomson, J. J., 18, 248, 272
thorium, 265
Tomonaga, 18, 103
Tonnelat, M. A., 40, 152
Torricelli, Evangelista, 232
Tournefort, Joseph P. de, 235
tracer elements, 275
Traité d'Energétique générale
(Duhem), 249
transmutation, of elements, 273
transuranic elements, 33

*Treatise on Analytical Me-
chanics* (Lagrance), 241
Treatise on Dynamics (d'Alembert), 240-242
trigger effects, 52-53
Trillat, Jean-Jacques, 79

Uhlenbeck, G. E., 15
uncertainty principle and relations, 3-13, 55, 97, 104,
122, 149, 175-176, 183
unified field theory, 151
uranium, 265; fission of, 269
u wave, 92-94, 111-114, 116-
122, 124, 148, 167-169, 173,
177-179

values, traditional, science and,
214-217
Vaucanson, Jacques de, 63
Verne, Jules, 191
vibration, 7-8
Vigier, Jean-Pierre, 42, 83, 101-
102, 104, 109, 113, 154,
166-167, 184
Ville, 55, 64
Voltaire, 106, 237, 243
v wave, 167-169, 176-177

Walter, Gray, 63, 67
wave mechanics, 16, 149; crystal structure and, 78;
cybernetics and, 55; de
Broglie's first researches
in, 87-92; dualism in, *see*
wave-particle dualism; history of, 156-160; inter-
pretation of, vii, 156-179;